*Dedicated to my friends, Scott Tiedke and Michael Klibaner,
gone too soon but never forgotten.*

- Ethan Sacks

*This one is for you, Dad.
Wherever you are...*

- Dalibor Talajić

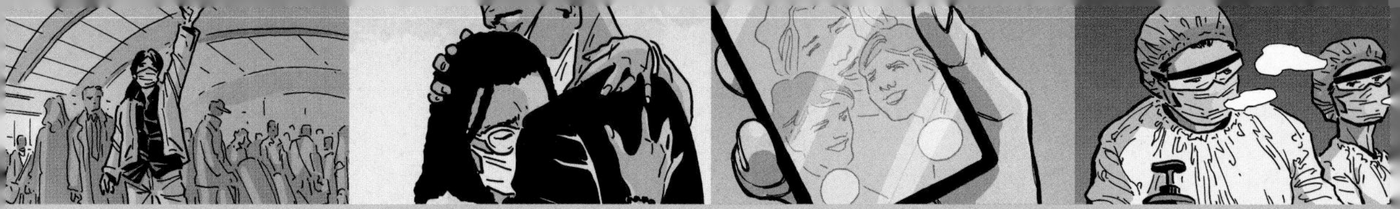

FOREWORD

by Alyssa Milano

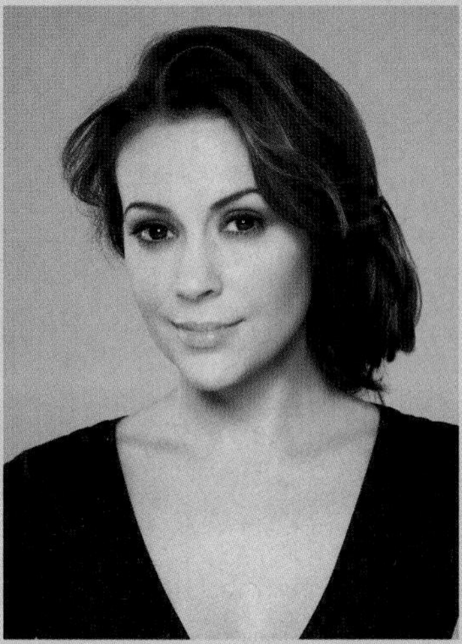

There is an illusion we all live with. It's part of what keeps society together, what keeps food on the shelves and people going to work, and gas in our cars, and each of us getting up every day and heading out into the world. The illusion is that we are *safe*. That we can breathe, and touch, and eat, and hook up, and visit our families and it will all be okay. That if we get sick, we get better.

That illusion is shattered.

It's taken me six days to write this foreword, these few hundred words. Exhaustion. The exhaustion is always there, pulling me backwards as I try to move forward. The brain fog and headaches make getting through most days a challenge that I thought I would never have to face. What was I doing in the fridge? What did Milo just ask me? Have I taken my meds? Each task, each bit of focus is ten times more expensive than it was before I had COVID.

But the worst is the fear.

I did not infect my family. My parents are safe. My children and husband are safe—from me.

But the fact that they have not been infected means they are *definitely* still vulnerable. I have nightmares of losing my mom, of my husband David in the hospital, of explaining to my kids the very worst news they would ever hear. As someone who already struggled with Generalized Anxiety Disorder, this fear adds an entirely new dimension of hell to daily life.

I've had to find new reasons to get out of bed. "Safe" is no longer enough.

Maybe that's true for all of us.

We saw it in the early days, when we stood on our balconies and cheered for the first responders and sang together in celebration of our common bond. Back before hundreds of thousands died and we believed we were going to power through, that optimism was the buoy that would keep us afloat on the roughest of seas. But optimism is not enough. It can face only so much proof that it is unwarranted. Optimism was buried in the graves of the more than a million people who have died from COVID. It is a ghost, haunting us.

Where we used to give each other bemused looks in grocery stores at the empty aisles of toilet paper, we now glare from behind our hidden faces, looking for the threat. We rightfully scorn those who would risk everyone else by not wearing a mask, unless we are one of those selfish masses, arrogant in our ignorance. We no longer sing, and we no longer cheer. We have lost that thing that brought us together in this. It has been cut in pieces by an incompetent response, a willfully stupid government, and the relentless toll of death and sickness and fear.

We are less than what we were.

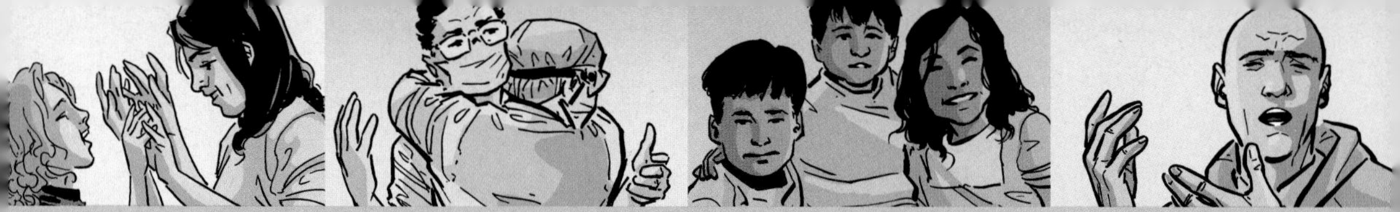

We are diminished by who we have lost. The sum of their absence is nearly as great as the sum of their presence was. The weight of their loss bends us over, hunched as though against a strong wind when we venture out into the world and see other people walking. We turn away. We wrap ourselves in separation. We find armor in loneliness. We all suffer. Many of us suffer needlessly, left without jobs and without income by a government that seems to simply not care. It didn't have to be this way, and that adds to the exhaustion. Anger—fury—is exhausting. And ever-present.

My hair is no longer falling out. For weeks, I would find it in great clumps when I brushed my hair. At first, I cried. Soon, I was numb. Another thing to endure in this crushing onslaught of things to endure. I couldn't imagine how I had any hair left and hoped I would be as brave and strong and beautiful as people like Ayanna Pressley, whose alopecia took her hair long before COVID took mine. I tried to find inspiration in the millions of cancer survivors and other strong and inspiring people who have endured.

But inspiration is difficult these days.

The stories that follow in this book are real. They touch on things that each of us have experienced or feared or seen as we struggled through the hellscape of 2020. I don't know if they are inspiring. What does inspiring even mean in the face of a pandemic? Can you be inspired to avoid a virus? I truly don't know. But I *do* know that the people we see in the pages that follow, the true stories told, the experiences that are recounted are *powerful*. I know that they connect to parts of us that have been wounded by COVID, by those we lost. I know that I cried when I read it.

If I've learned anything in a life of acting and activism, it is this: stories *matter*. Stories might not be the thing that lifts us out of the pandemic, but they will be the things that allow us to reconnect after. They will be the touchstone that help us build back up, better than we were before. They will help us remember what we have lost and find our way back to who we were before. I know that my life is richer for knowing that the people who are spotlighted here existed in the world, and that their stories will be guiding us to whatever normal looks like in 2021 and beyond.

I would normally end a foreword suggesting that the reader enjoy the stories that follow. That is not the right word here. I don't think you will enjoy them, although the art is wonderfully crafted and the writing is expert. The stories are not a balm. Do not enjoy them, but do *experience* them. Allow them to penetrate into your most protected places, to resonate in your soul. To create a memory imprint that will carry them through generations. Tell them to your kids, and your grandkids, when they are old enough to know. These stories have become all of us. We carry them into the new world.

And until we get there, we endure.

- A.M. October 5, 2020.

“The stories that follow in this book are real. They touch on things that each of us have experienced or feared or seen as we struggled through the hellscape of 2020.”

CHAPTER 1
A NURSE'S ANGUISH IN THE ICU

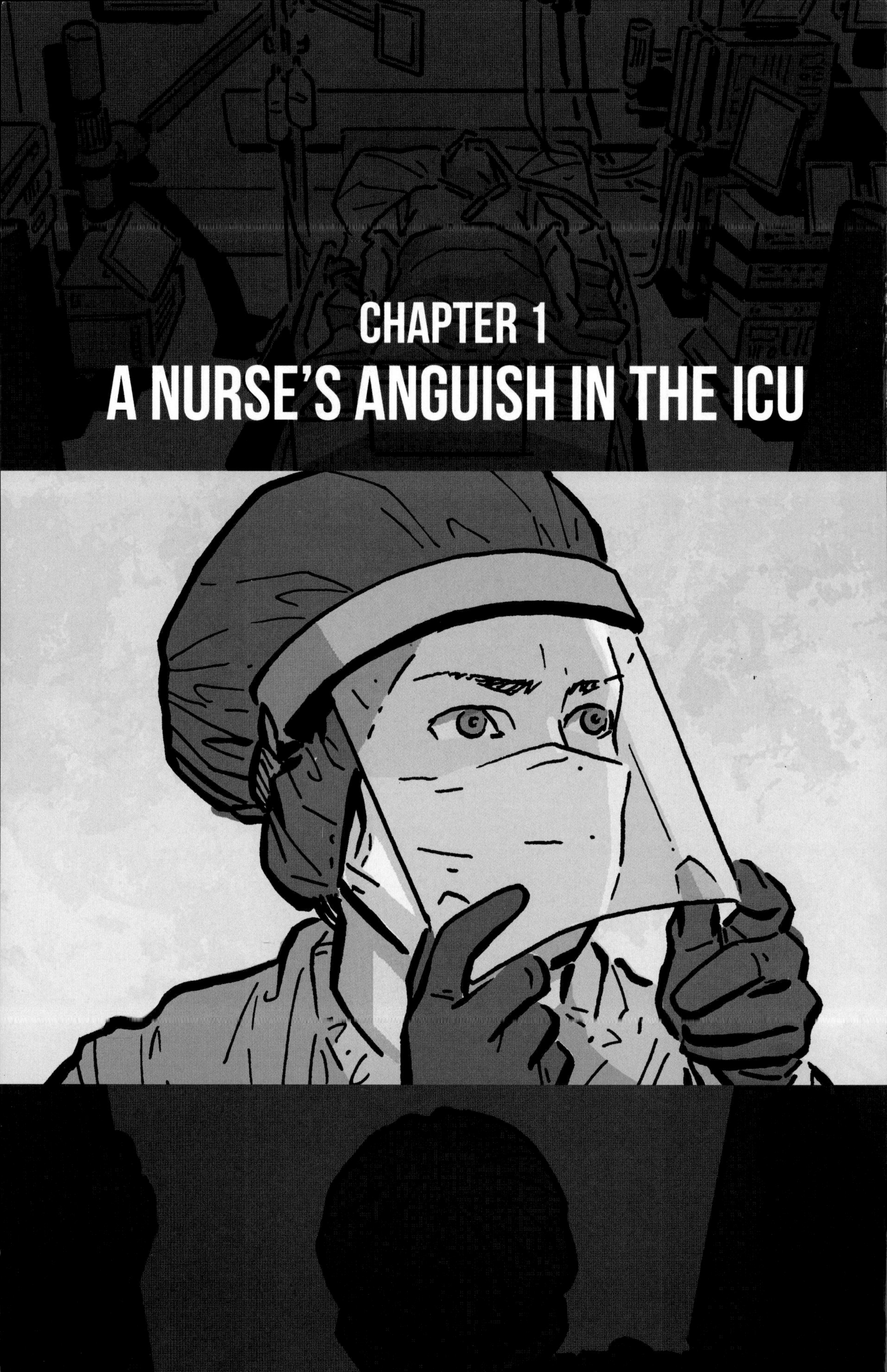

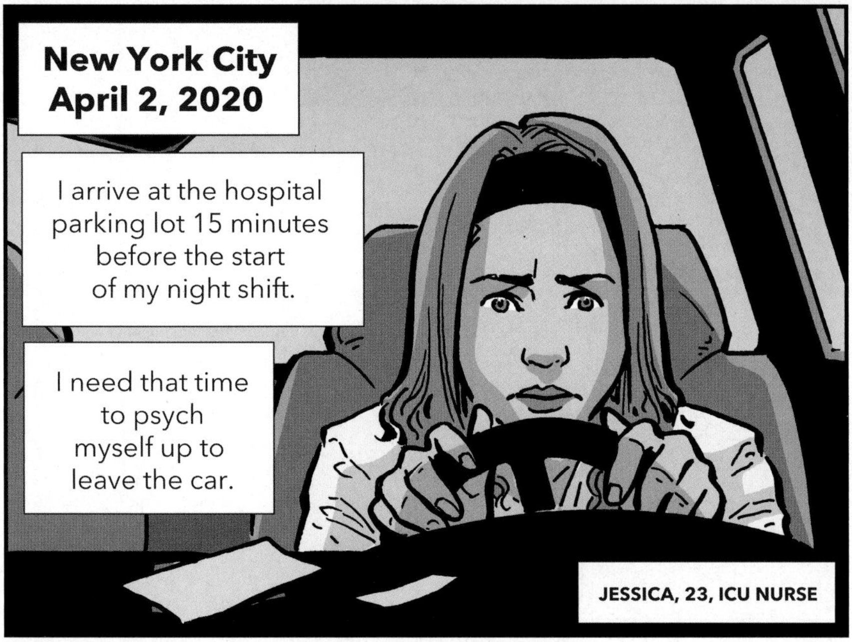
New York City
April 2, 2020
I arrive at the hospital parking lot 15 minutes before the start of my night shift.
I need that time to psych myself up to leave the car.
JESSICA, 23, ICU NURSE

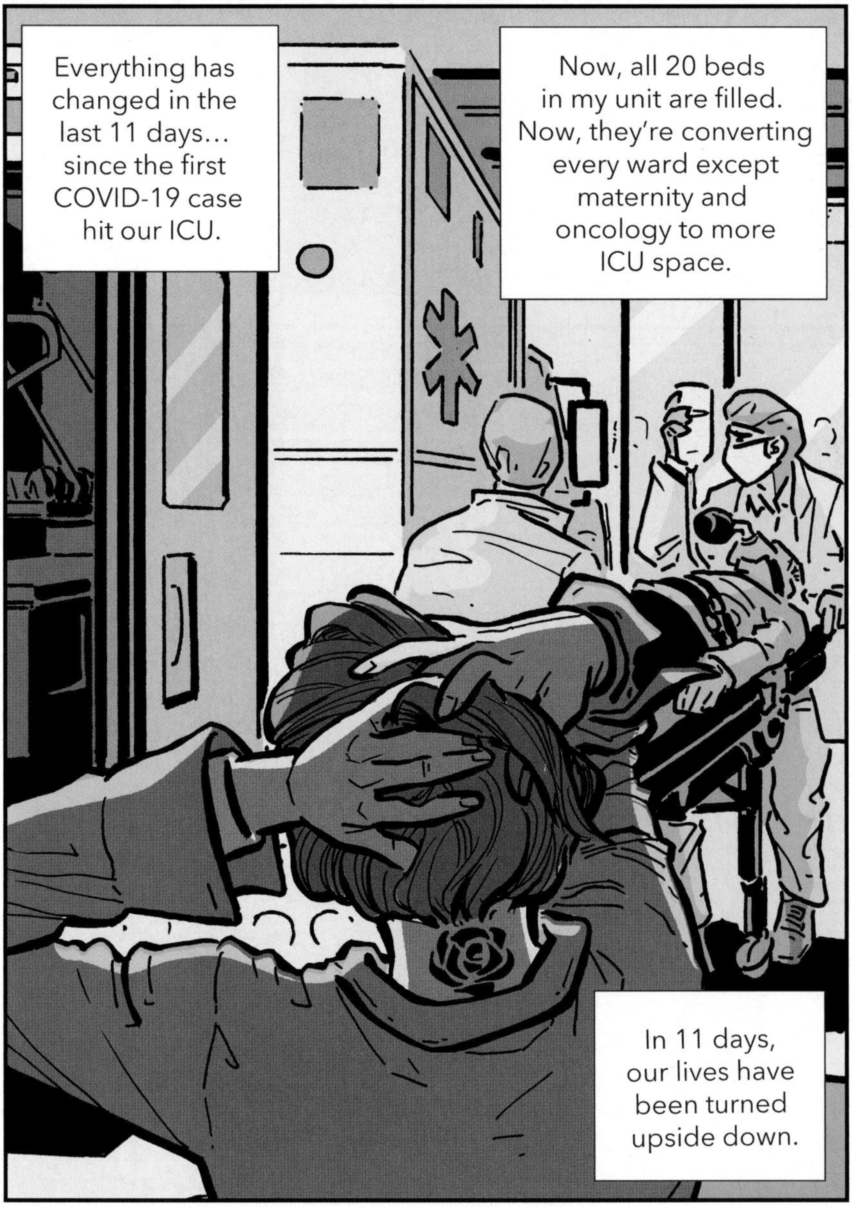
Everything has changed in the last 11 days… since the first COVID-19 case hit our ICU.
Now, all 20 beds in my unit are filled. Now, they're converting every ward except maternity and oncology to more ICU space.
In 11 days, our lives have been turned upside down.

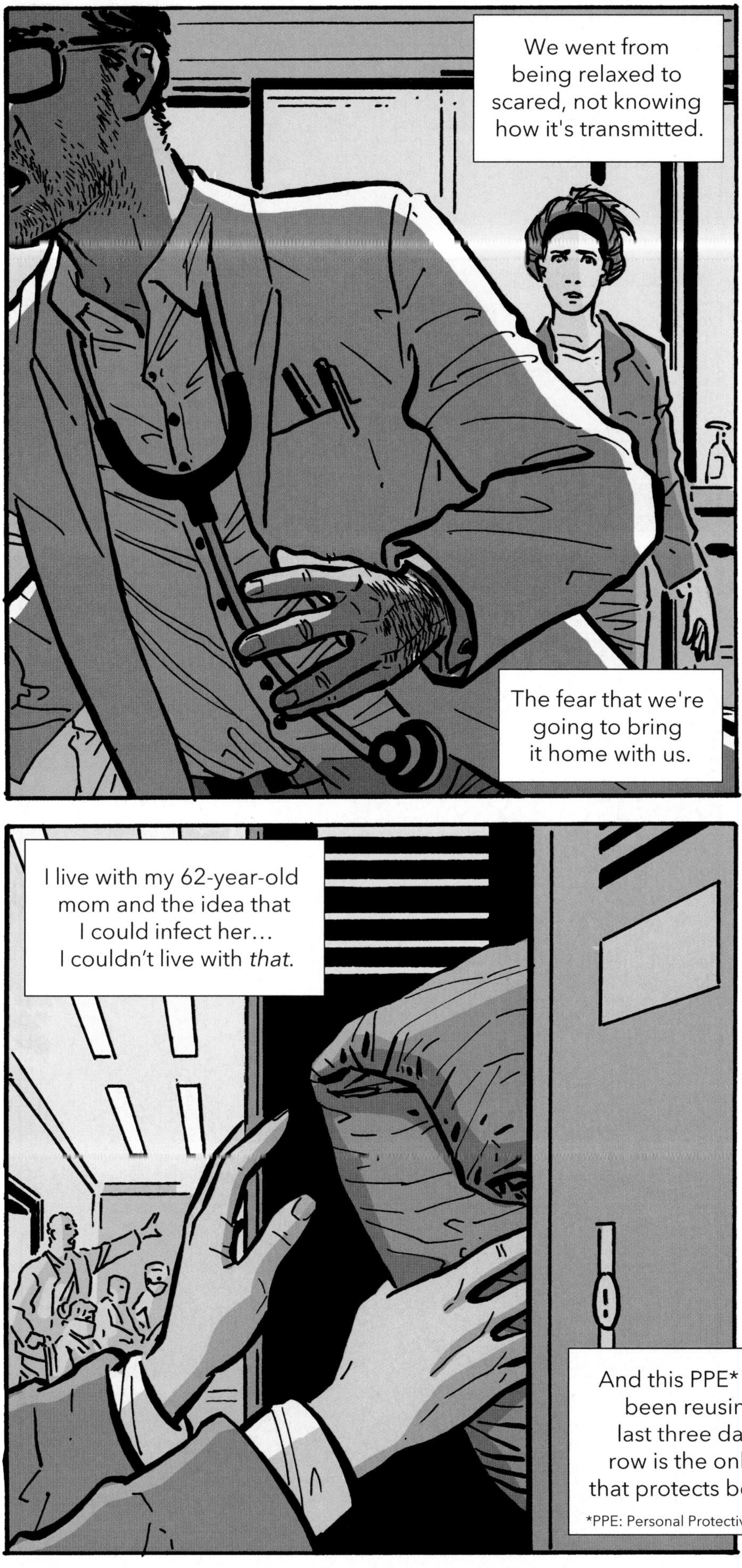
We went from being relaxed to scared, not knowing how it's transmitted.
The fear that we're going to bring it home with us.
I live with my 62-year-old mom and the idea that I could infect her… I couldn't live with *that*.
And this PPE* that I've been reusing the last three days in a row is the only thing that protects both of us.
*PPE: Personal Protective Equipment

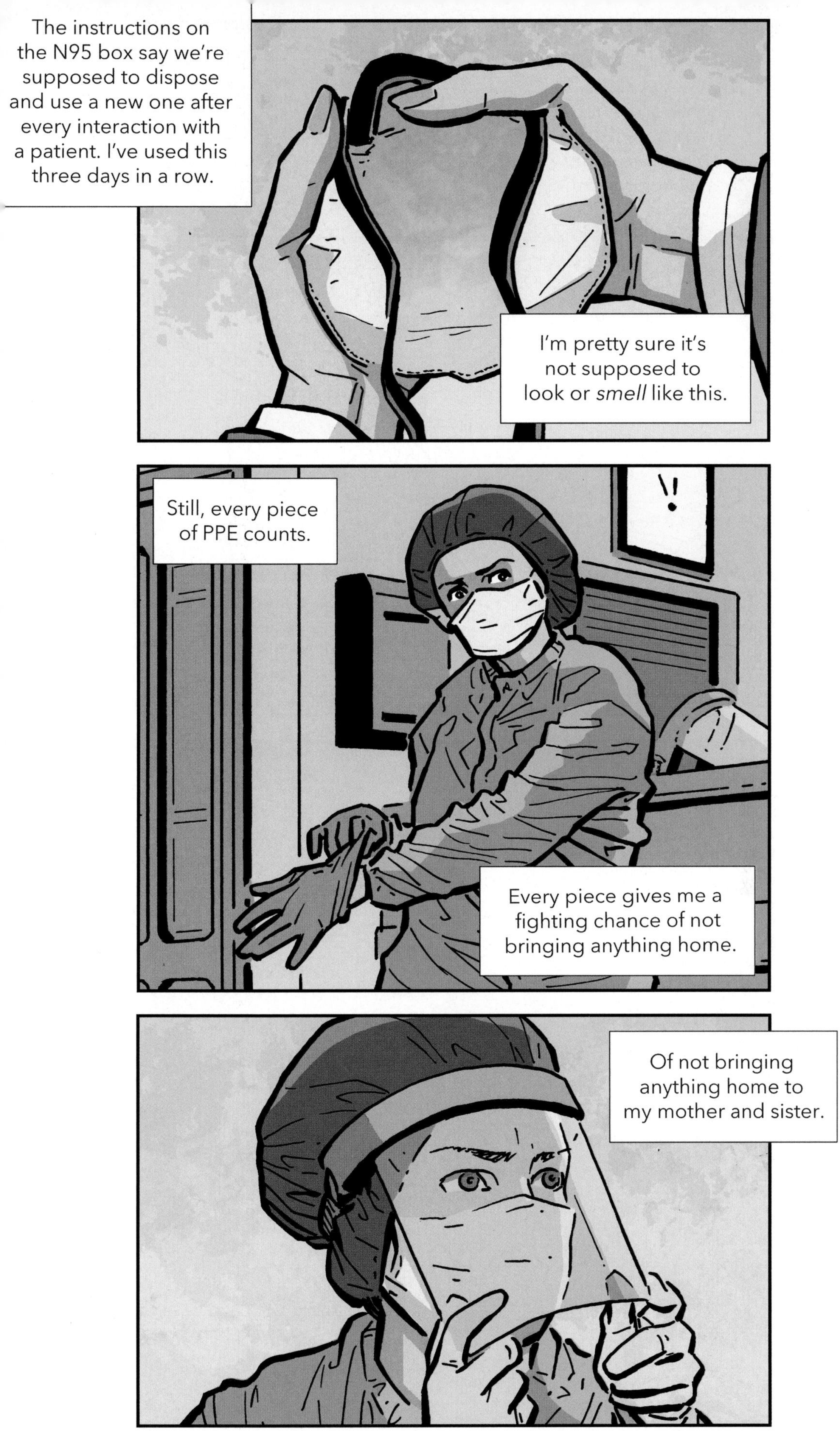

The instructions on the N95 box say we're supposed to dispose and use a new one after every interaction with a patient. I've used this three days in a row.
I'm pretty sure it's not supposed to look or *smell* like this.
Still, every piece of PPE counts.
Every piece gives me a fighting chance of not bringing anything home.
Of not bringing anything home to my mother and sister.

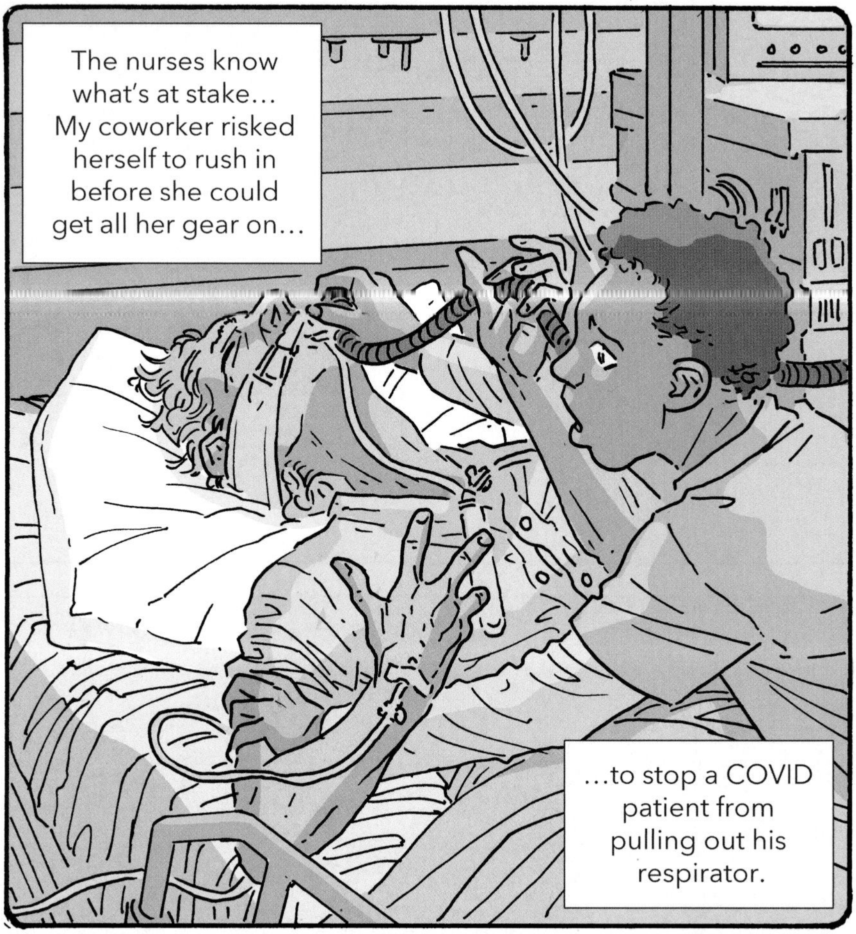
The nurses know what's at stake… My coworker risked herself to rush in before she could get all her gear on…
…to stop a COVID patient from pulling out his respirator.

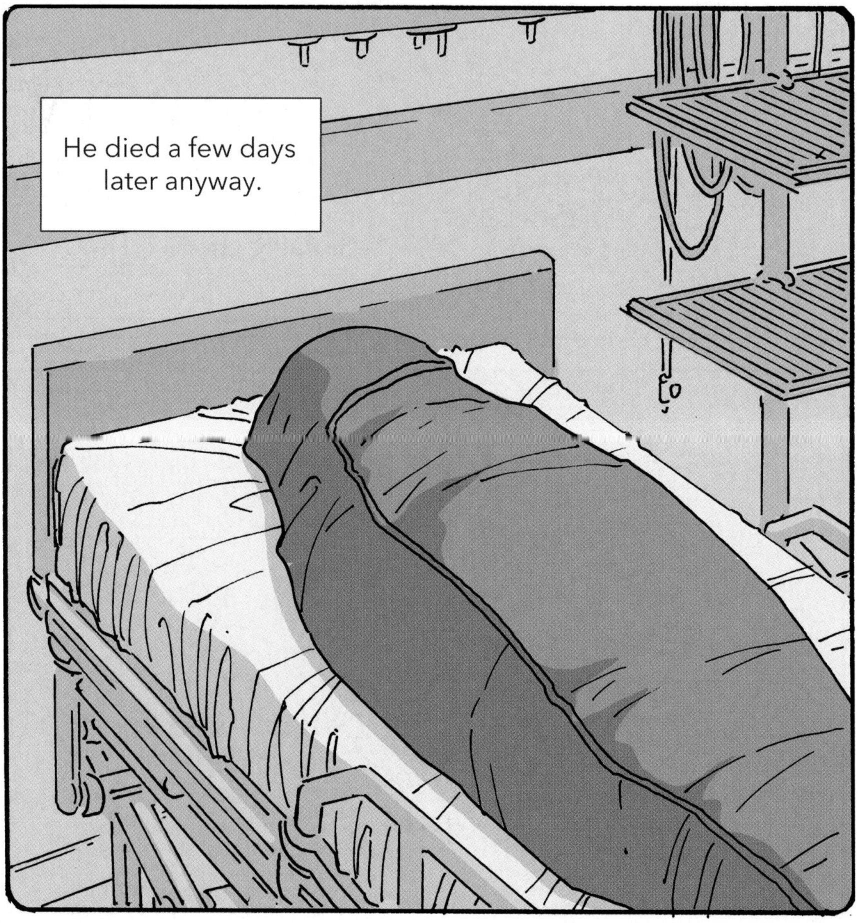
He died a few days later anyway.

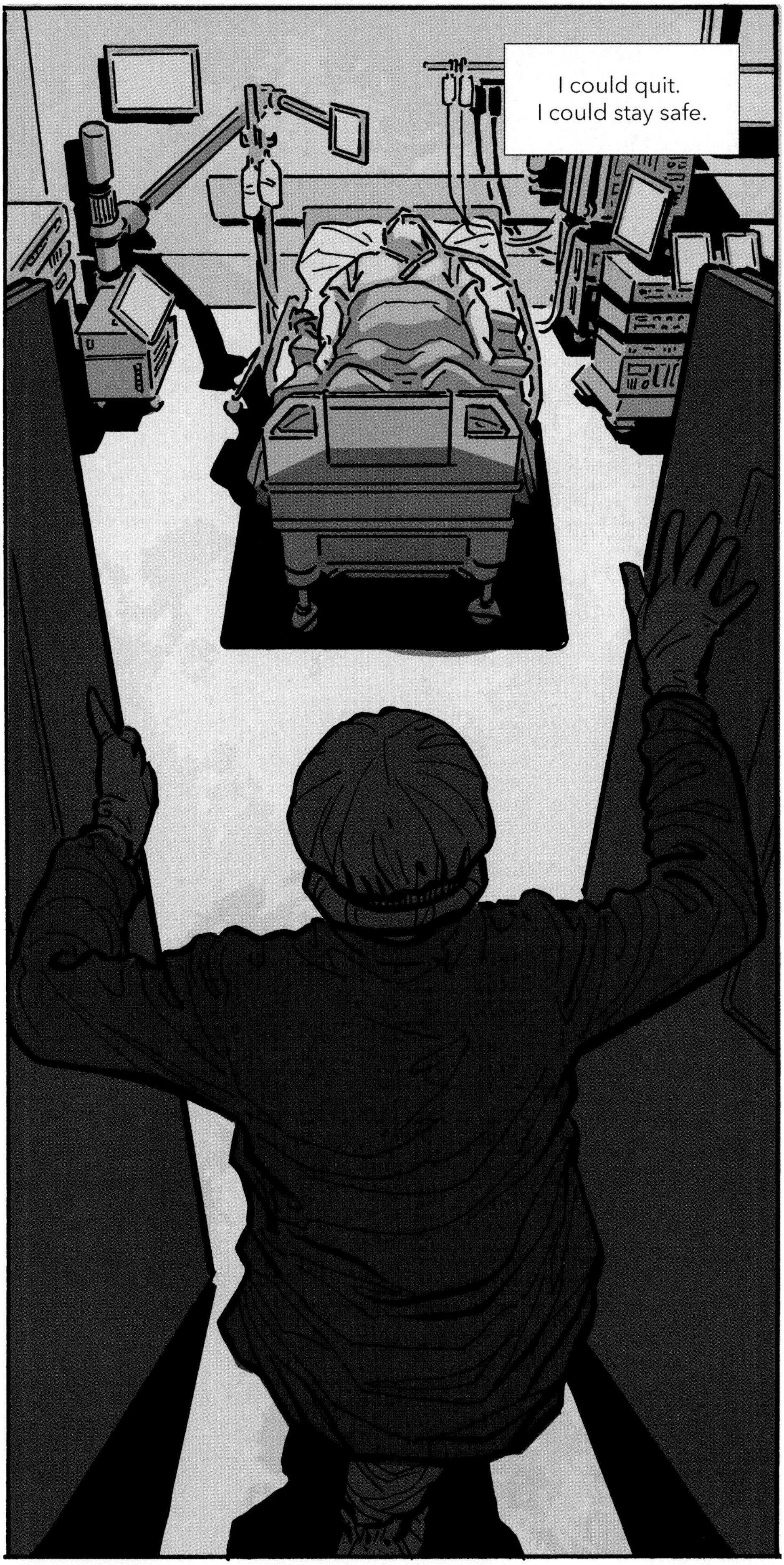
I could quit.
I could stay safe.

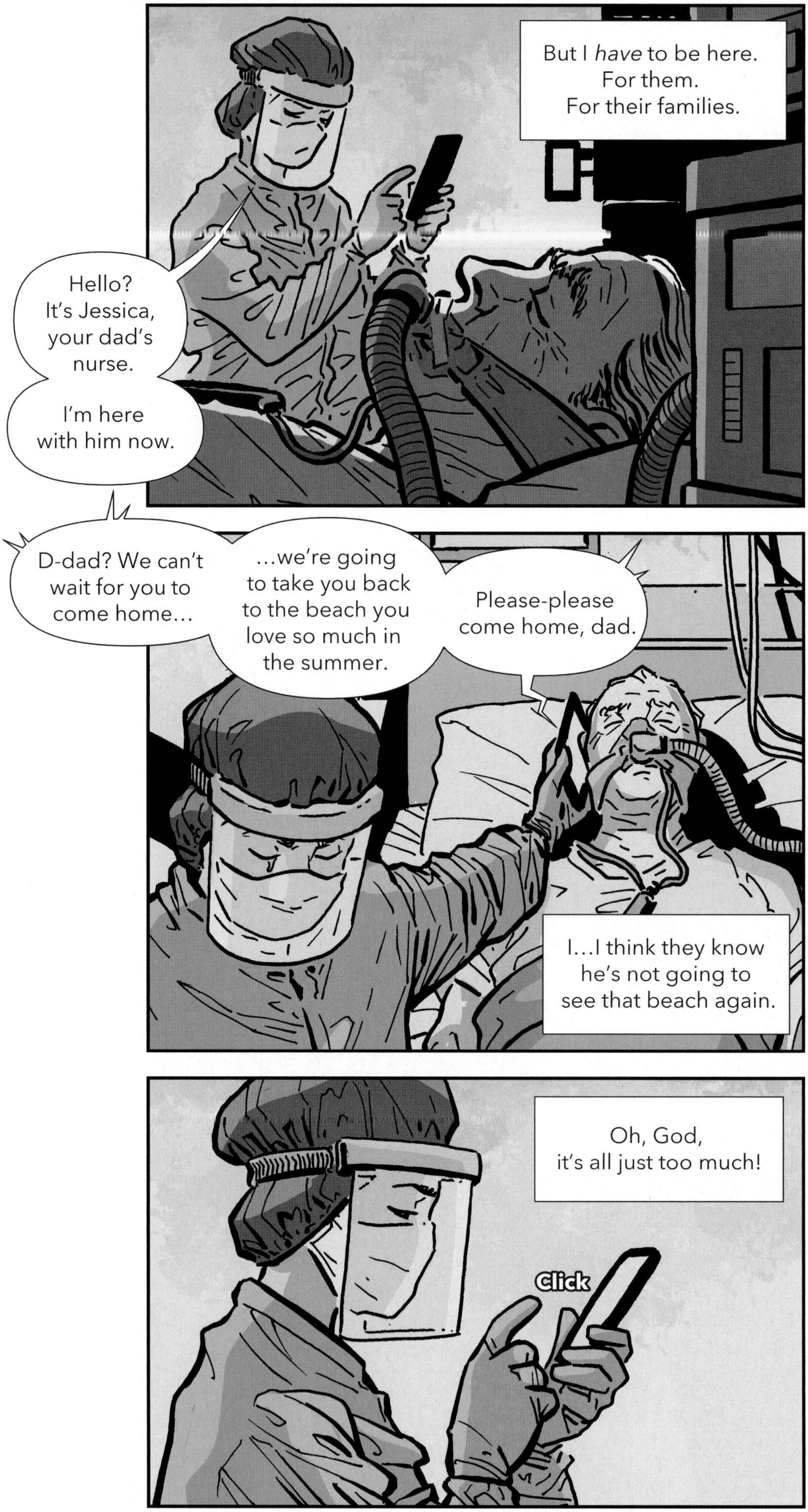
But I *have* to be here. For them. For their families.
Hello? It's Jessica, your dad's nurse.
I'm here with him now.
D-dad? We can't wait for you to come home...
...we're going to take you back to the beach you love so much in the summer.
Please-please come home, dad.
I...I think they know he's not going to see that beach again.
Oh, God, it's all just too much!
Click

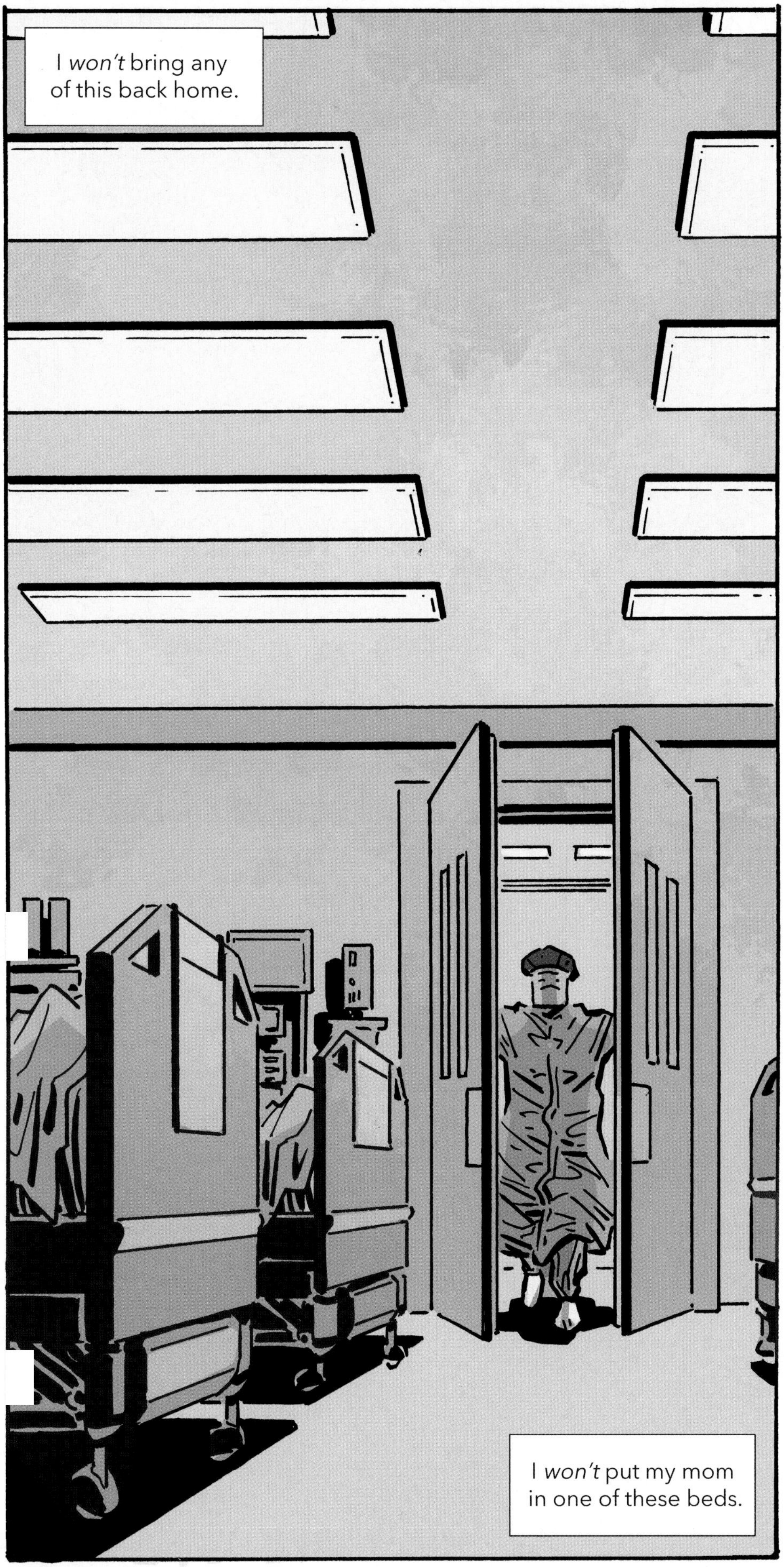
I *won't* bring any of this back home.
I *won't* put my mom in one of these beds.

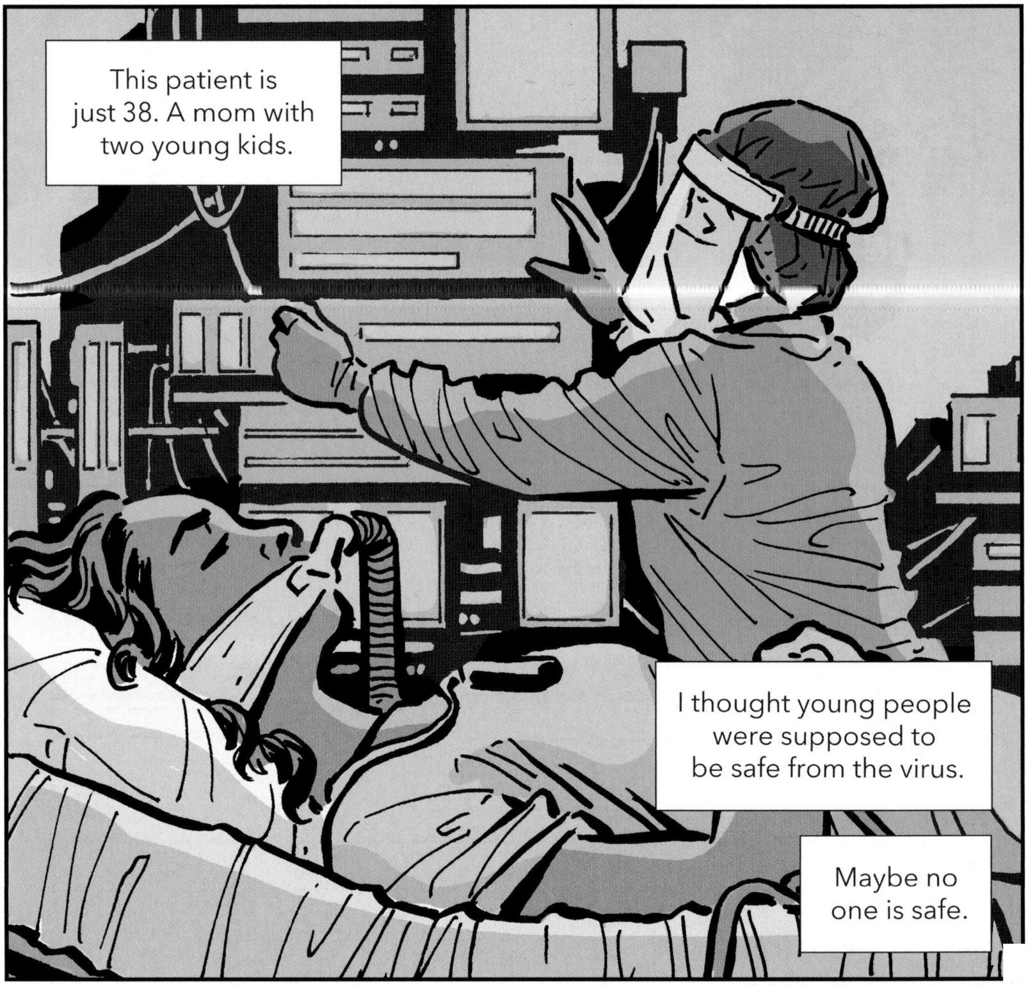
This patient is just 38. A mom with two young kids.
I thought young people were supposed to be safe from the virus.
Maybe no one is safe.

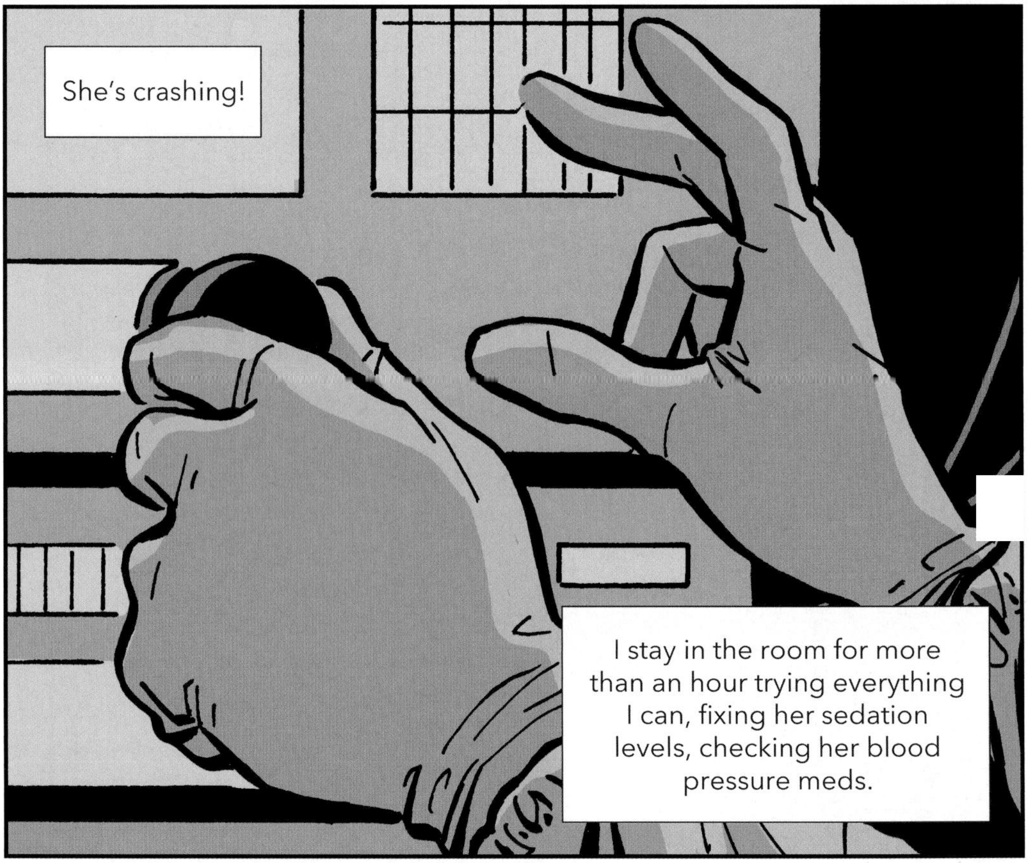
She's crashing!
I stay in the room for more than an hour trying everything I can, fixing her sedation levels, checking her blood pressure meds.

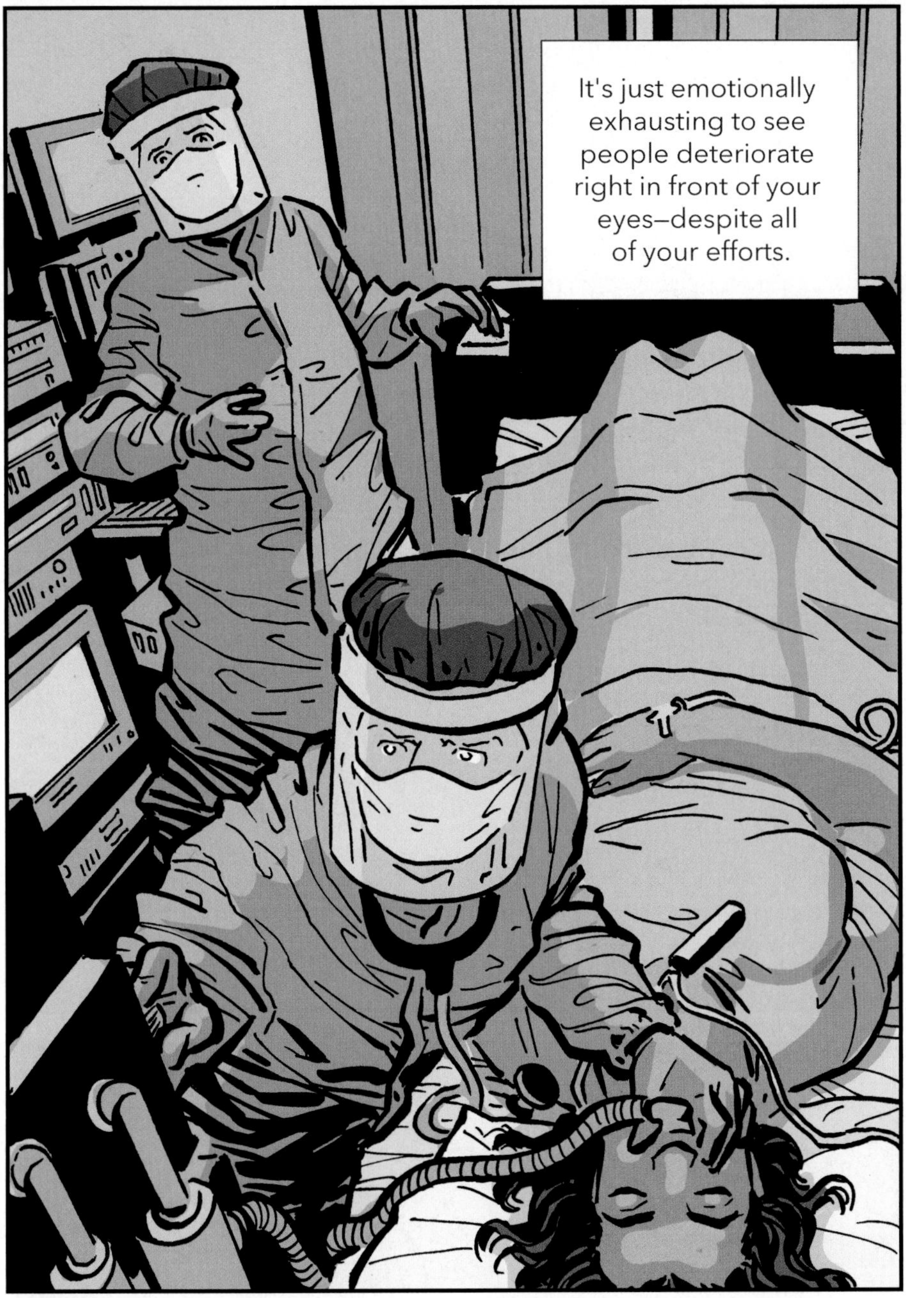
It's just emotionally exhausting to see people deteriorate right in front of your eyes—despite all of your efforts.

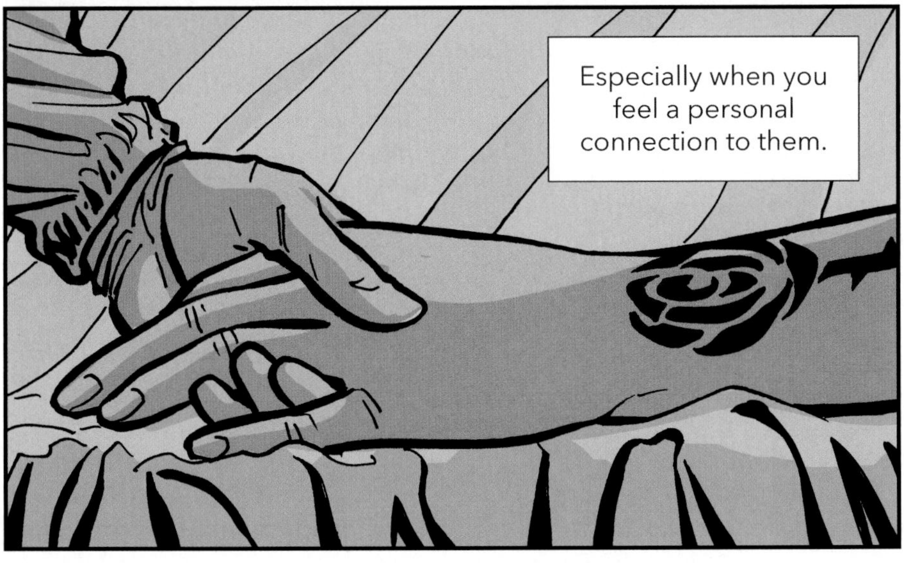
Especially when you feel a personal connection to them.

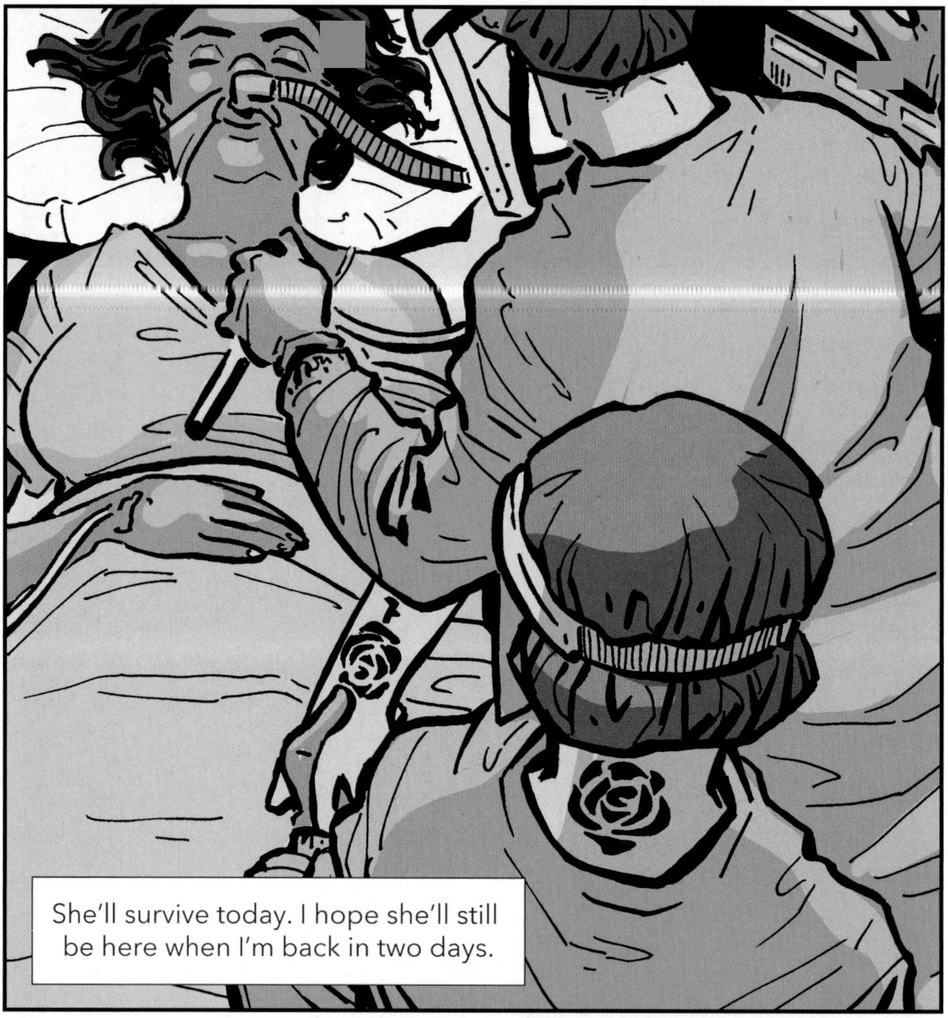
She'll survive today. I hope she'll still be here when I'm back in two days.

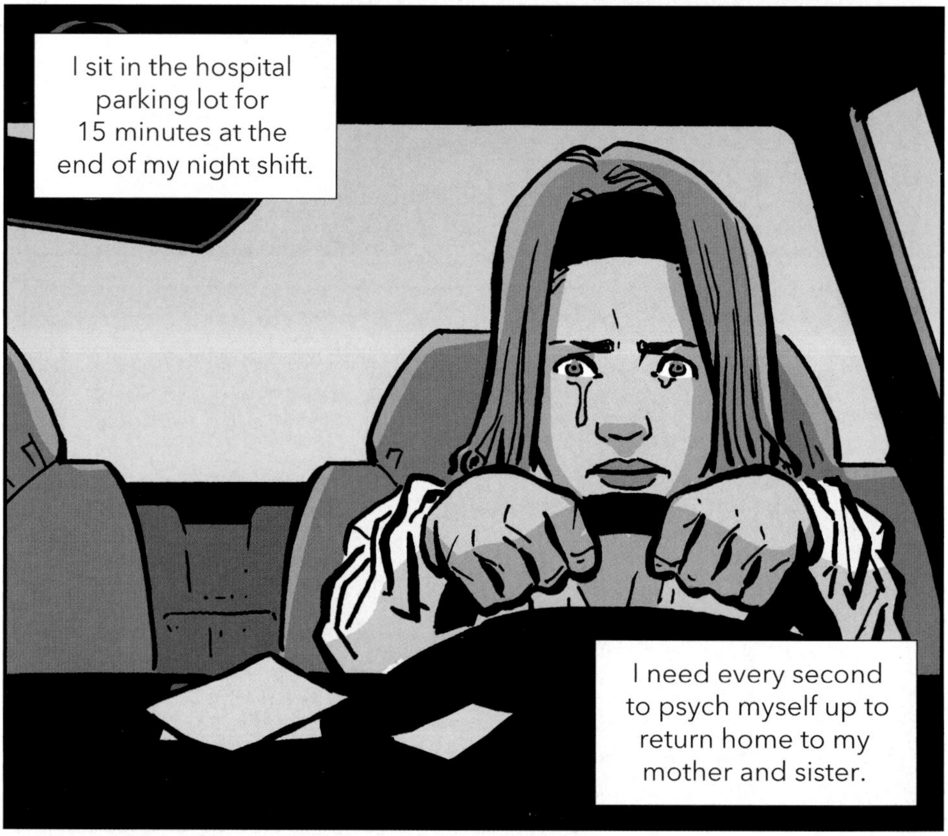
I sit in the hospital parking lot for 15 minutes at the end of my night shift.
I need every second to psych myself up to return home to my mother and sister.

CHAPTER 2
‘I THINK THIS VIRUS IS TRYING TO KILL ME’

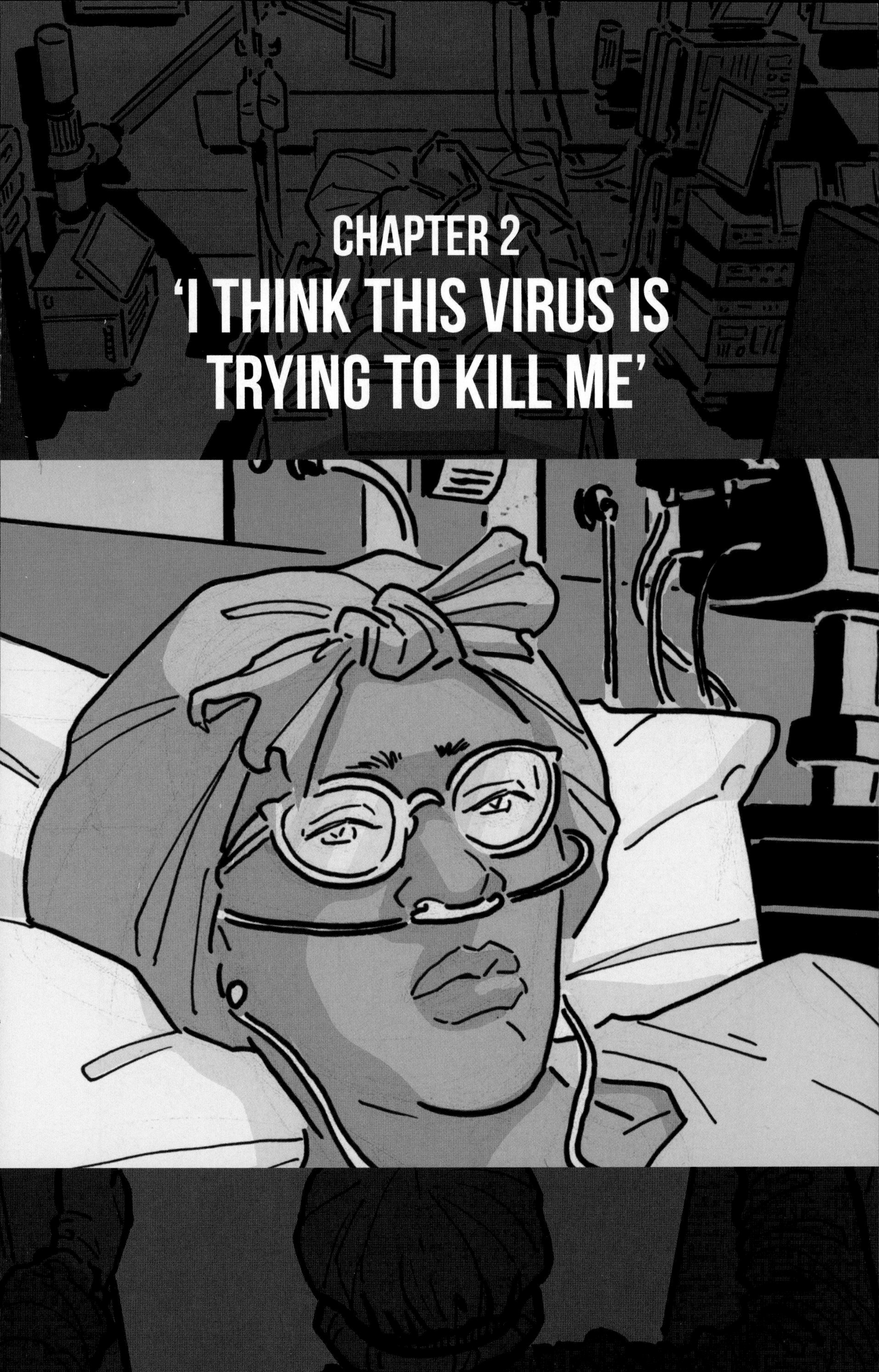

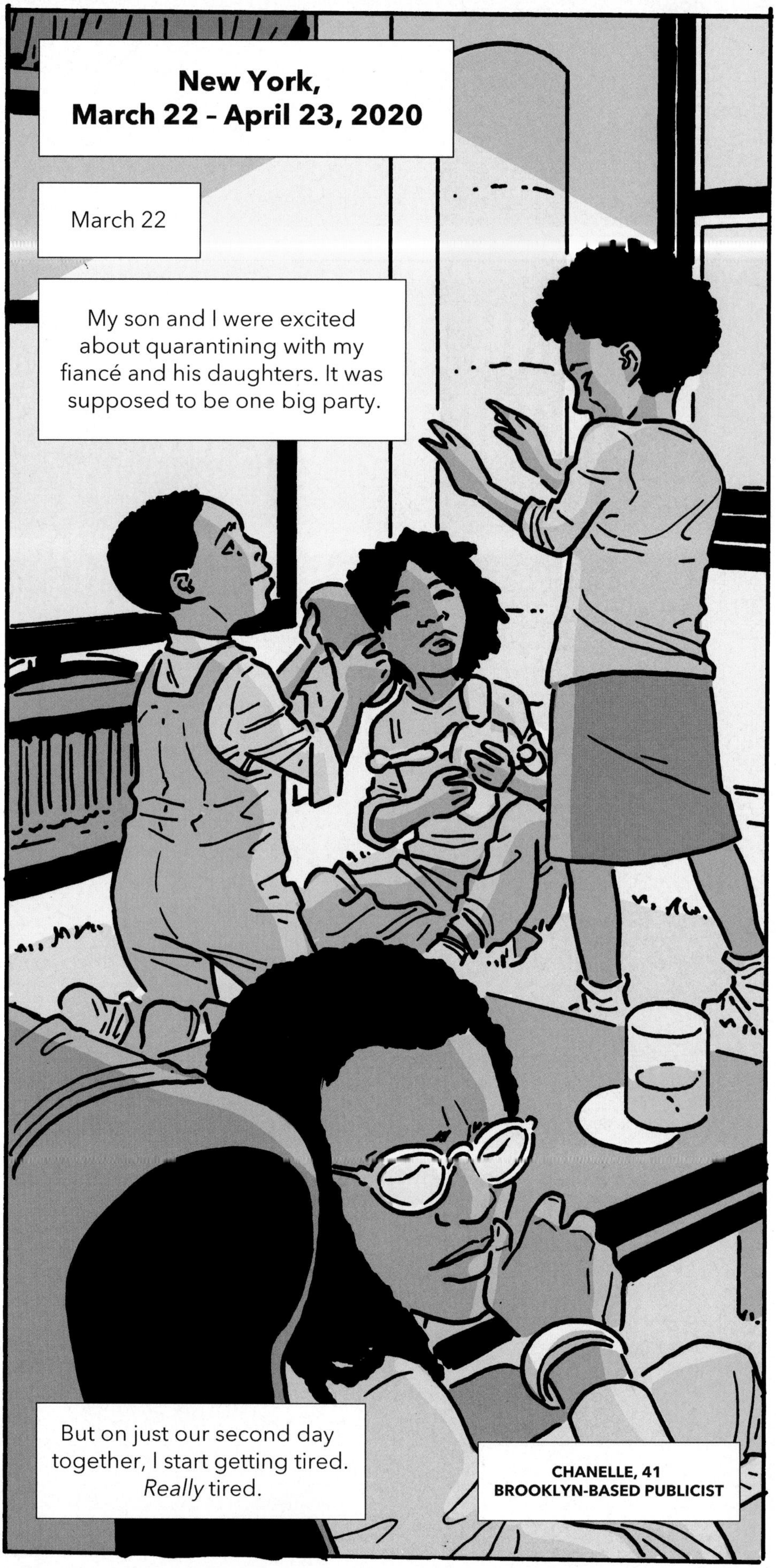

New York,
March 22 – April 23, 2020
March 22
My son and I were excited about quarantining with my fiancé and his daughters. It was supposed to be one big party.
But on just our second day together, I start getting tired. *Really* tired.
CHANELLE, 41
BROOKLYN-BASED PUBLICIST

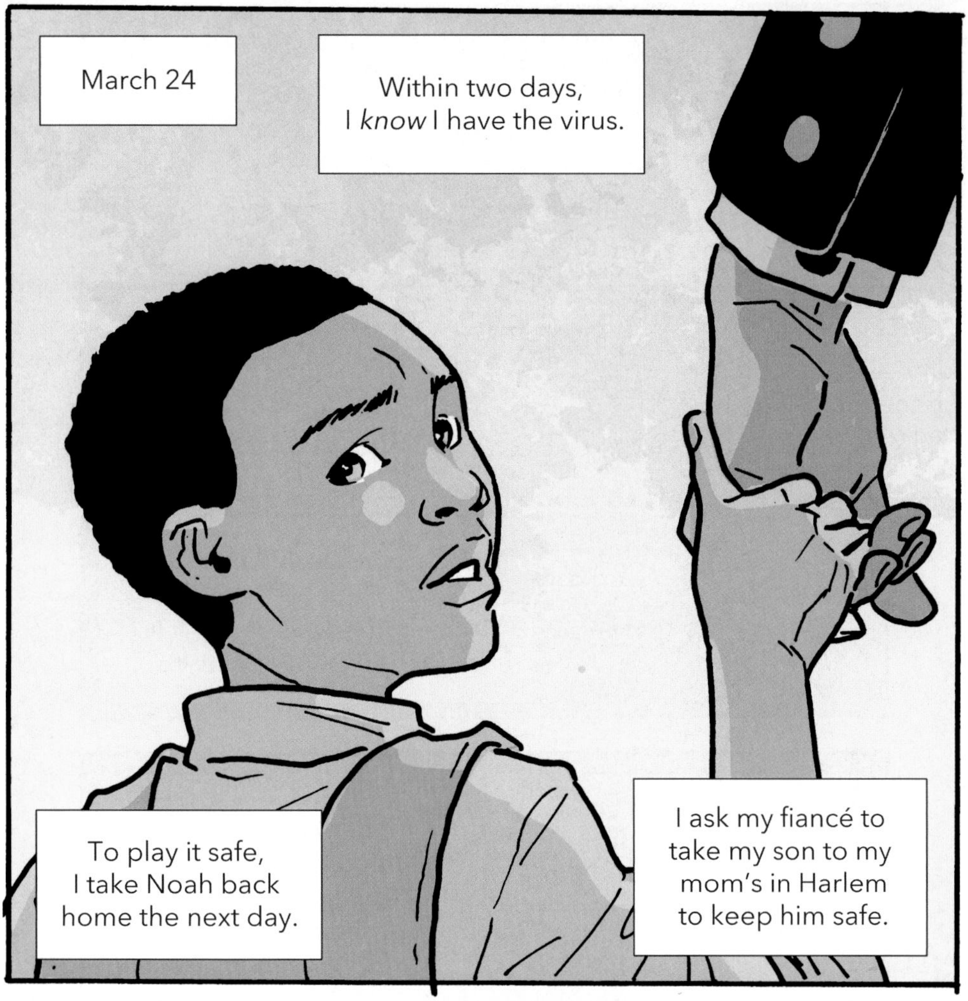
March 24
Within two days, I *know* I have the virus.
To play it safe, I take Noah back home the next day.
I ask my fiancé to take my son to my mom's in Harlem to keep him safe.

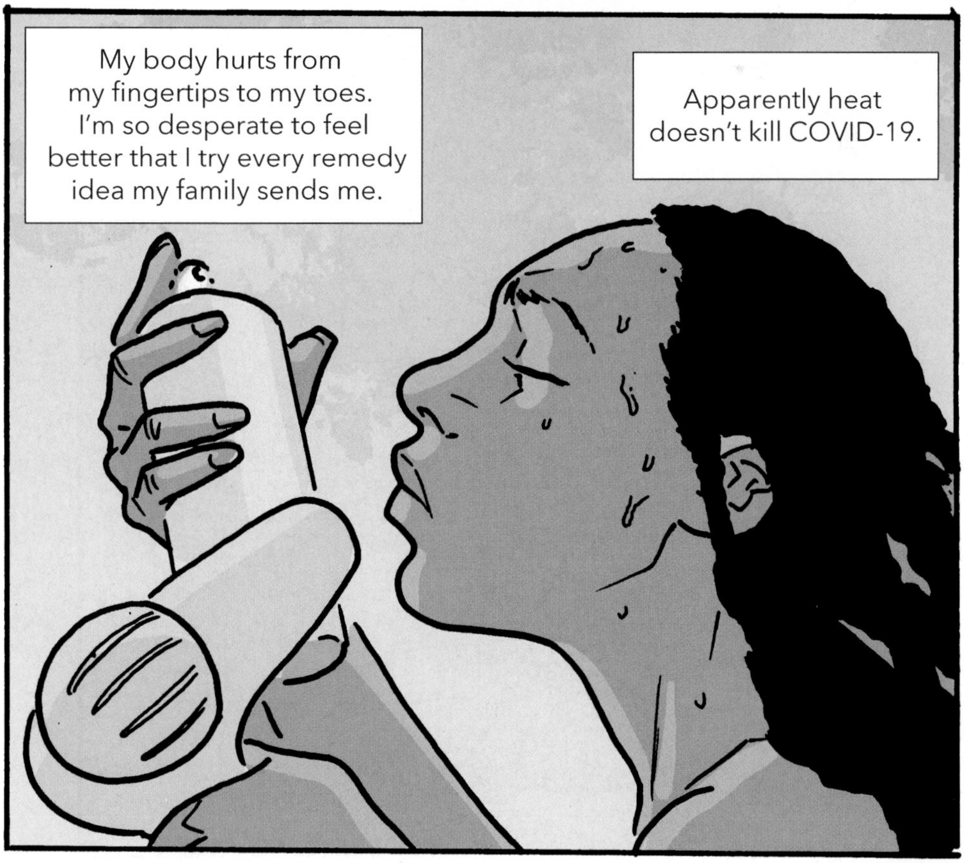
My body hurts from my fingertips to my toes. I'm so desperate to feel better that I try every remedy idea my family sends me.
Apparently heat doesn't kill COVID-19.

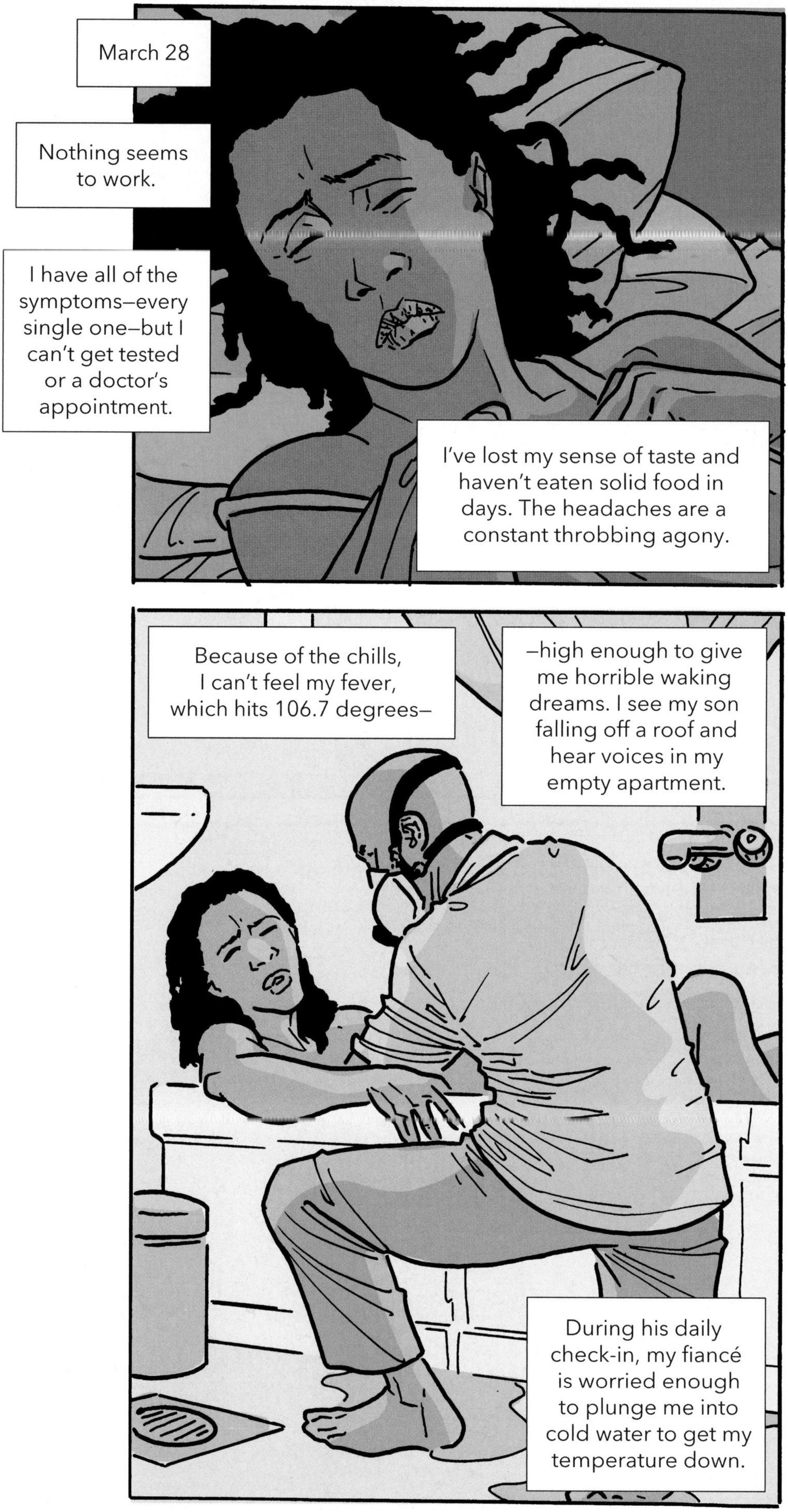
March 28
Nothing seems to work.
I have all of the symptoms—every single one—but I can't get tested or a doctor's appointment.
I've lost my sense of taste and haven't eaten solid food in days. The headaches are a constant throbbing agony.
Because of the chills, I can't feel my fever, which hits 106.7 degrees—
—high enough to give me horrible waking dreams. I see my son falling off a roof and hear voices in my empty apartment.
During his daily check-in, my fiancé is worried enough to plunge me into cold water to get my temperature down.

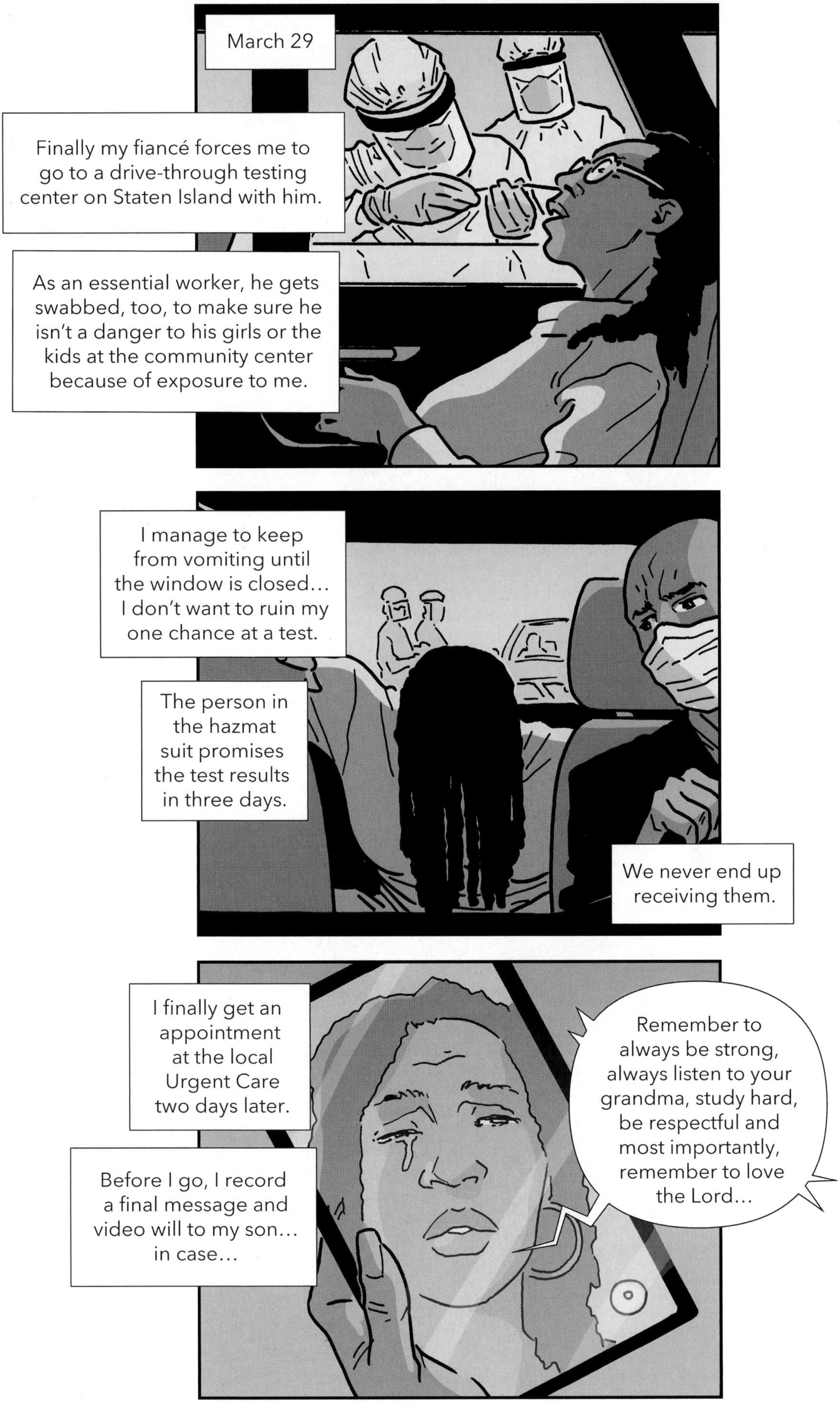
March 29
Finally my fiancé forces me to go to a drive-through testing center on Staten Island with him.
As an essential worker, he gets swabbed, too, to make sure he isn't a danger to his girls or the kids at the community center because of exposure to me.
I manage to keep from vomiting until the window is closed... I don't want to ruin my one chance at a test.
The person in the hazmat suit promises the test results in three days.
We never end up receiving them.
I finally get an appointment at the local Urgent Care two days later.
Before I go, I record a final message and video will to my son... in case...
Remember to always be strong, always listen to your grandma, study hard, be respectful and most importantly, remember to love the Lord...

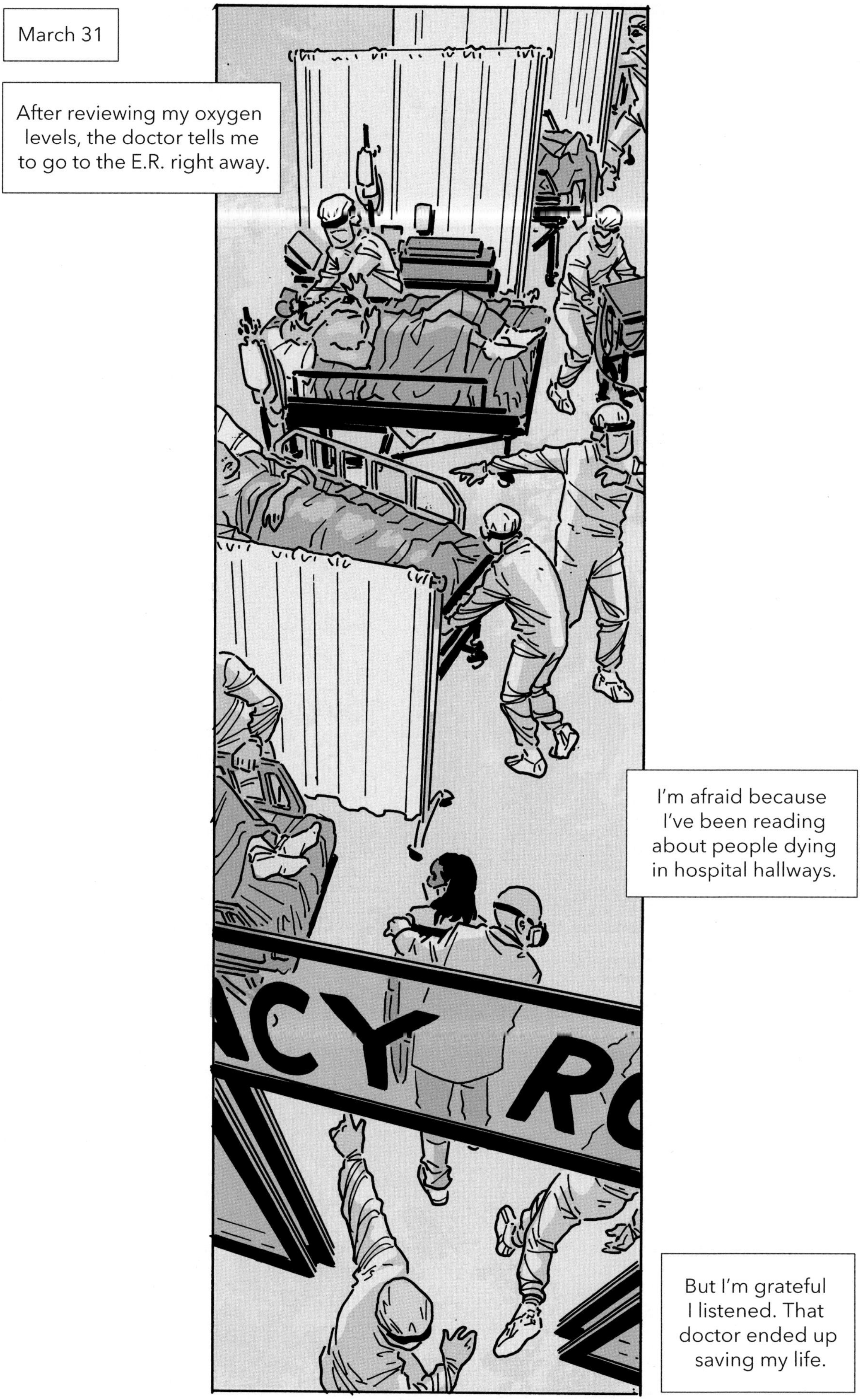
March 31
After reviewing my oxygen levels, the doctor tells me to go to the E.R. right away.
I'm afraid because I've been reading about people dying in hospital hallways.
But I'm grateful I listened. That doctor ended up saving my life.

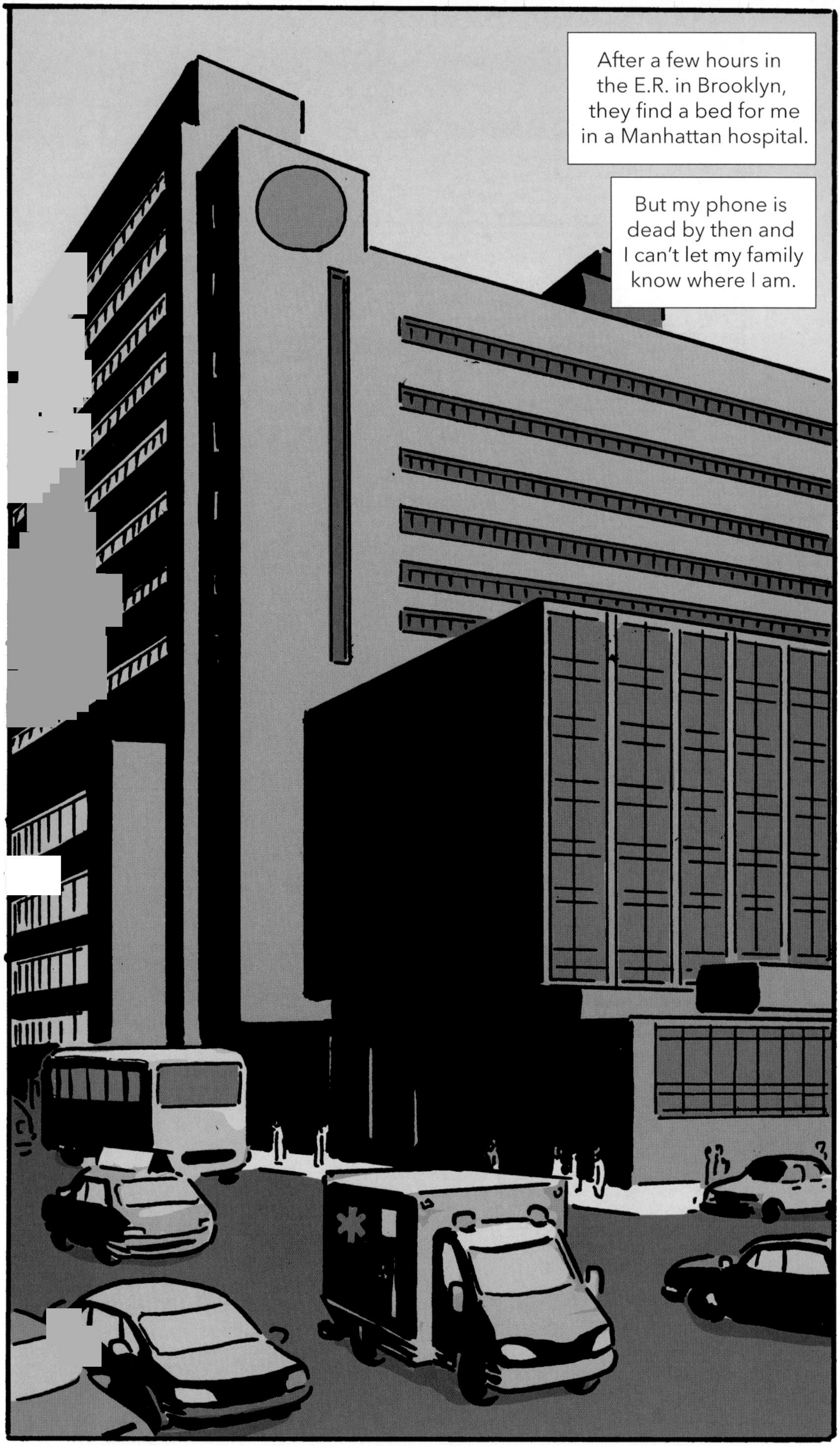
After a few hours in the E.R. in Brooklyn, they find a bed for me in a Manhattan hospital.
But my phone is dead by then and I can't let my family know where I am.

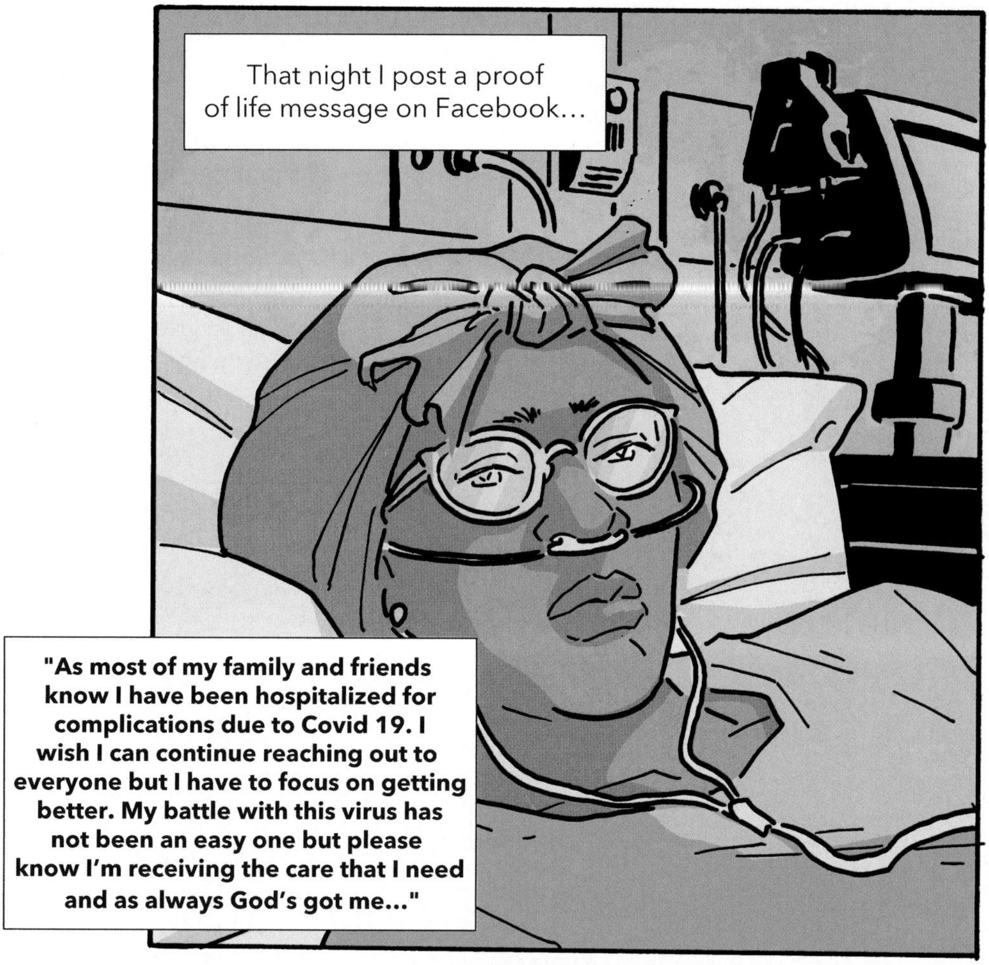
That night I post a proof of life message on Facebook…
"As most of my family and friends know I have been hospitalized for complications due to Covid 19. I wish I can continue reaching out to everyone but I have to focus on getting better. My battle with this virus has not been an easy one but please know I'm receiving the care that I need and as always God's got me..."

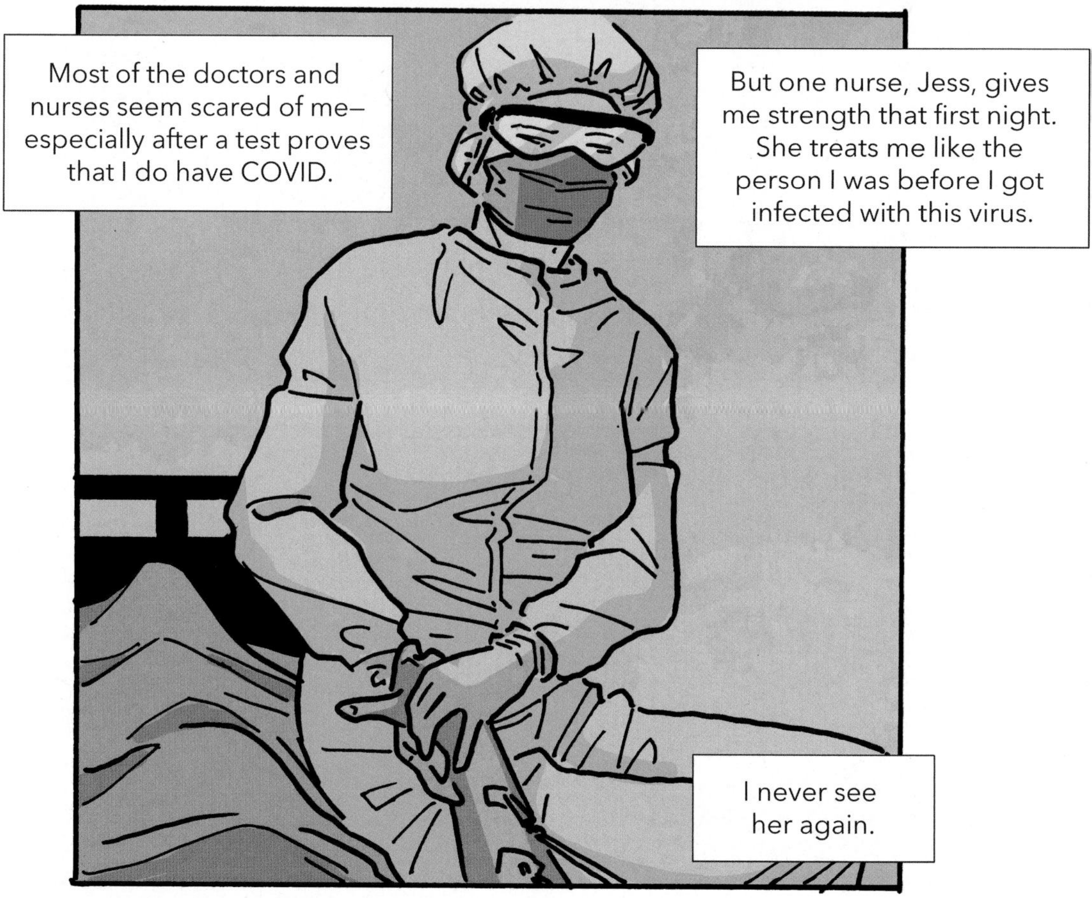
Most of the doctors and nurses seem scared of me—especially after a test proves that I do have COVID.
But one nurse, Jess, gives me strength that first night. She treats me like the person I was before I got infected with this virus.
I never see her again.

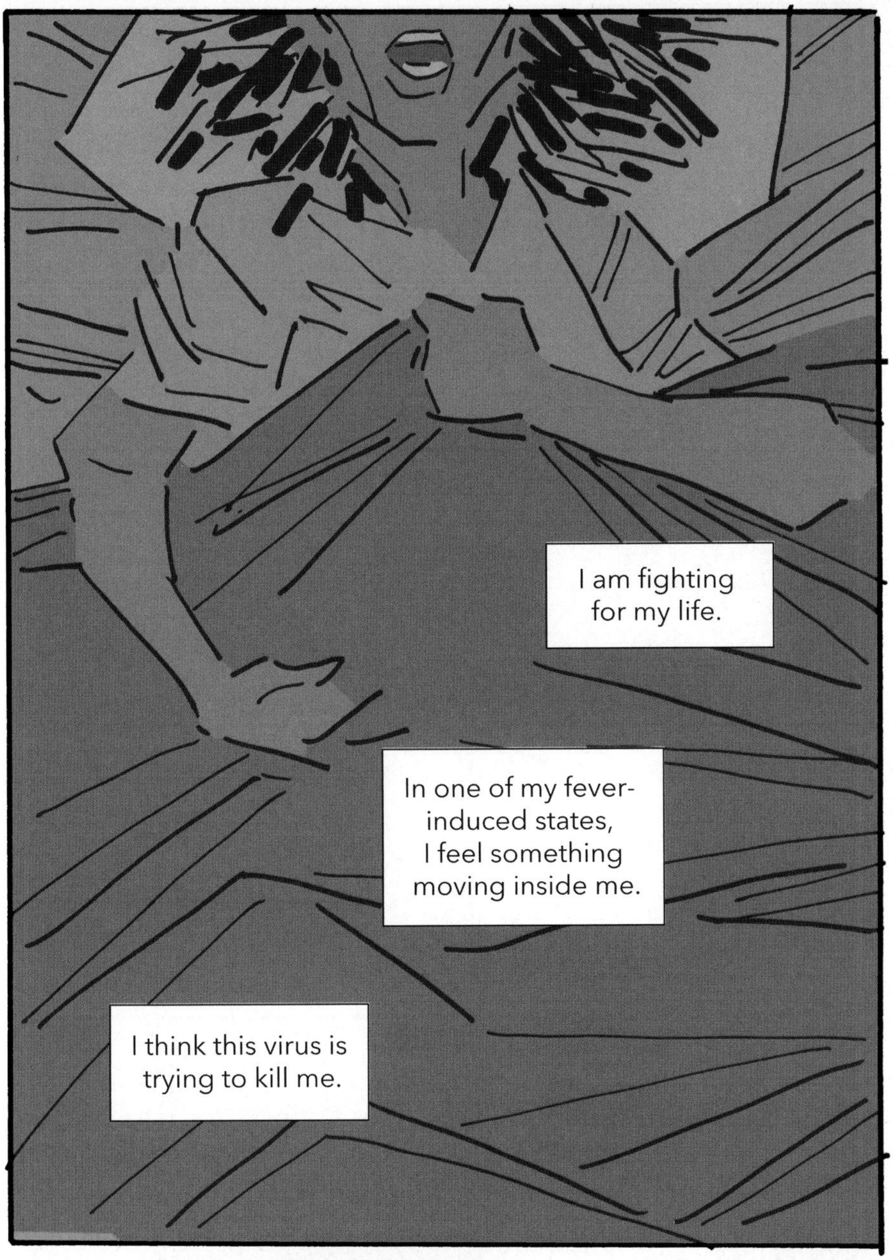
I am fighting
for my life.
In one of my fever-
induced states,
I feel something
moving inside me.
I think this virus is
trying to kill me.

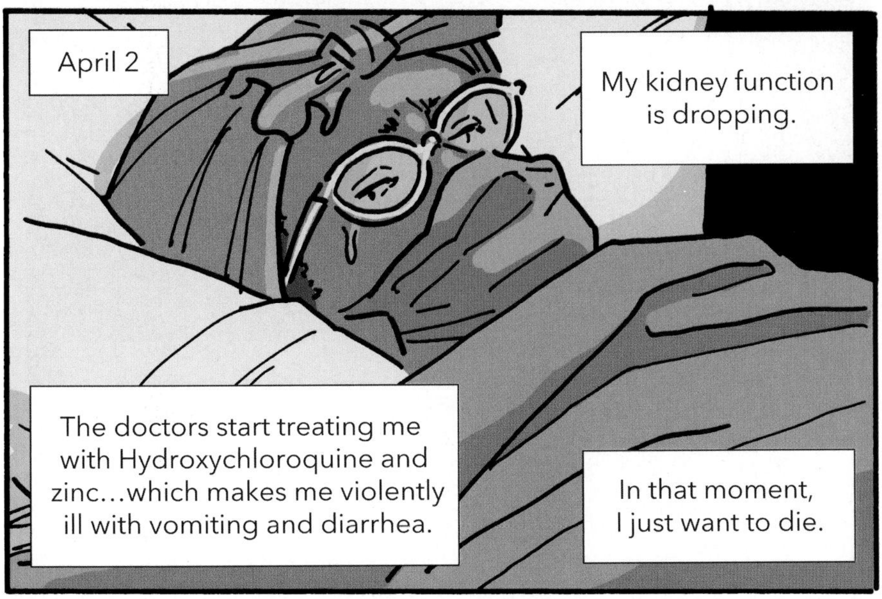
April 2
My kidney function
is dropping.
The doctors start treating me
with Hydroxychloroquine and
zinc…which makes me violently
ill with vomiting and diarrhea.
In that moment,
I just want to die.

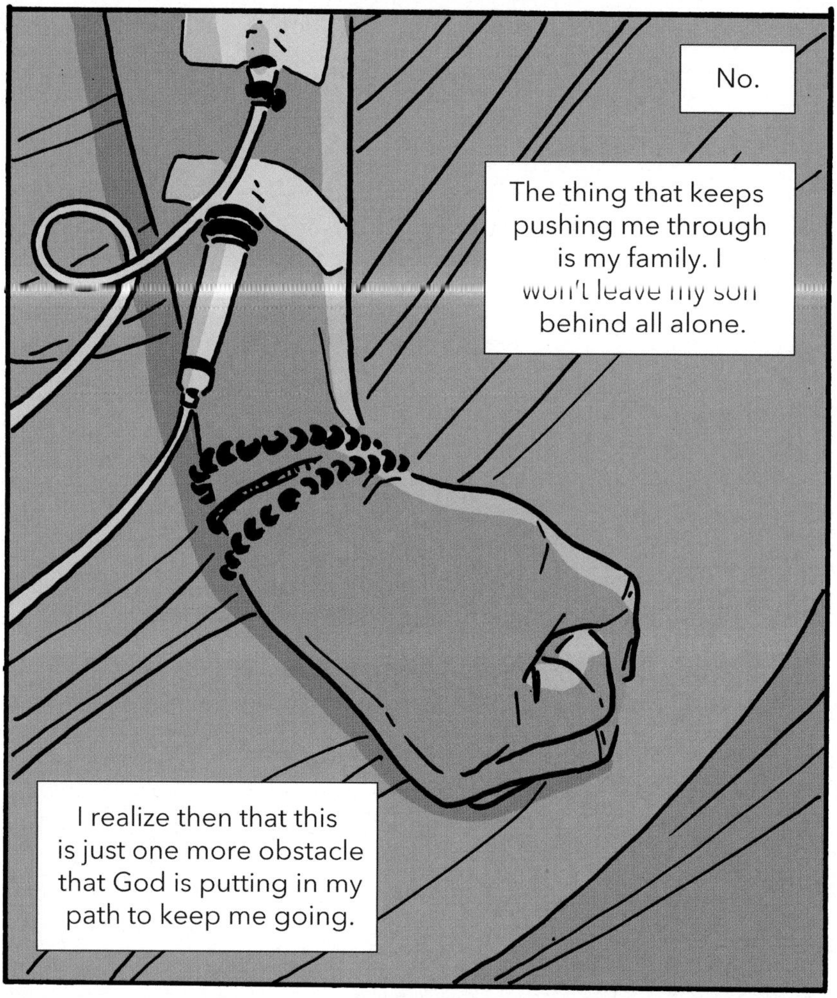
No.
The thing that keeps pushing me through is my family. I won't leave my son behind all alone.
I realize then that this is just one more obstacle that God is putting in my path to keep me going.

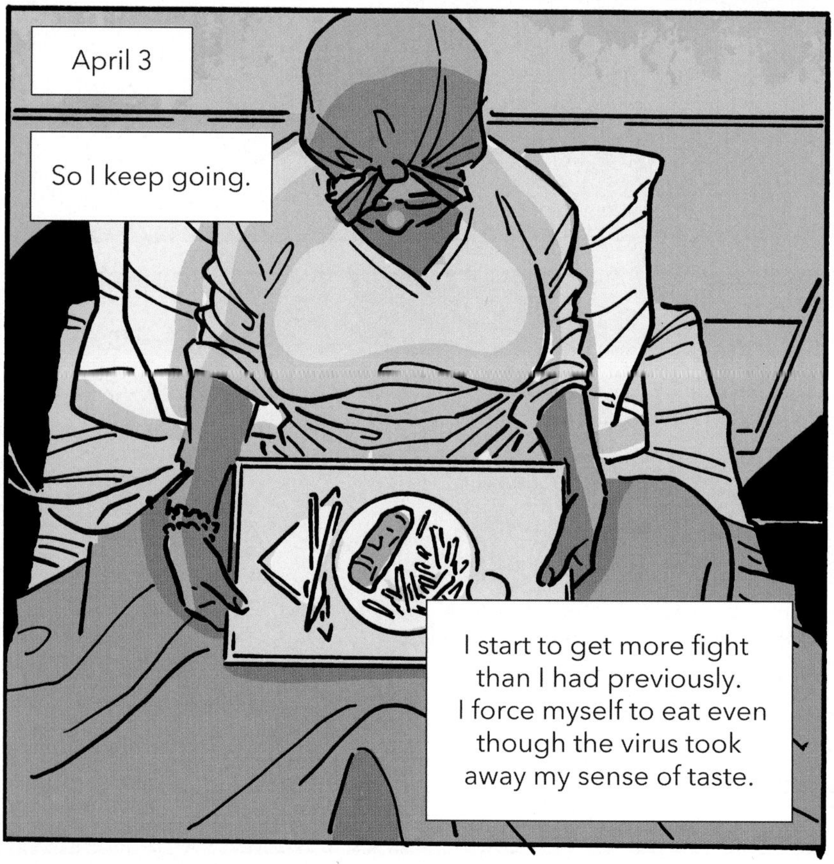
April 3
So I keep going.
I start to get more fight than I had previously. I force myself to eat even though the virus took away my sense of taste.

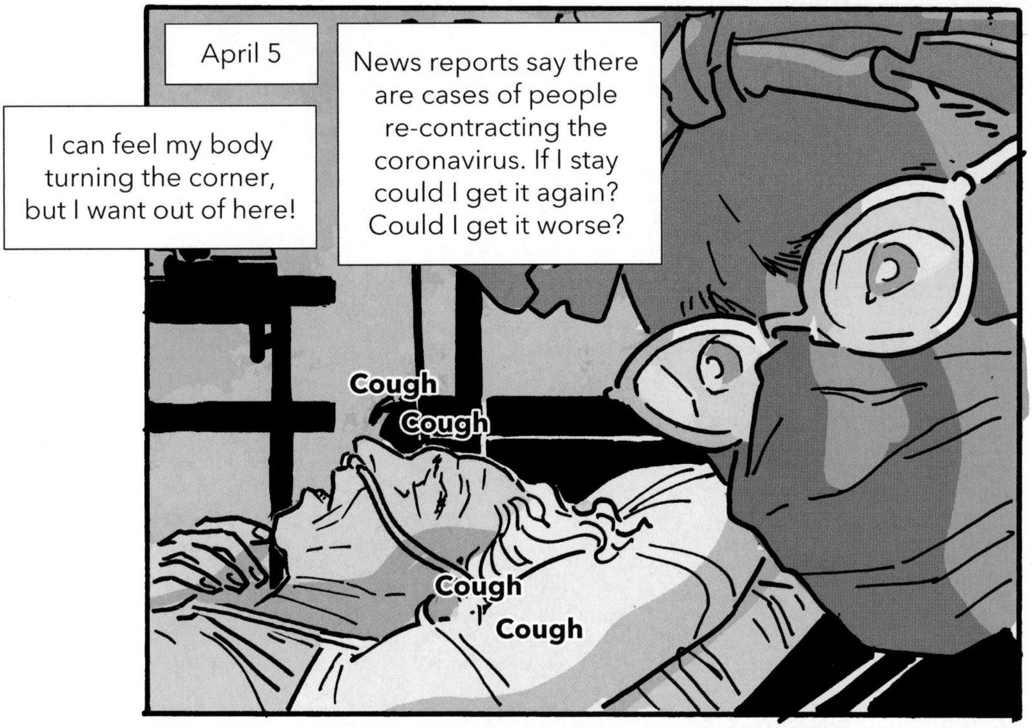
April 5
I can feel my body turning the corner, but I want out of here!
News reports say there are cases of people re-contracting the coronavirus. If I stay could I get it again? Could I get it worse?
Cough
Cough
Cough
Cough

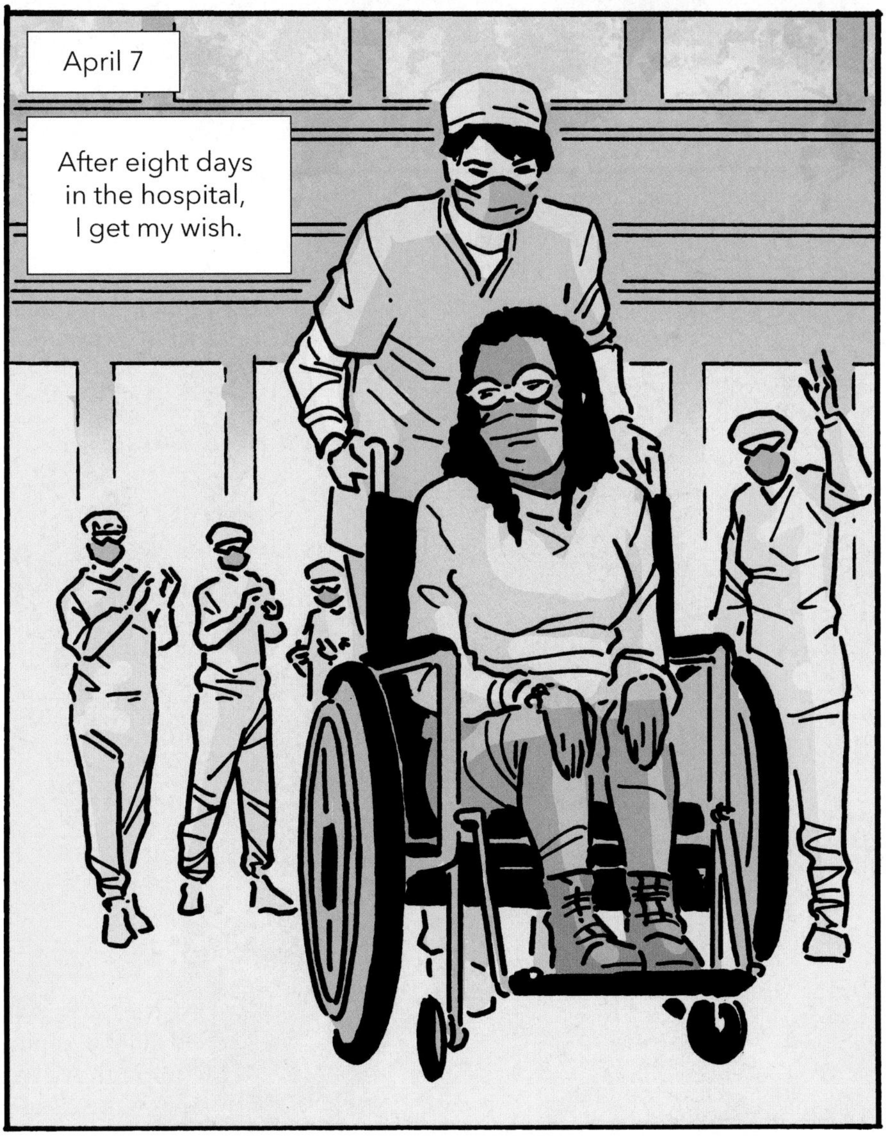
April 7
After eight days in the hospital, I get my wish.

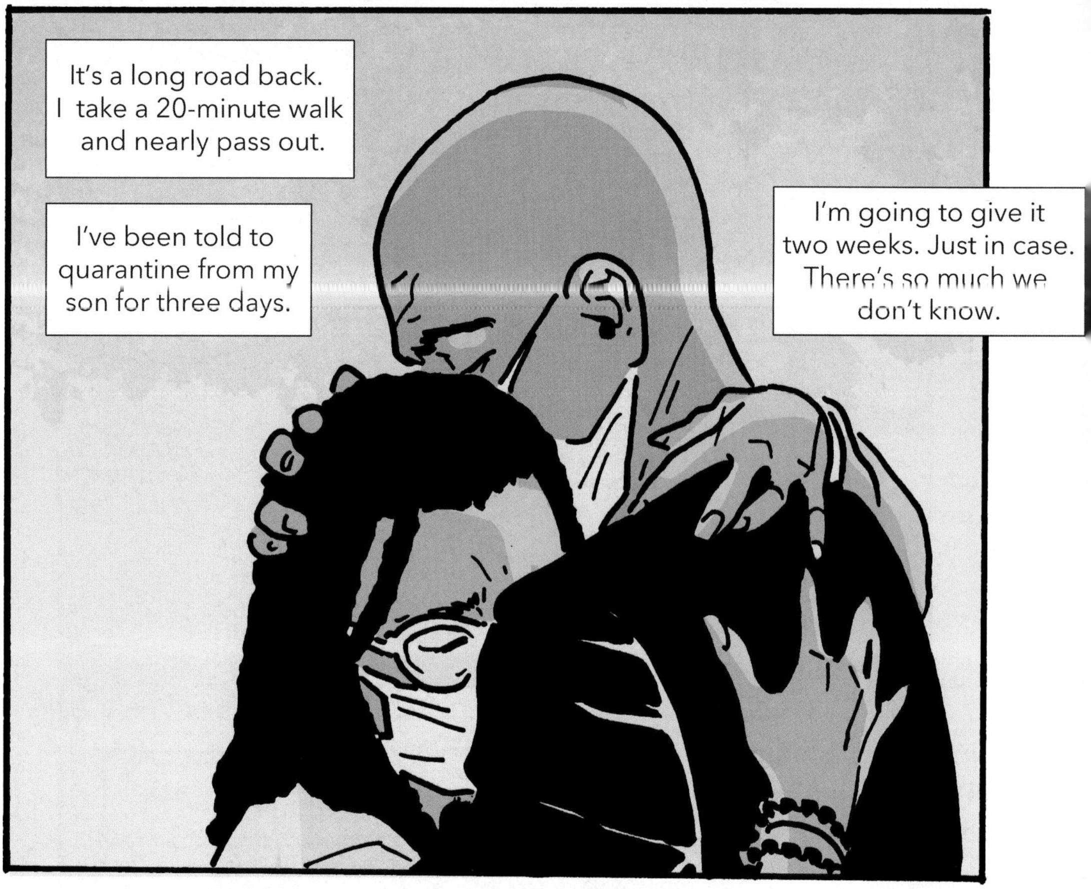
It's a long road back.
I take a 20-minute walk and nearly pass out.
I've been told to quarantine from my son for three days.
I'm going to give it two weeks. Just in case. There's so much we don't know.

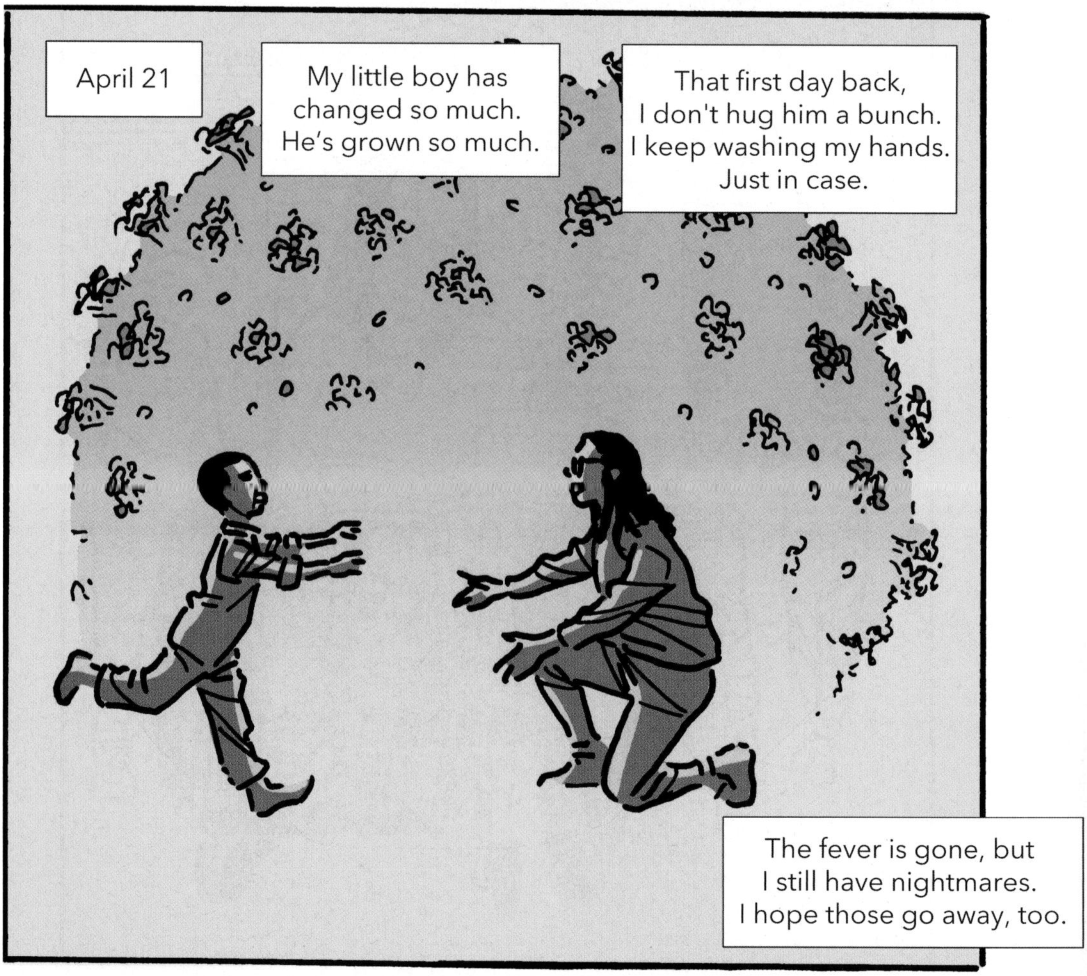
April 21
My little boy has changed so much. He's grown so much.
That first day back, I don't hug him a bunch. I keep washing my hands. Just in case.
The fever is gone, but I still have nightmares. I hope those go away, too.

CHAPTER 3

AN OPERA SINGER'S VOICE CARRIES DURING QUARANTINE

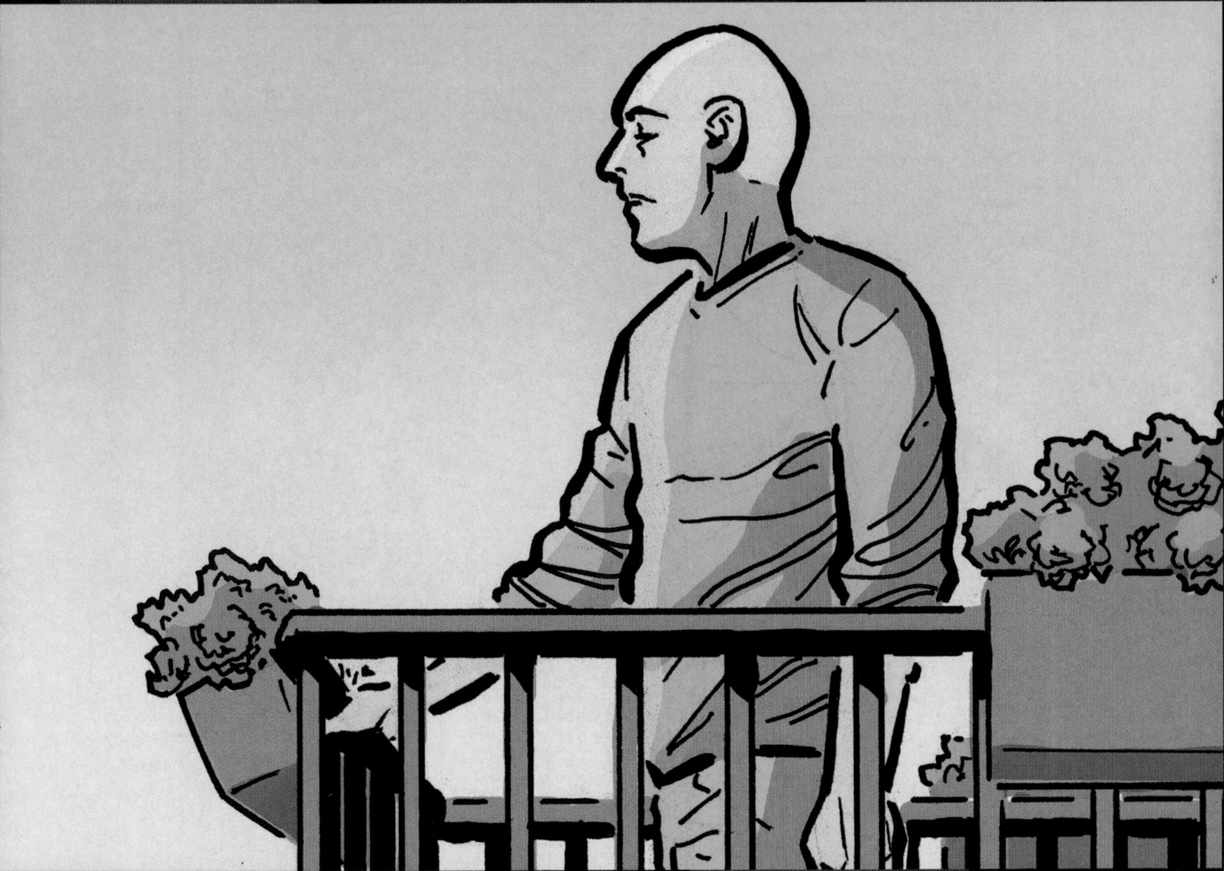

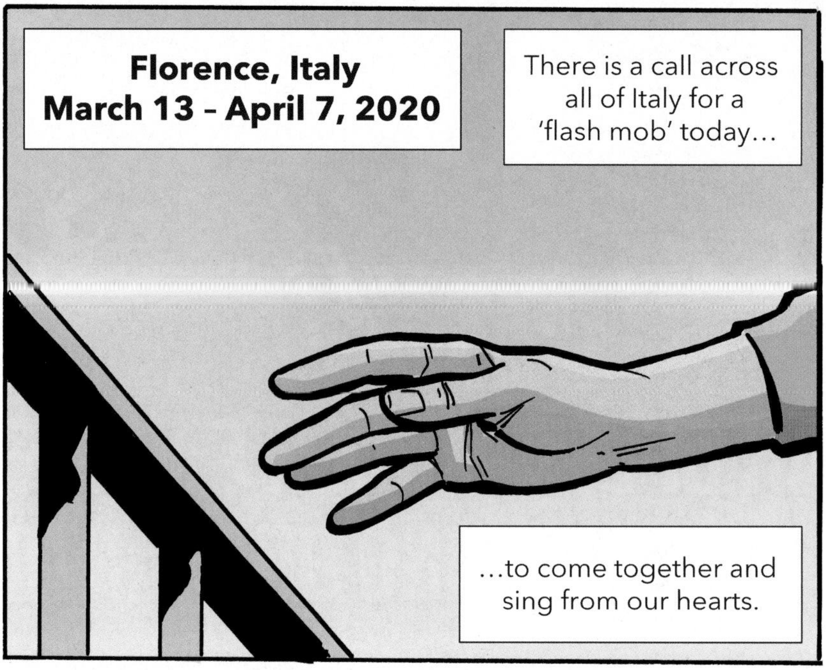
Florence, Italy
March 13 – April 7, 2020
There is a call across all of Italy for a 'flash mob' today…
…to come together and sing from our hearts.

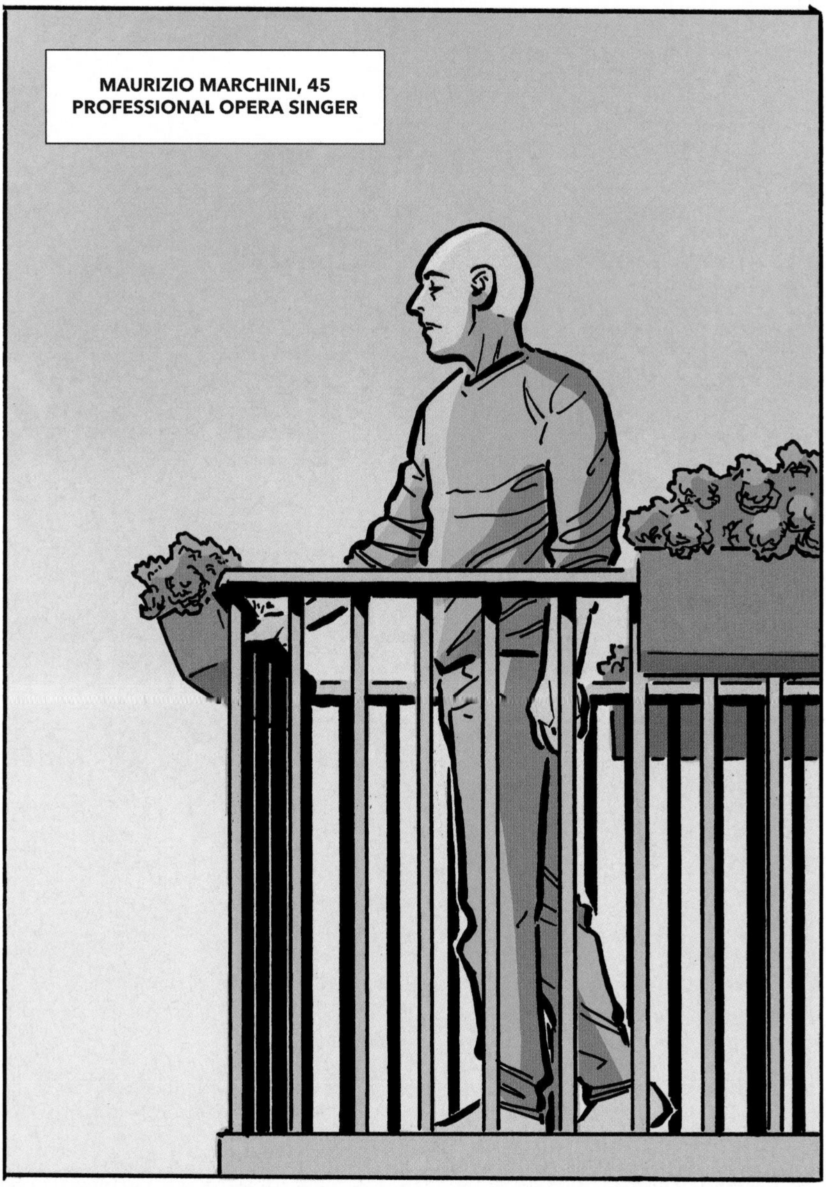
MAURIZIO MARCHINI, 45
PROFESSIONAL OPERA SINGER

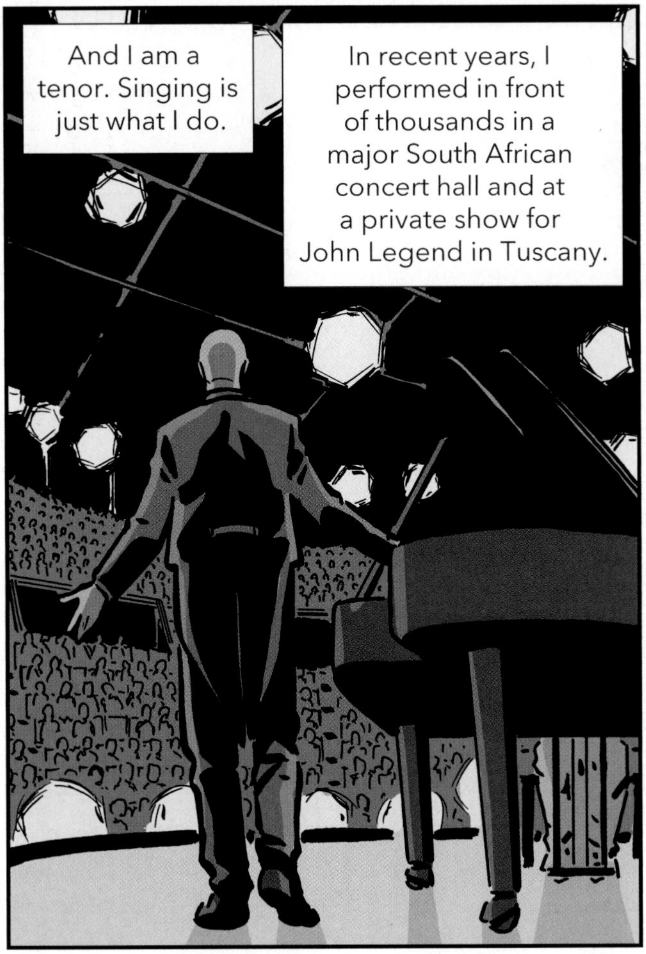
And I am a tenor. Singing is just what I do.
In recent years, I performed in front of thousands in a major South African concert hall and at a private show for John Legend in Tuscany.

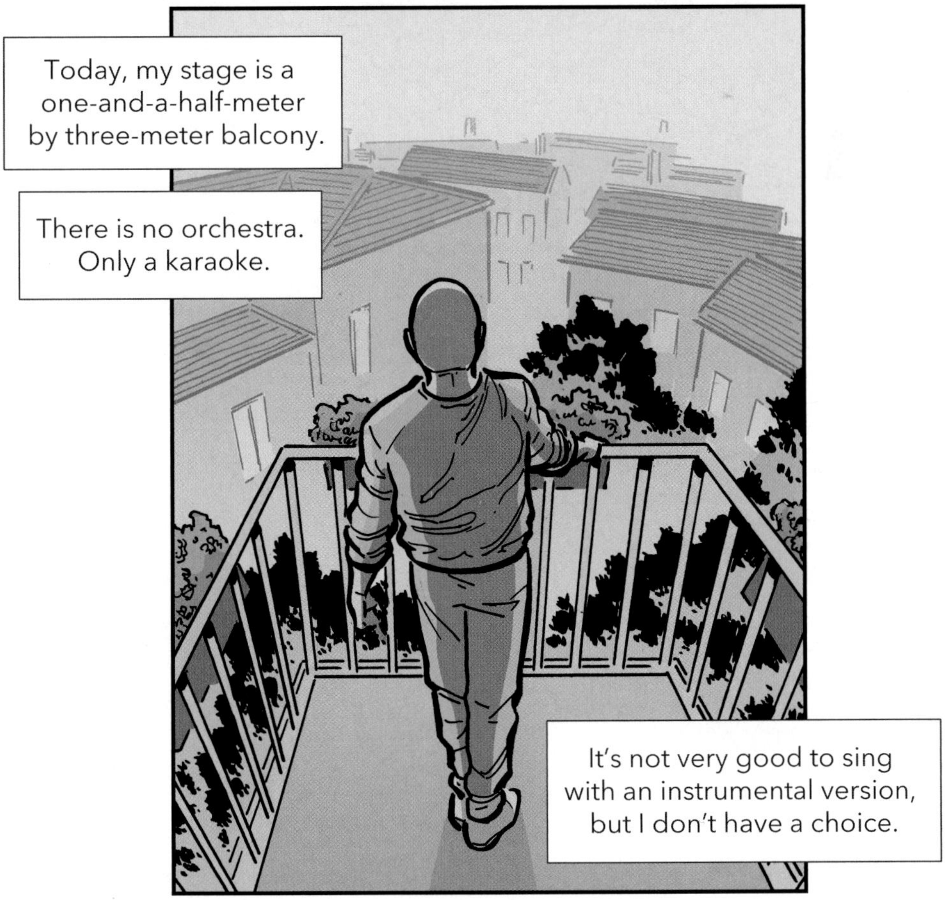
Today, my stage is a one-and-a-half-meter by three-meter balcony.
There is no orchestra. Only a karaoke.
It's not very good to sing with an instrumental version, but I don't have a choice.

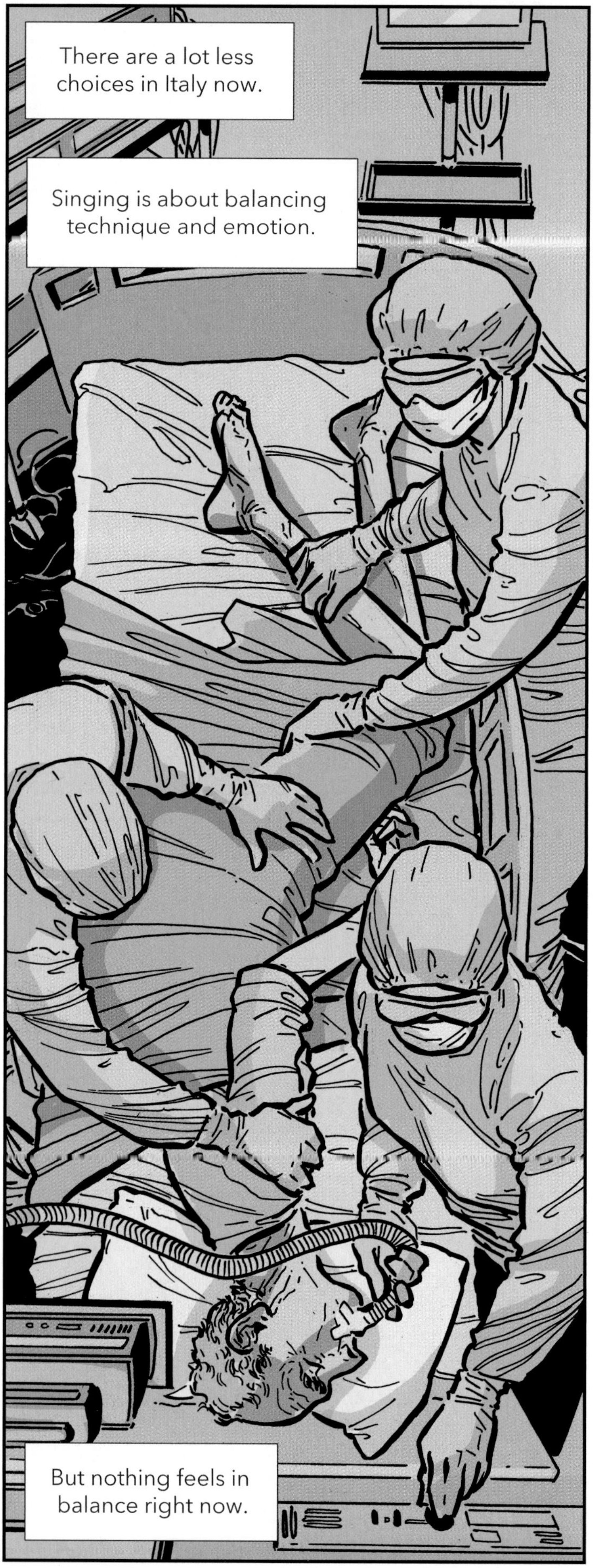
There are a lot less choices in Italy now.
Singing is about balancing technique and emotion.
But nothing feels in balance right now.

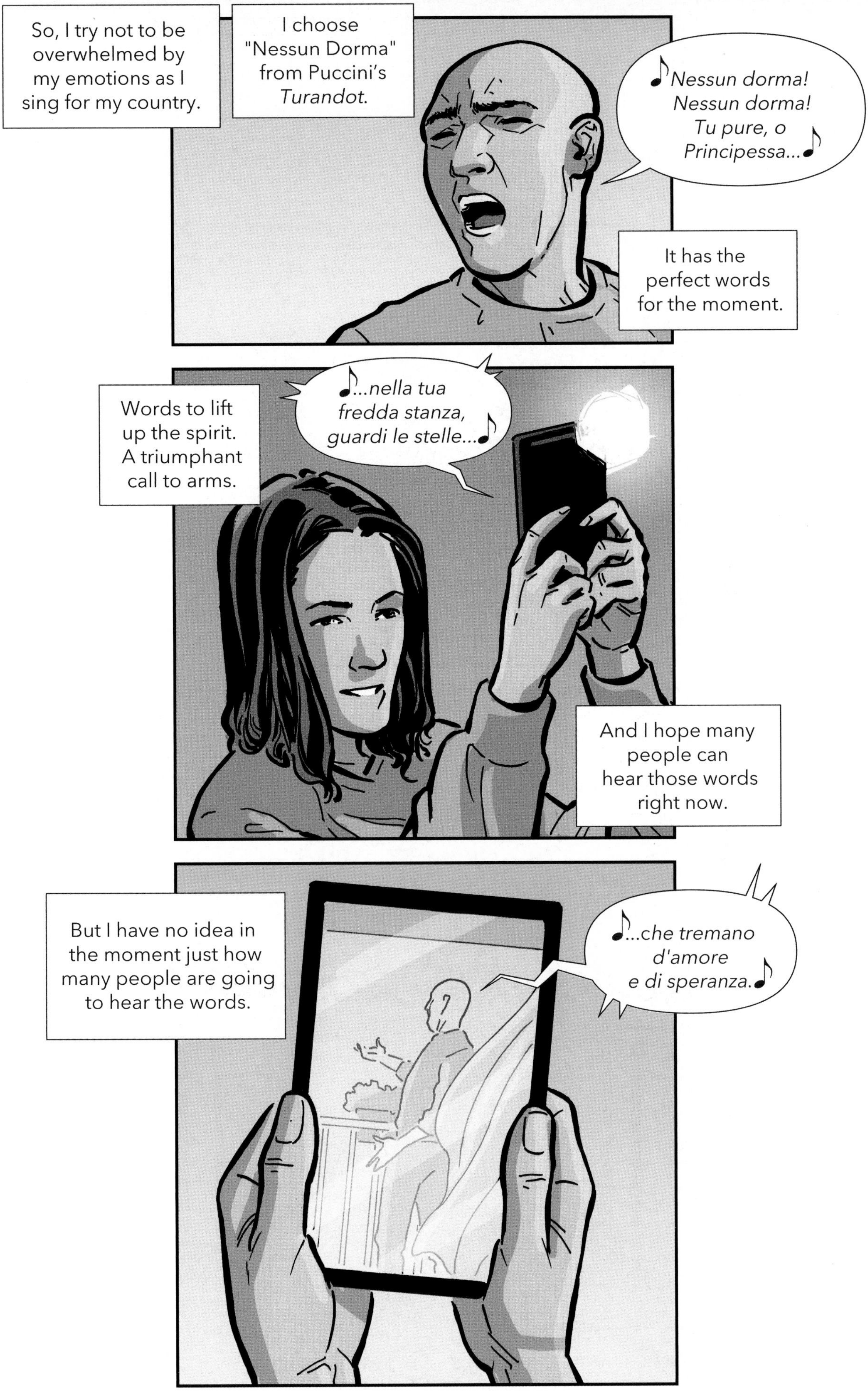
So, I try not to be overwhelmed by my emotions as I sing for my country.
I choose "Nessun Dorma" from Puccini's *Turandot*.
♪*Nessun dorma! Nessun dorma! Tu pure, o Principessa...*♪
It has the perfect words for the moment.
Words to lift up the spirit. A triumphant call to arms.
♪*...nella tua fredda stanza, guardi le stelle...*♪
And I hope many people can hear those words right now.
But I have no idea in the moment just how many people are going to hear the words.
♪*...che tremano d'amore e di speranza.*♪

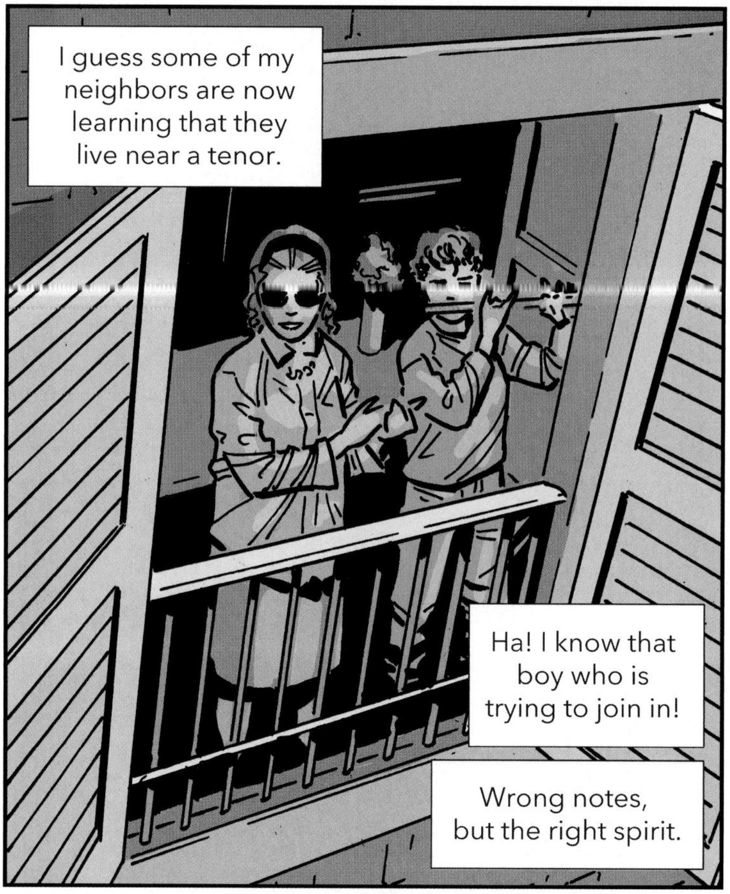
I guess some of my neighbors are now learning that they live near a tenor.
Ha! I know that boy who is trying to join in!
Wrong notes, but the right spirit.

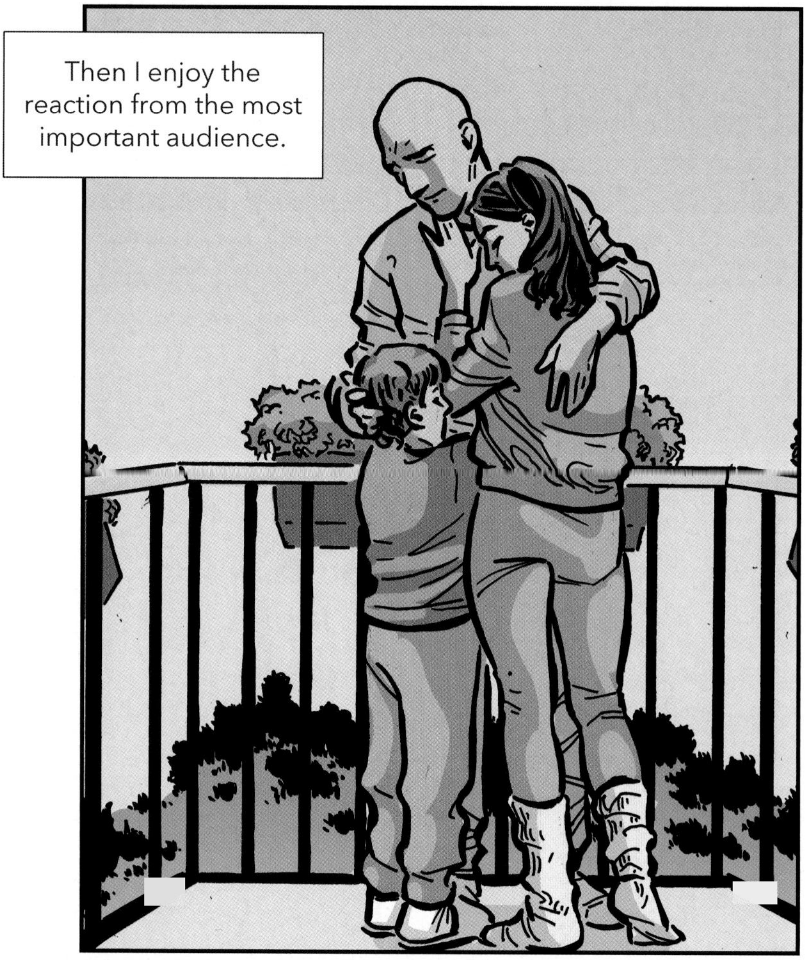
Then I enjoy the reaction from the most important audience.

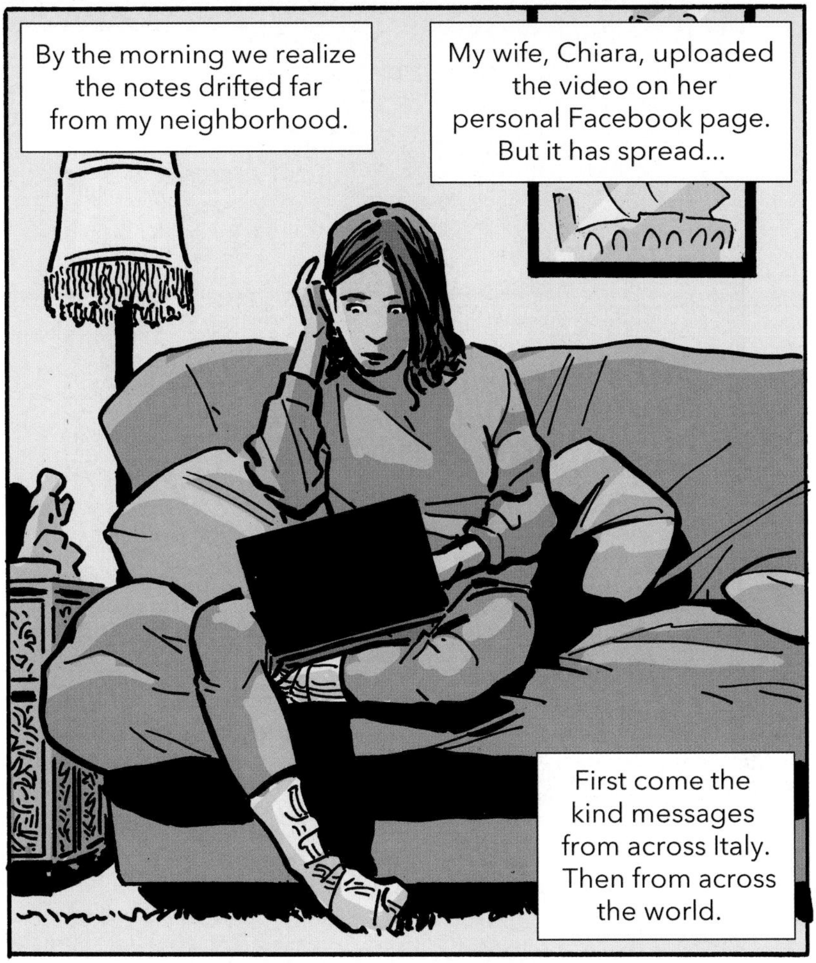
By the morning we realize the notes drifted far from my neighborhood.
My wife, Chiara, uploaded the video on her personal Facebook page. But it has spread...
First come the kind messages from across Italy. Then from across the world.

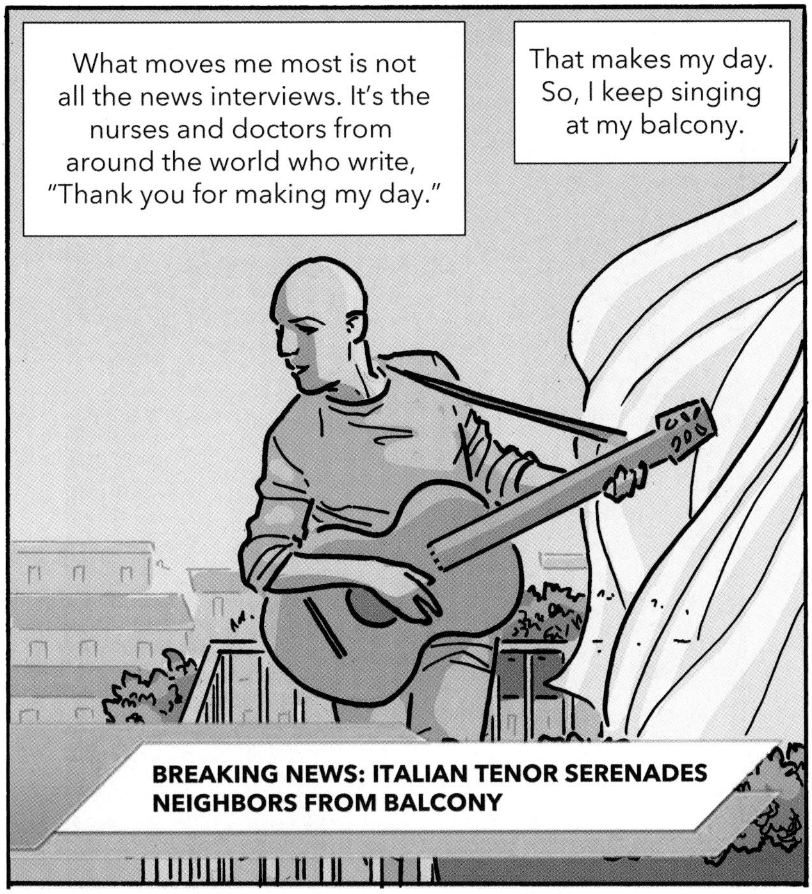
What moves me most is not all the news interviews. It's the nurses and doctors from around the world who write, "Thank you for making my day."
That makes my day. So, I keep singing at my balcony.
BREAKING NEWS: ITALIAN TENOR SERENADES NEIGHBORS FROM BALCONY

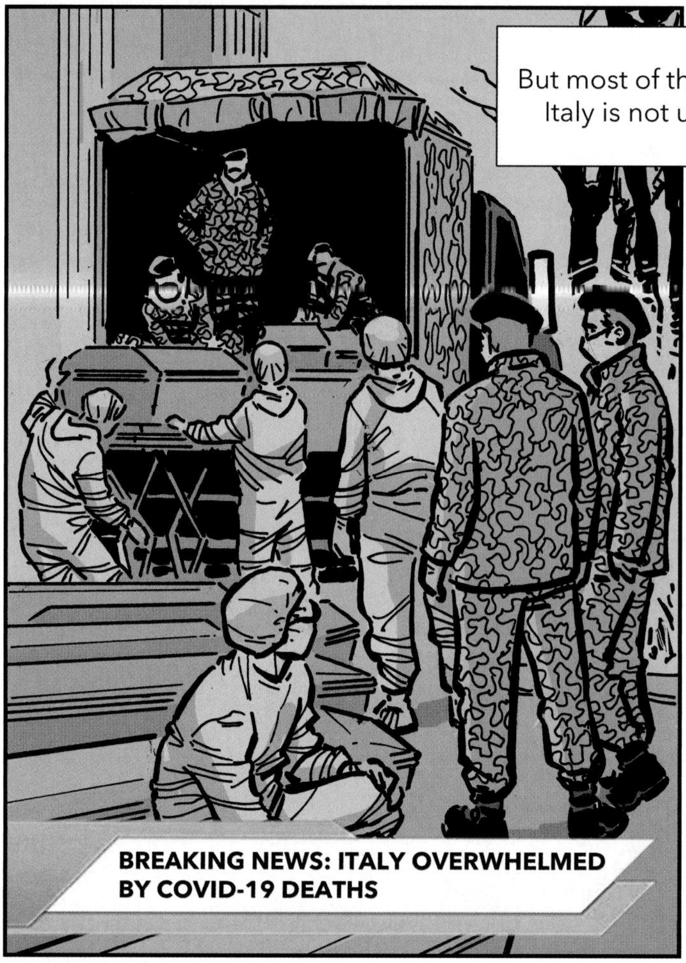
But most of the news in Italy is not uplifting.
BREAKING NEWS: ITALY OVERWHELMED BY COVID-19 DEATHS

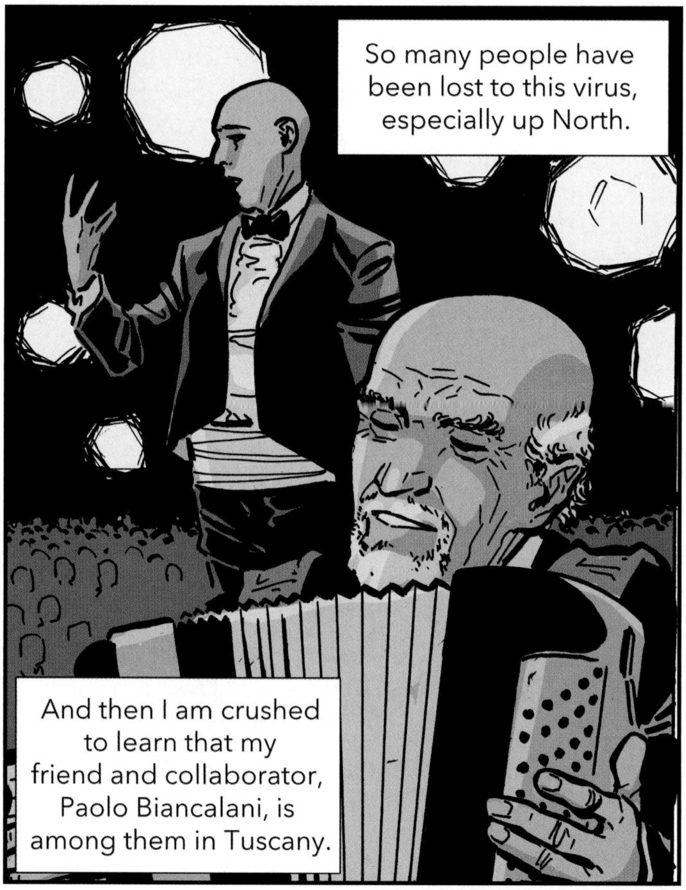
So many people have been lost to this virus, especially up North.
And then I am crushed to learn that my friend and collaborator, Paolo Biancalani, is among them in Tuscany.

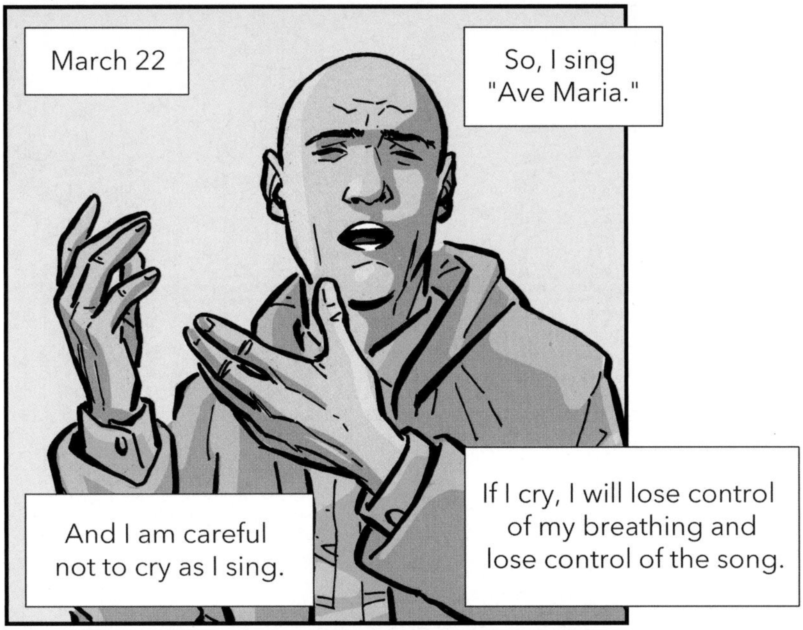
March 22
So, I sing "Ave Maria."
And I am careful not to cry as I sing.
If I cry, I will lose control of my breathing and lose control of the song.

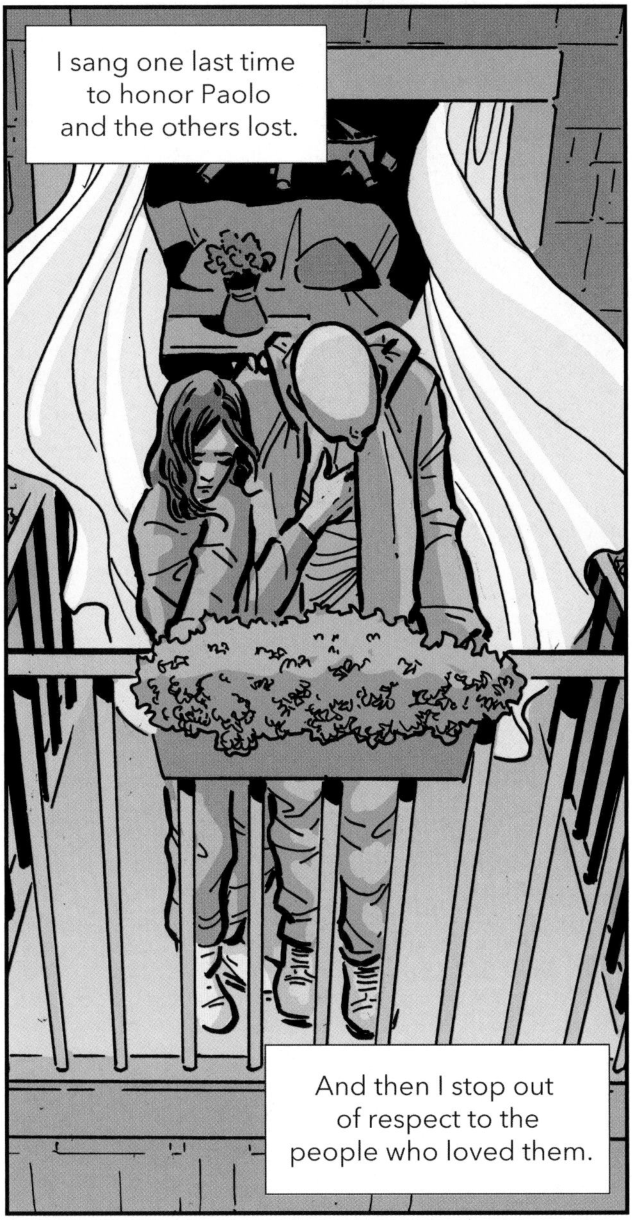
I sang one last time to honor Paolo and the others lost.
And then I stop out of respect to the people who loved them.

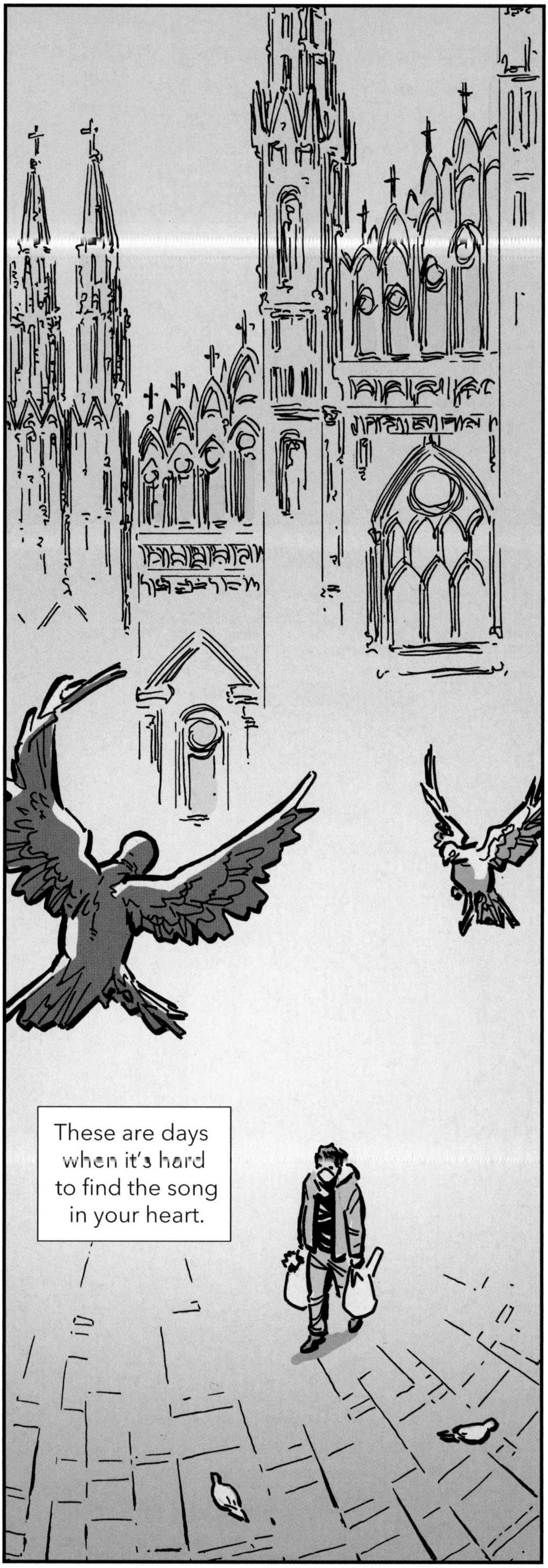
These are days when it's hard to find the song in your heart.

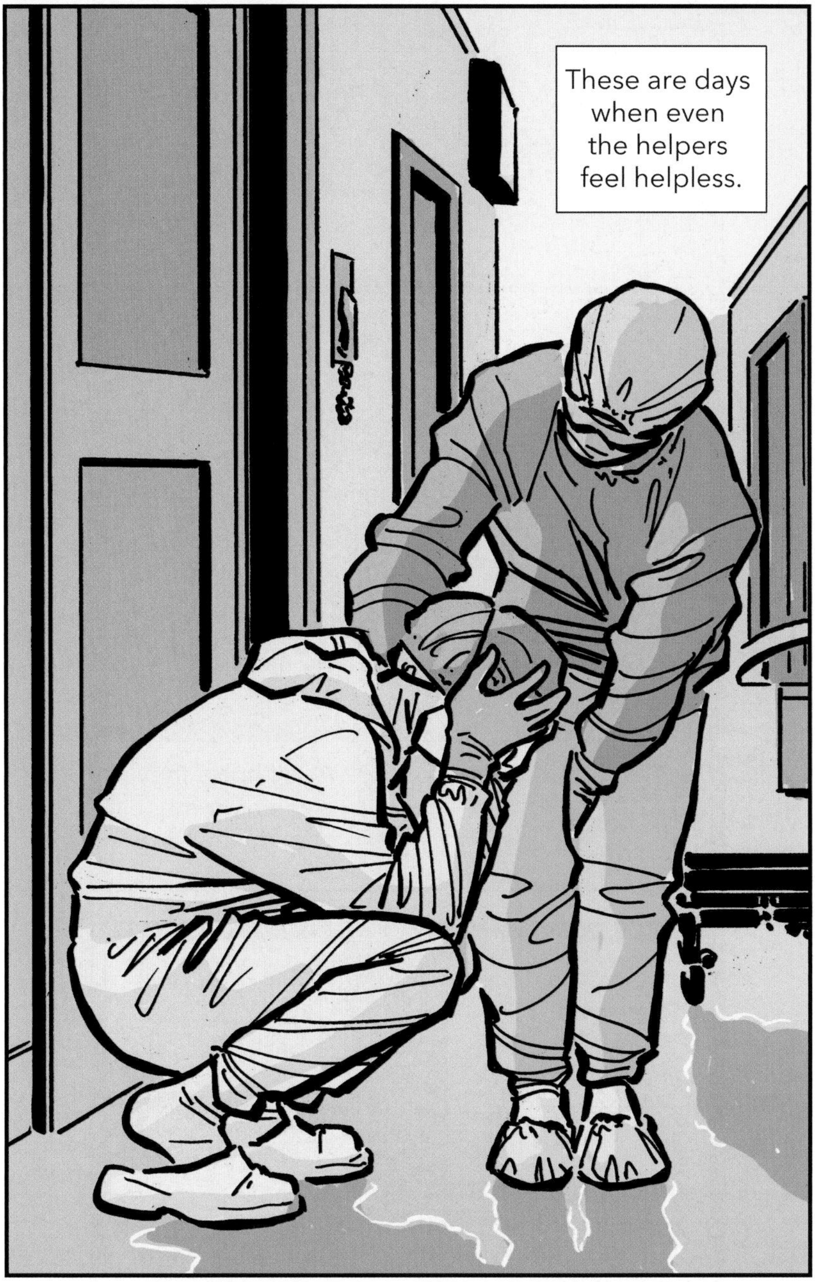
These are days when even the helpers feel helpless.

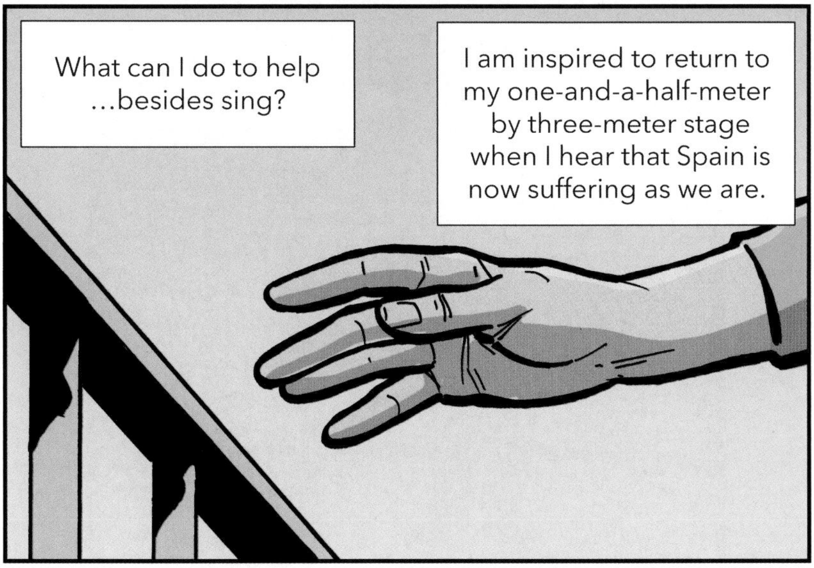
What can I do to help ...besides sing?
I am inspired to return to my one-and-a-half-meter by three-meter stage when I hear that Spain is now suffering as we are.

April 7
So, I sing them the Spanish song, "Granada."
And I hope they can hear me from my balcony.

I think the next time I will sing "Nessun Dorma" it will be in front of a live audience in a concert hall.
Only then I will know we have come full circle.

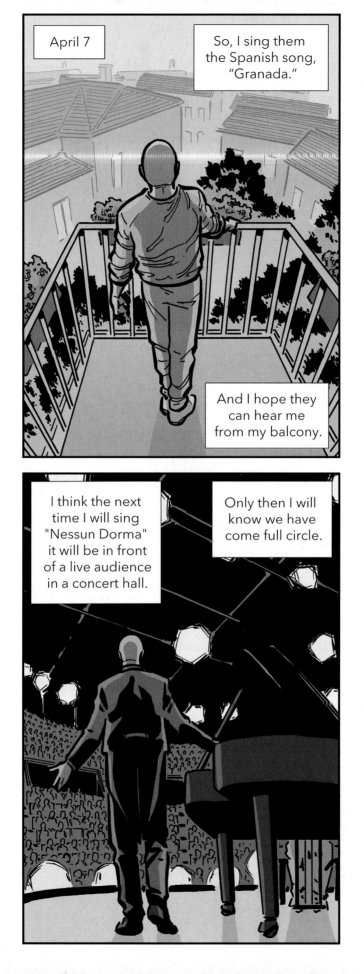

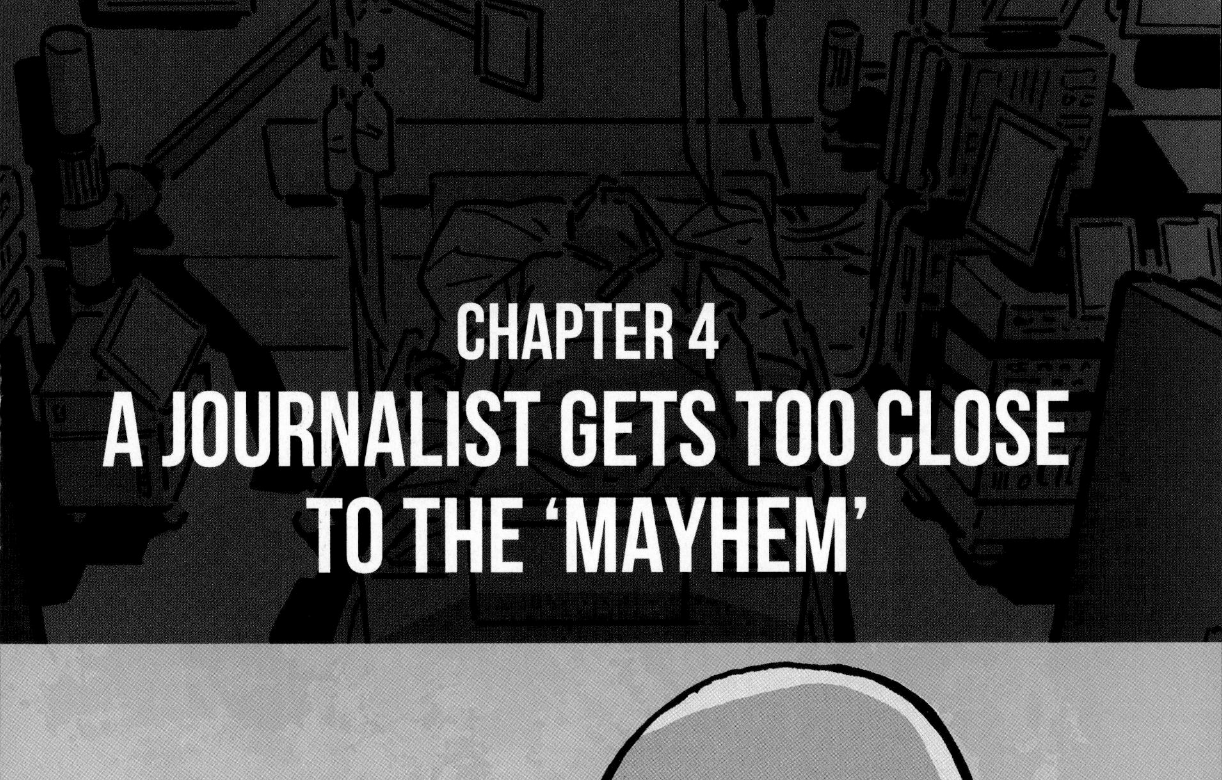

CHAPTER 4
A JOURNALIST GETS TOO CLOSE TO THE 'MAYHEM'

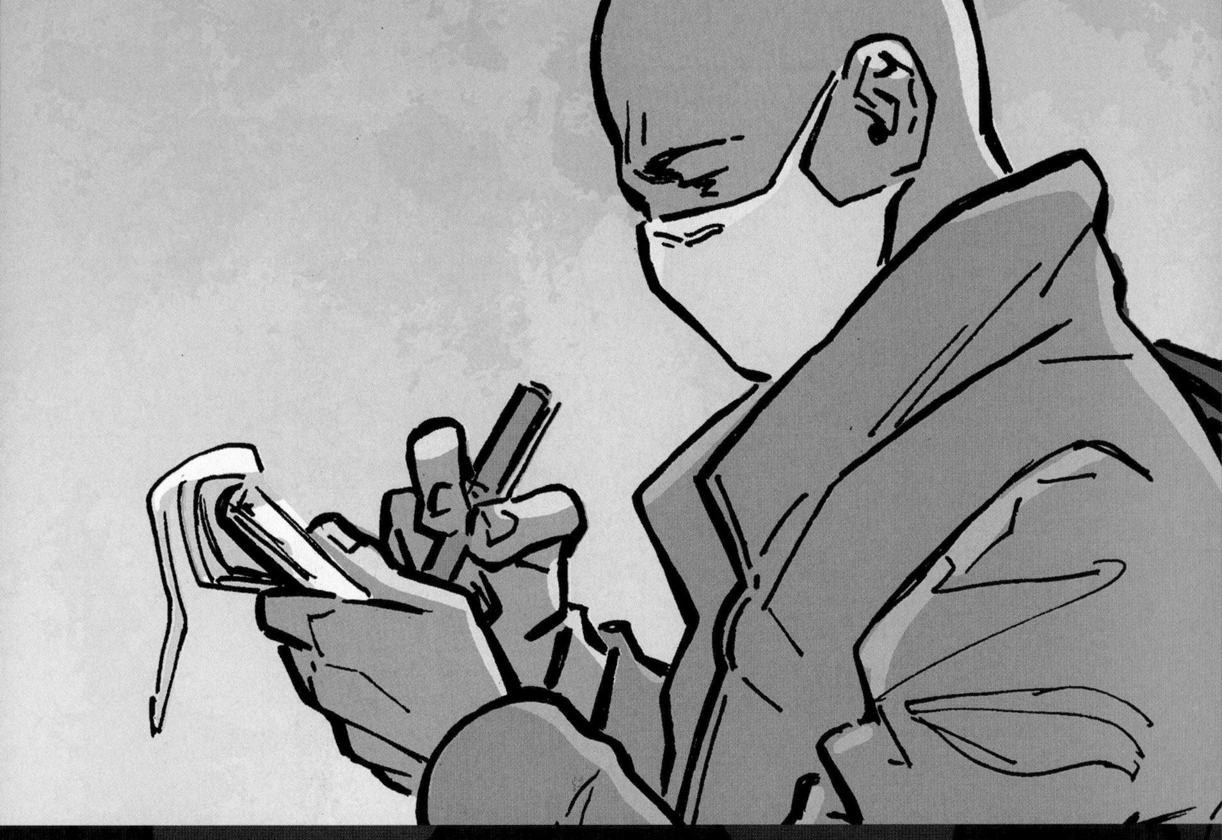

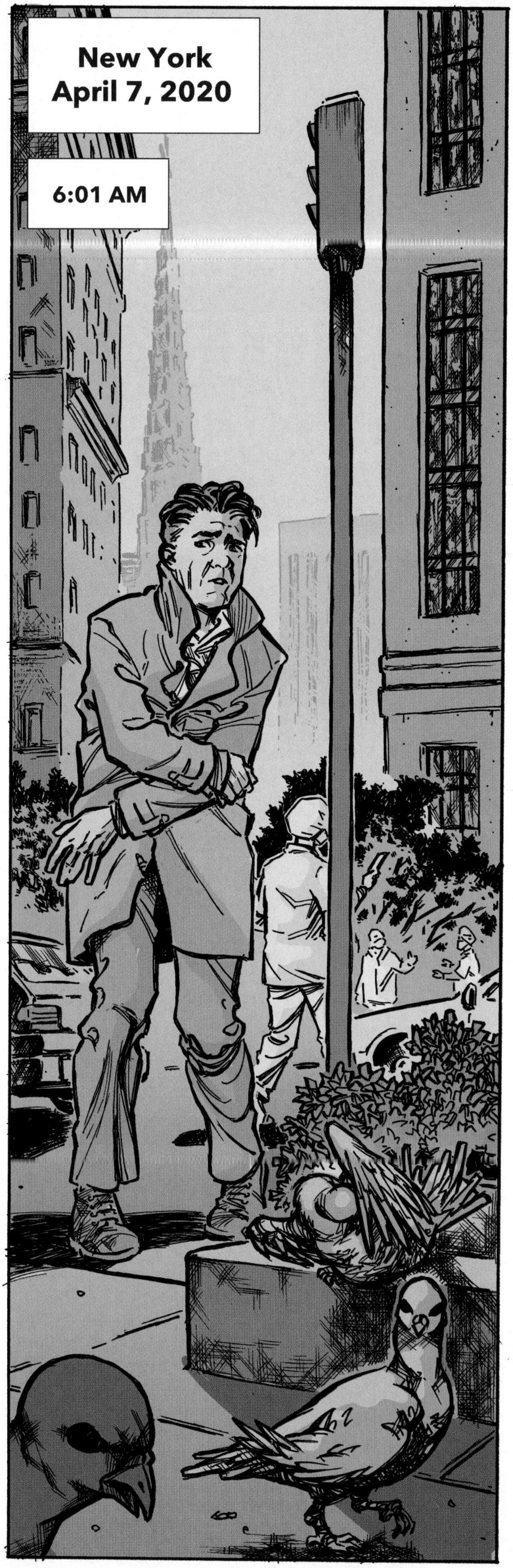
New York
April 7, 2020
6:01 AM

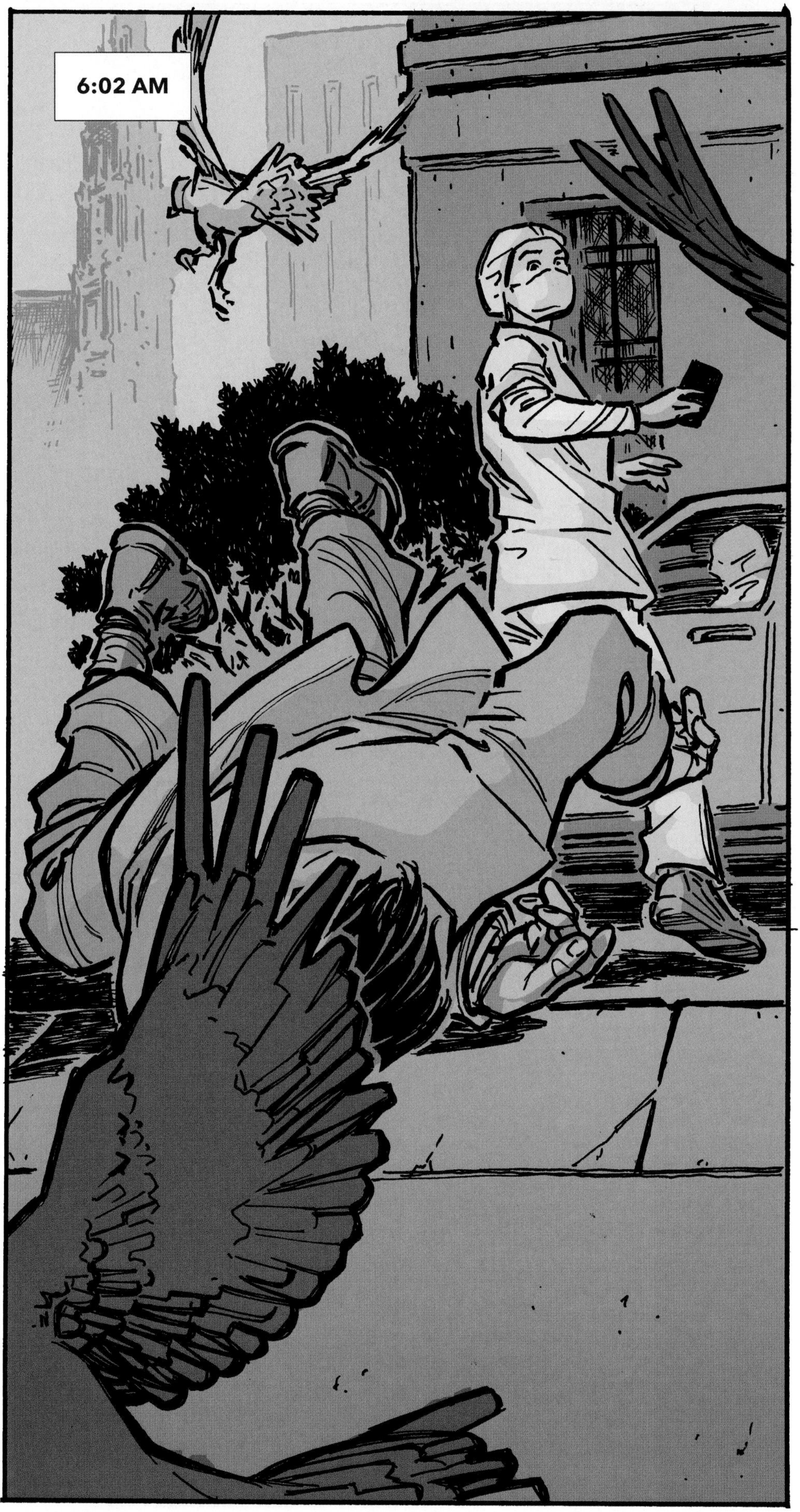
6:02 AM

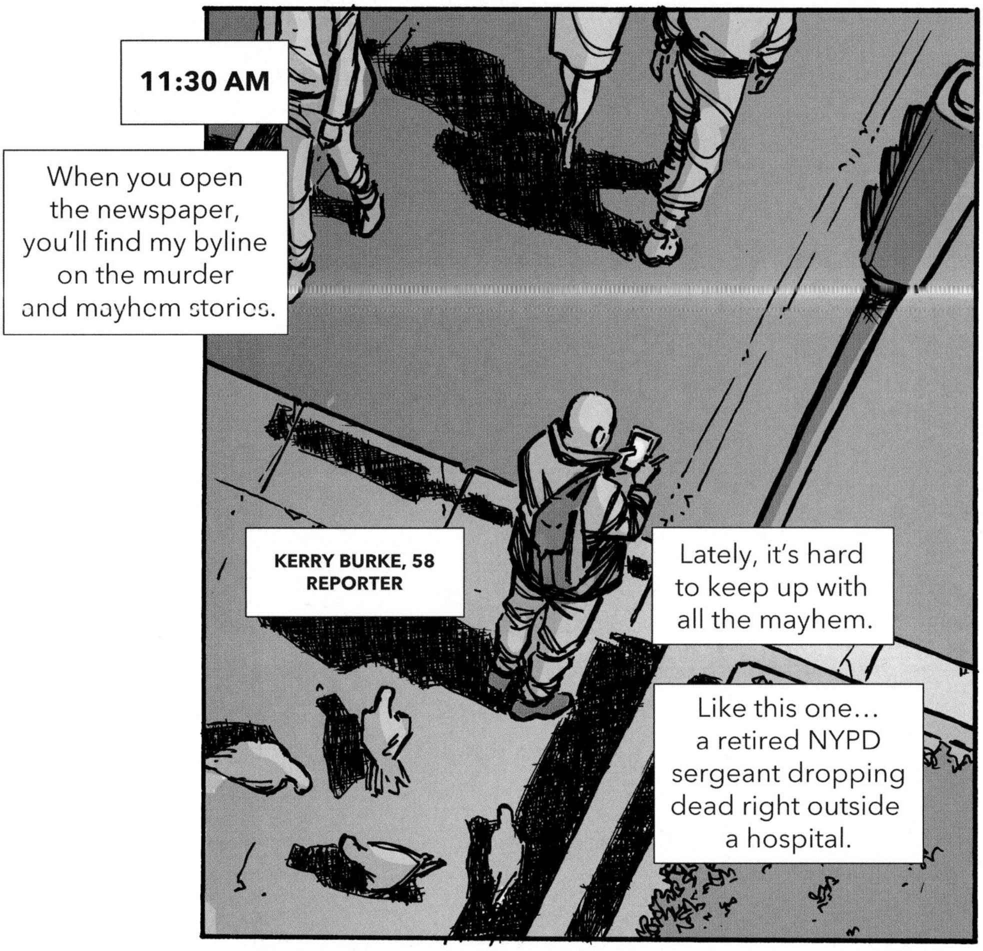
11:30 AM
When you open the newspaper, you'll find my byline on the murder and mayhem stories.
KERRY BURKE, 58
REPORTER
Lately, it's hard to keep up with all the mayhem.
Like this one… a retired NYPD sergeant dropping dead right outside a hospital.

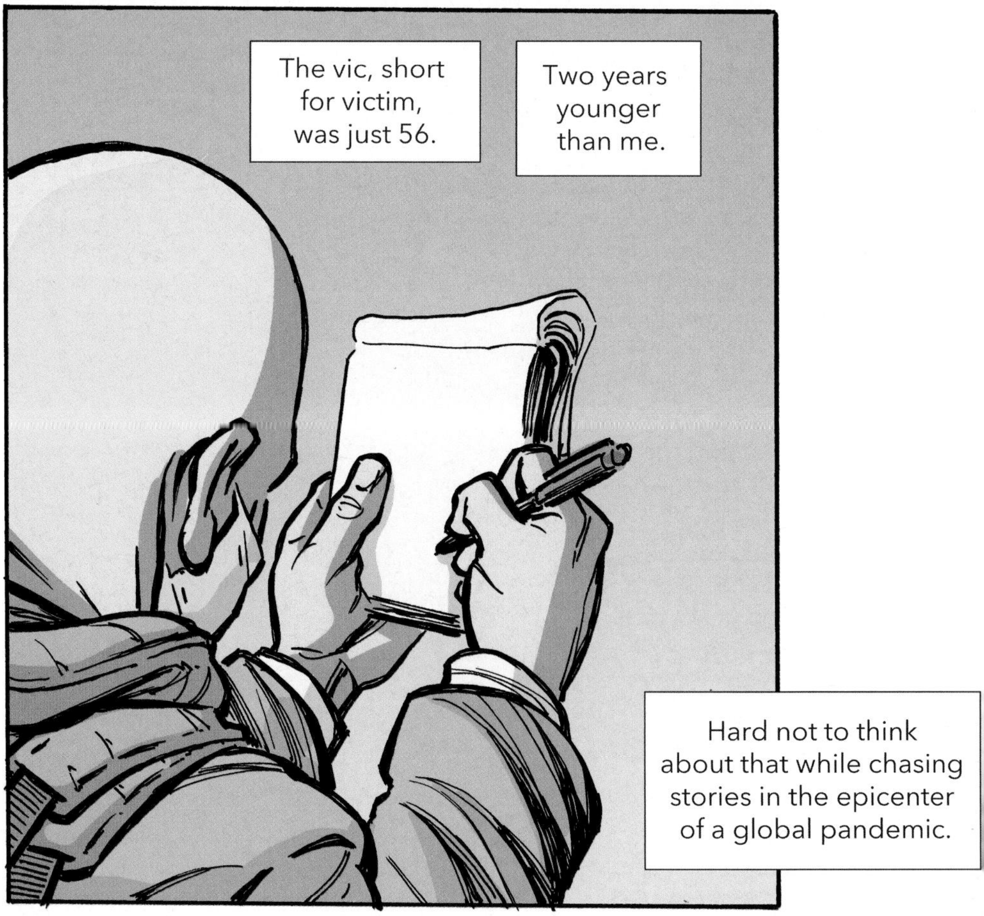
The vic, short for victim, was just 56.
Two years younger than me.
Hard not to think about that while chasing stories in the epicenter of a global pandemic.

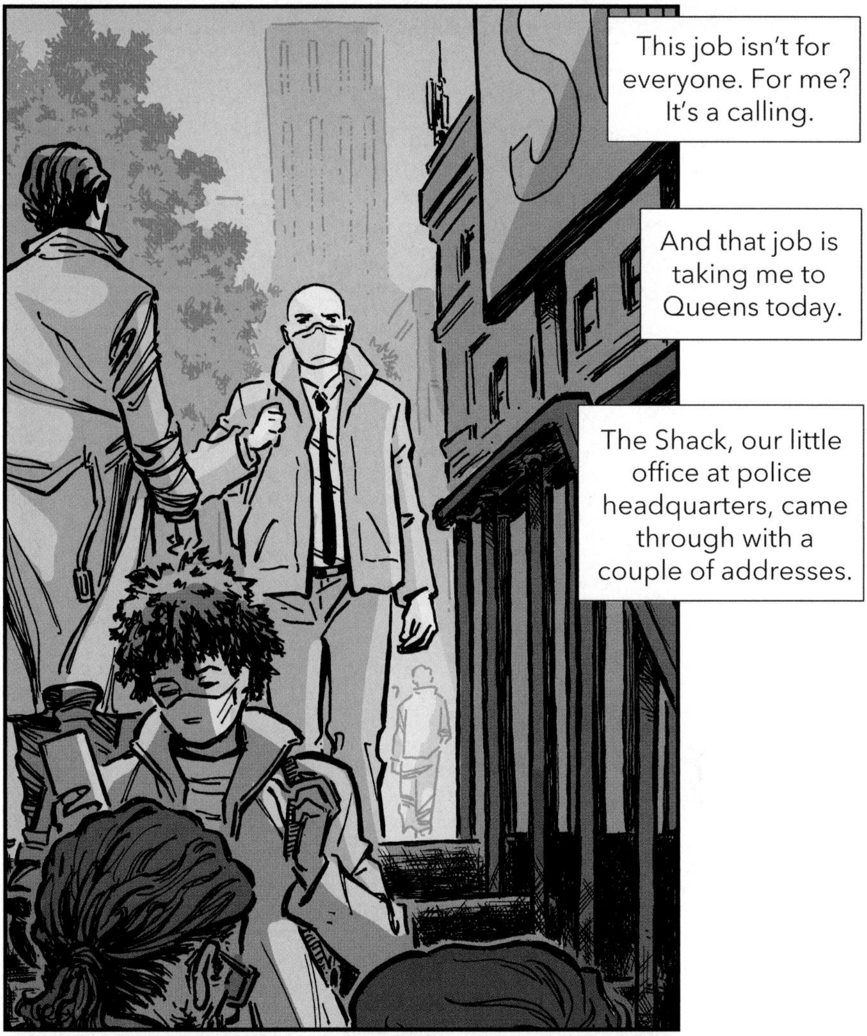
This job isn't for everyone. For me? It's a calling.
And that job is taking me to Queens today.
The Shack, our little office at police headquarters, came through with a couple of addresses.

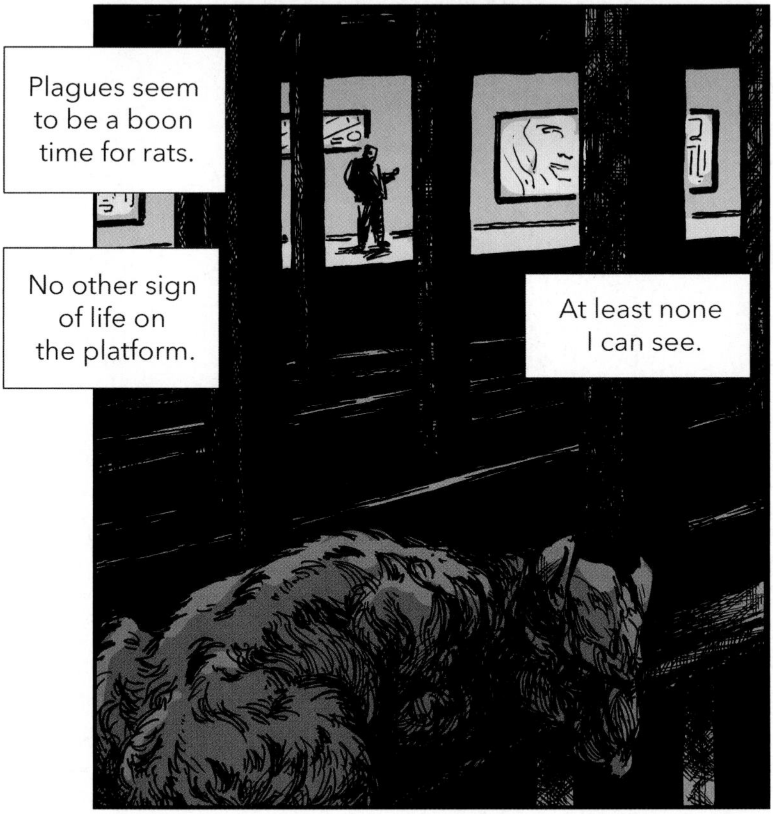
Plagues seem to be a boon time for rats.
No other sign of life on the platform.
At least none I can see.

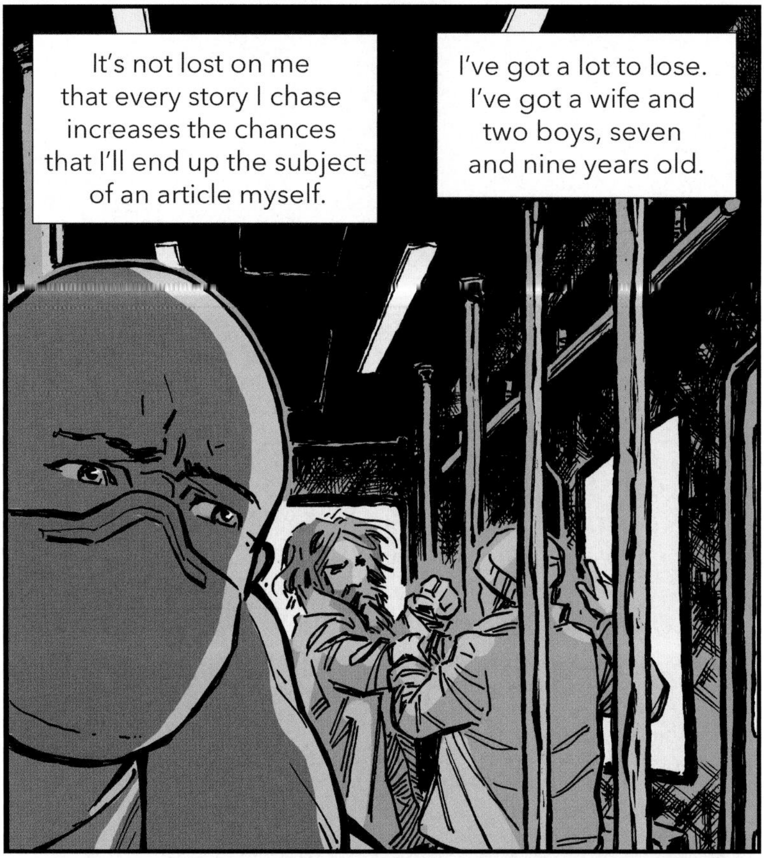
It's not lost on me that every story I chase increases the chances that I'll end up the subject of an article myself.
I've got a lot to lose. I've got a wife and two boys, seven and nine years old.

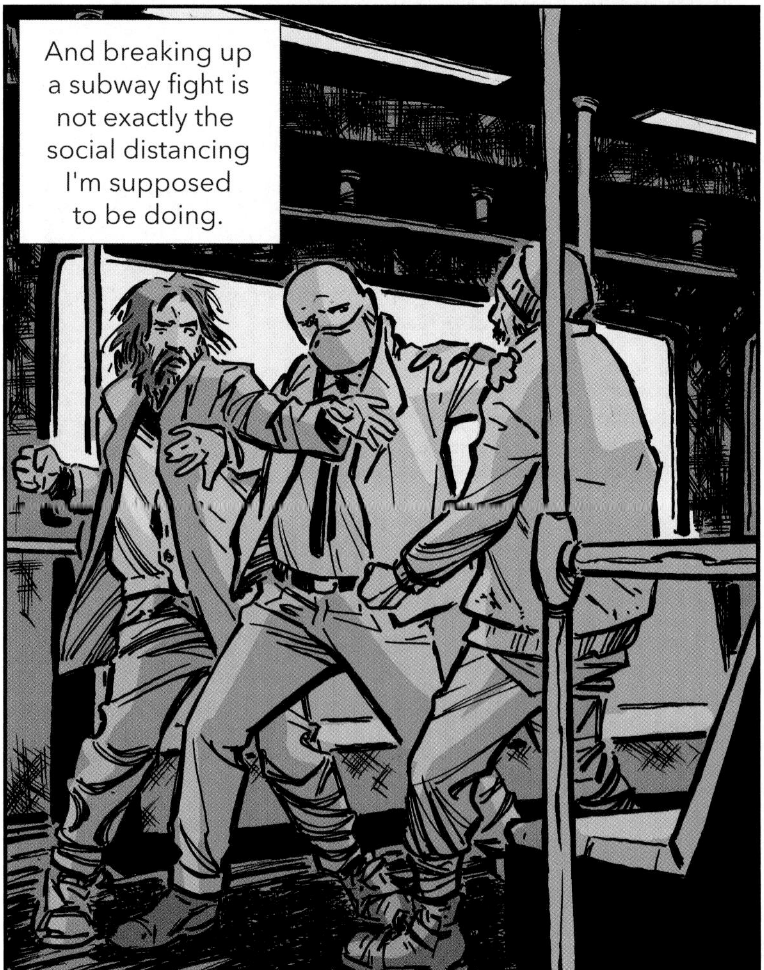
And breaking up a subway fight is not exactly the social distancing I'm supposed to be doing.

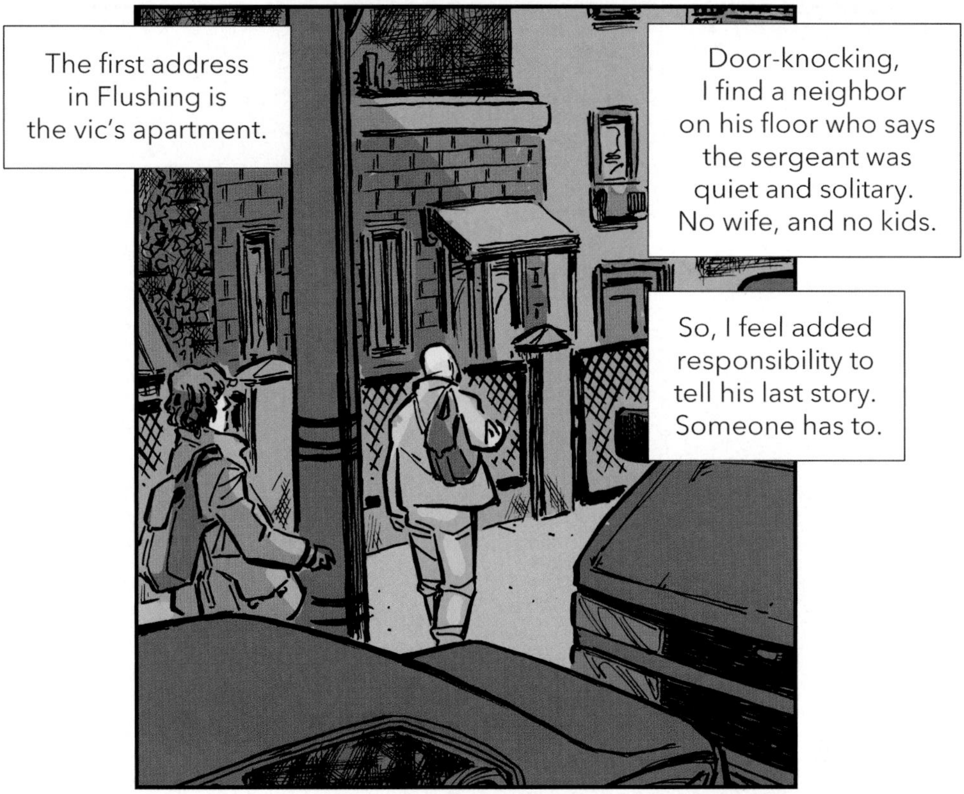
The first address in Flushing is the vic's apartment.
Door-knocking, I find a neighbor on his floor who says the sergeant was quiet and solitary. No wife, and no kids.
So, I feel added responsibility to tell his last story. Someone has to.

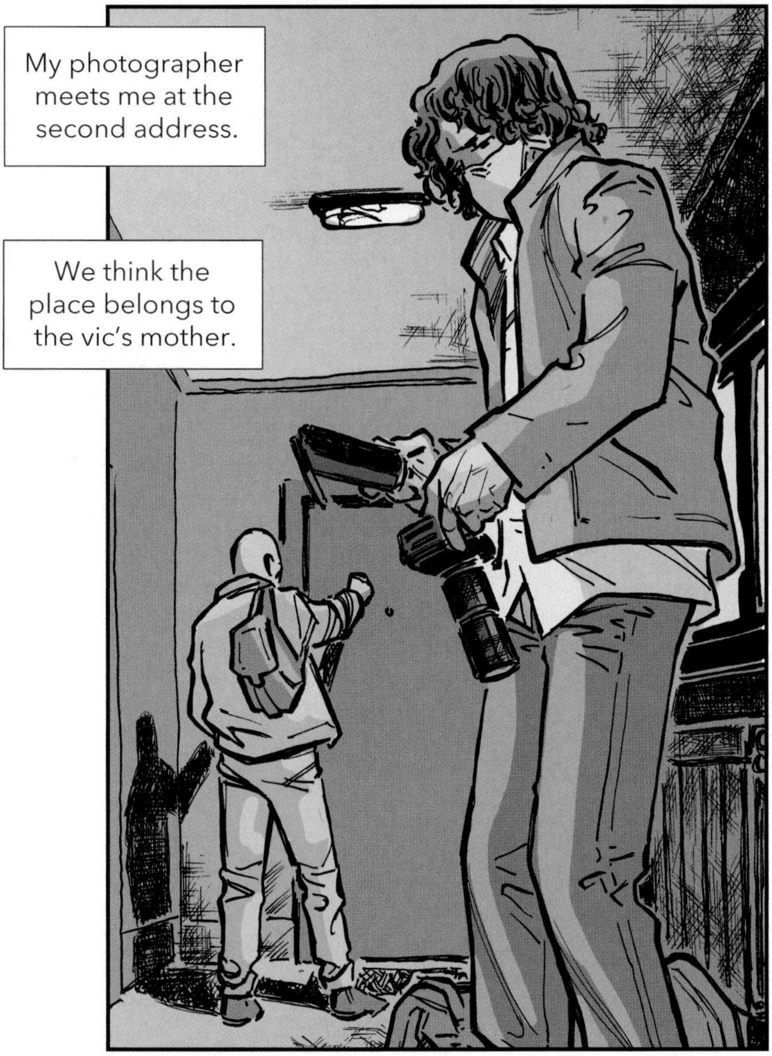
My photographer meets me at the second address.
We think the place belongs to the vic's mother.

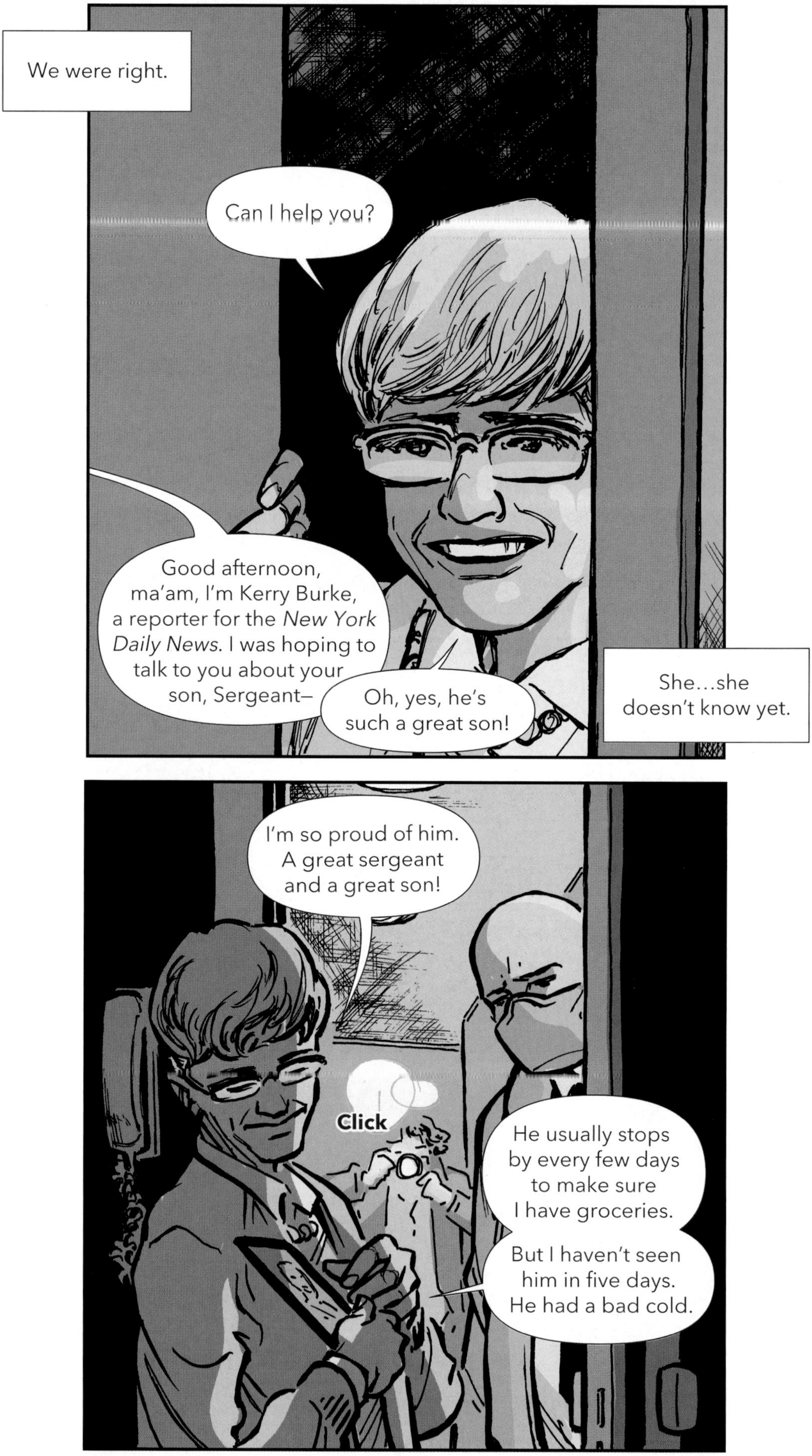
We were right.
Can I help you?
Good afternoon, ma'am, I'm Kerry Burke, a reporter for the *New York Daily News*. I was hoping to talk to you about your son, Sergeant–
Oh, yes, he's such a great son!
She…she doesn't know yet.
I'm so proud of him. A great sergeant and a great son!
Click
He usually stops by every few days to make sure I have groceries.
But I haven't seen him in five days. He had a bad cold.

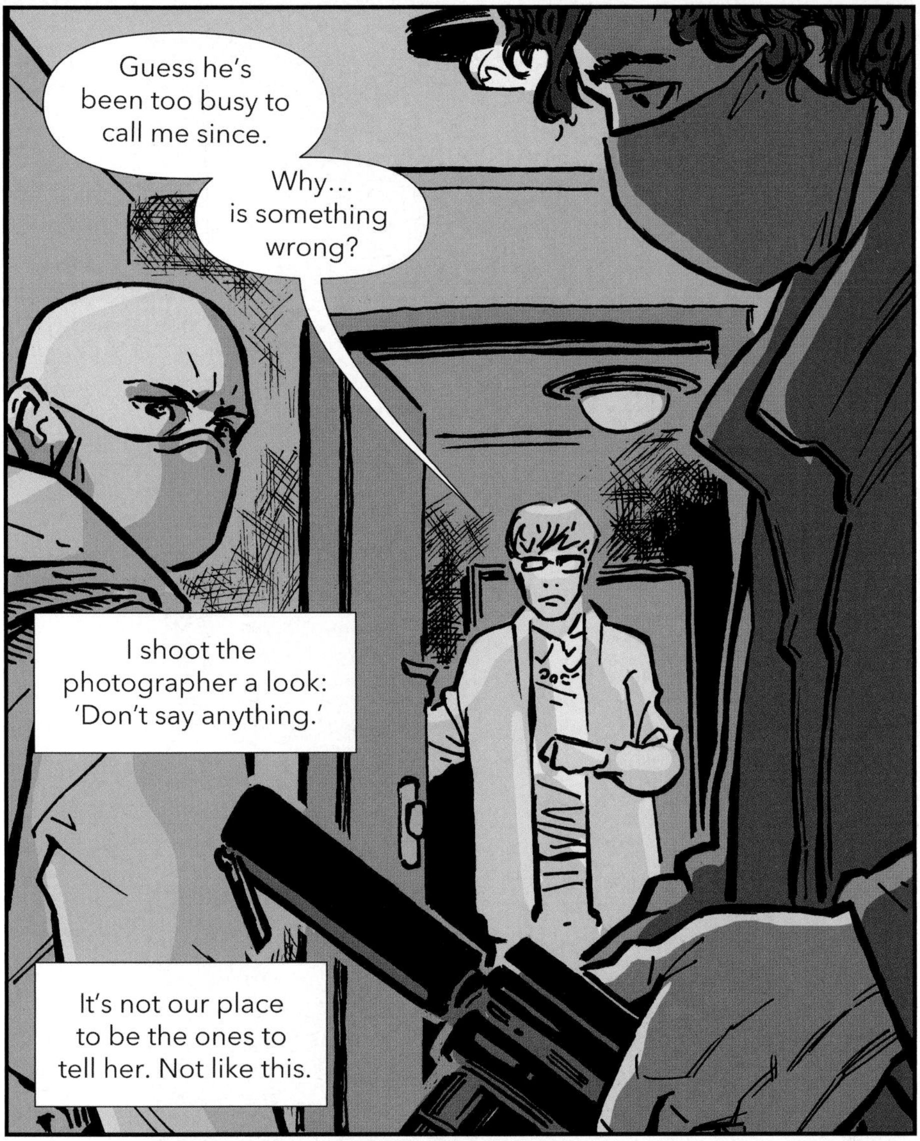
Guess he's been too busy to call me since.
Why… is something wrong?
I shoot the photographer a look: 'Don't say anything.'
It's not our place to be the ones to tell her. Not like this.

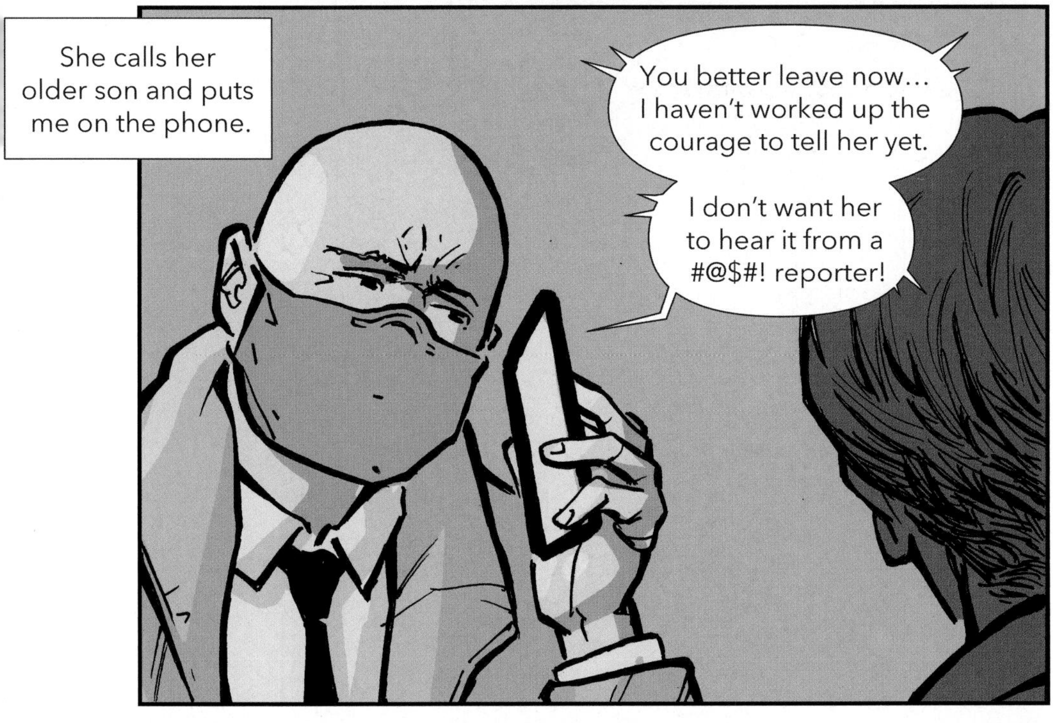
She calls her older son and puts me on the phone.
You better leave now… I haven't worked up the courage to tell her yet.
I don't want her to hear it from a #@$#! reporter!

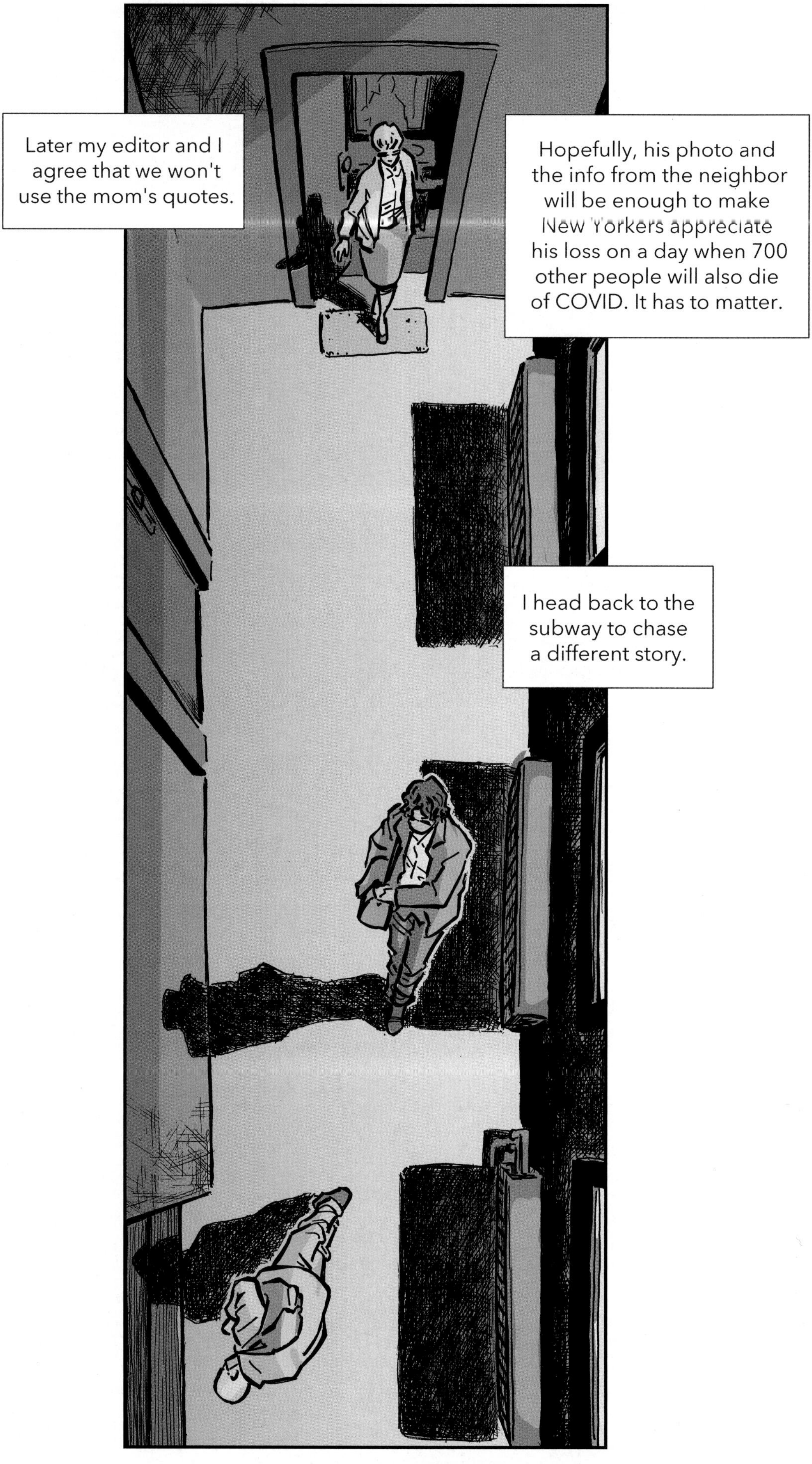
Later my editor and I agree that we won't use the mom's quotes.
Hopefully, his photo and the info from the neighbor will be enough to make New Yorkers appreciate his loss on a day when 700 other people will also die of COVID. It has to matter.
I head back to the subway to chase a different story.

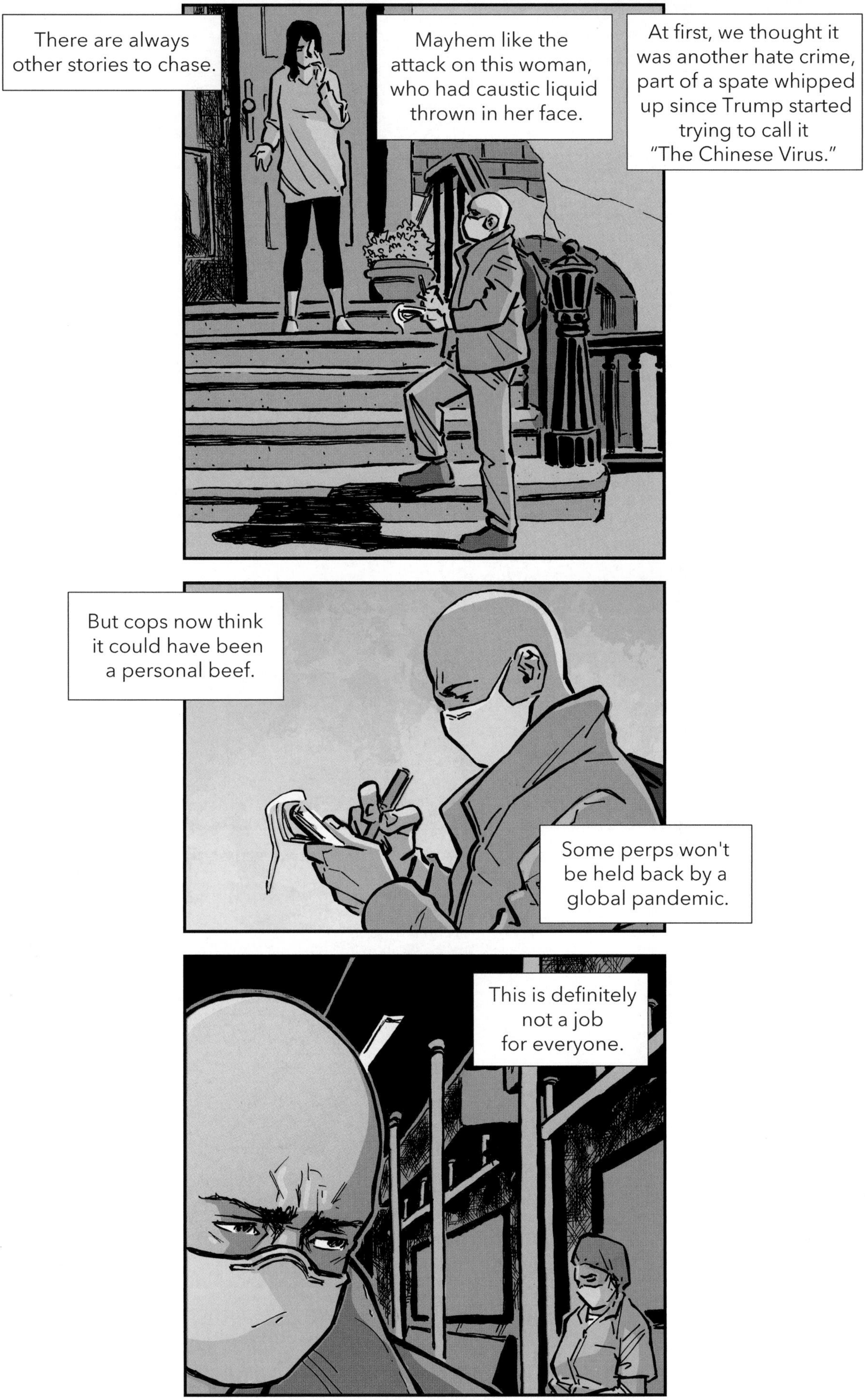
There are always other stories to chase.
Mayhem like the attack on this woman, who had caustic liquid thrown in her face.
At first, we thought it was another hate crime, part of a spate whipped up since Trump started trying to call it "The Chinese Virus."
But cops now think it could have been a personal beef.
Some perps won't be held back by a global pandemic.
This is definitely not a job for everyone.

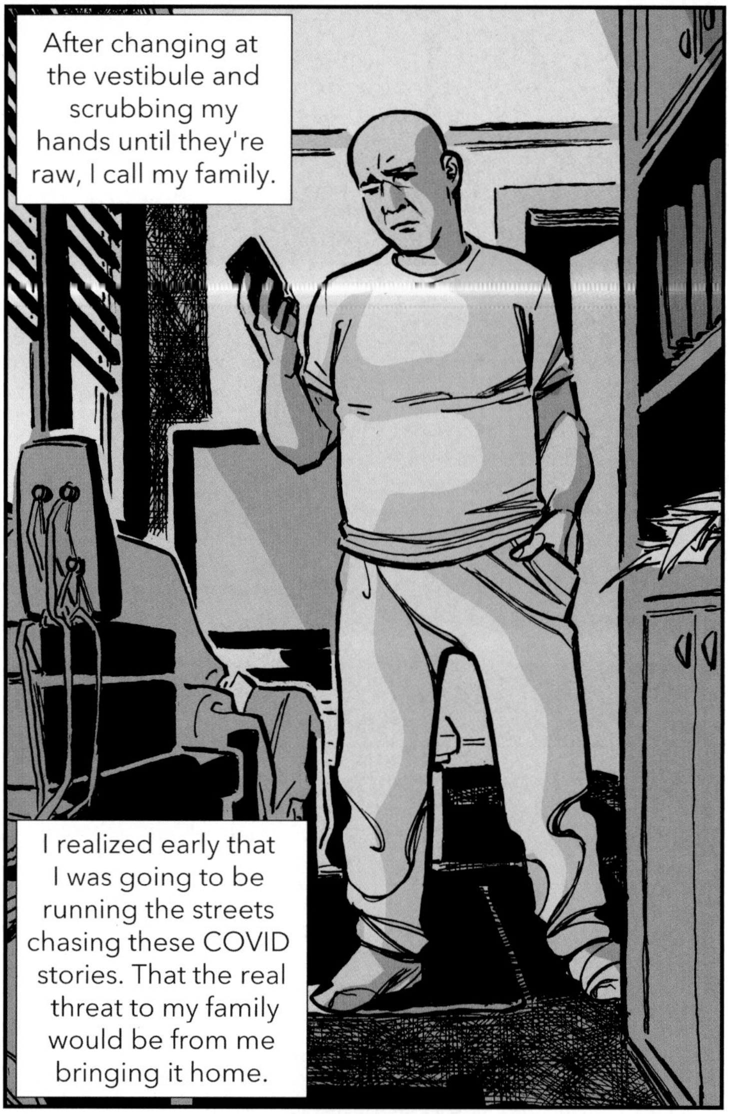
After changing at the vestibule and scrubbing my hands until they're raw, I call my family.
I realized early that I was going to be running the streets chasing these COVID stories. That the real threat to my family would be from me bringing it home.

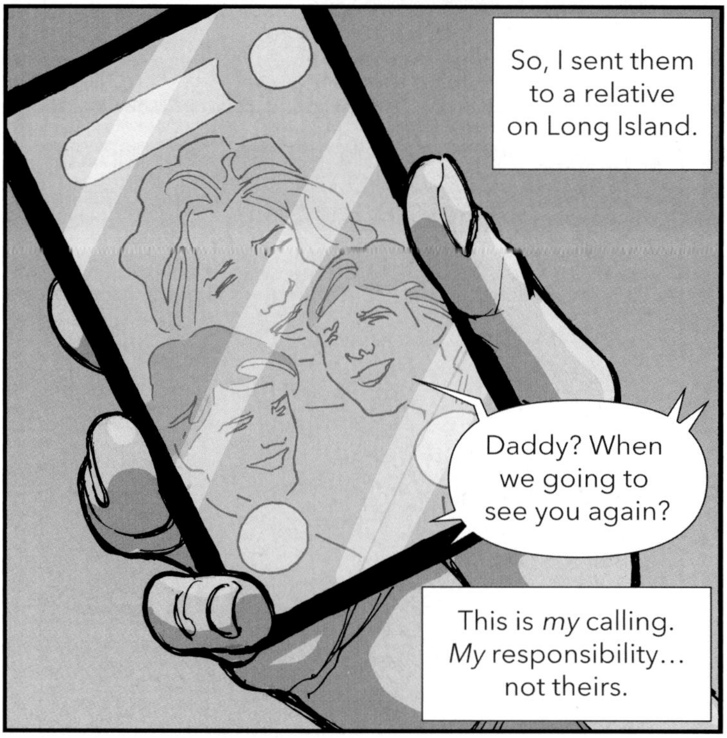
So, I sent them to a relative on Long Island.
Daddy? When we going to see you again?
This is *my* calling. *My* responsibility... not theirs.

CHAPTER 5
LOCKED DOWN IN WUHAN DURING COVID'S PEAK

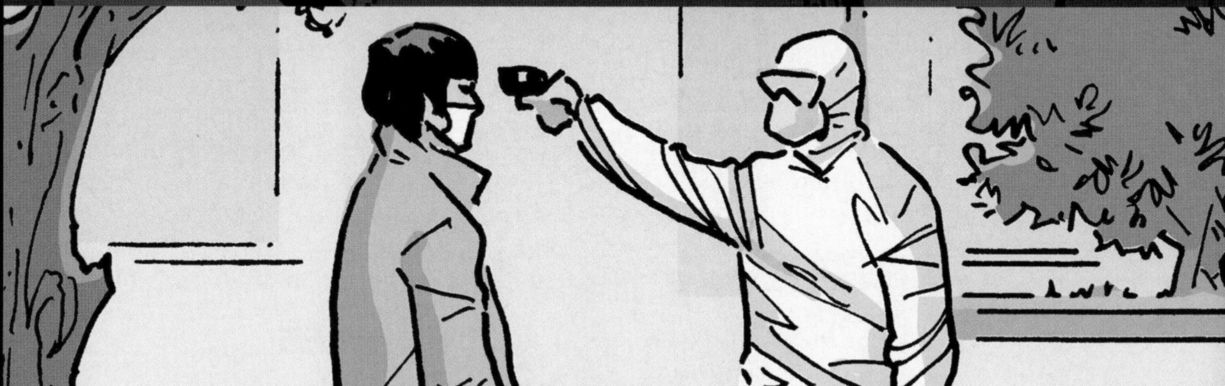

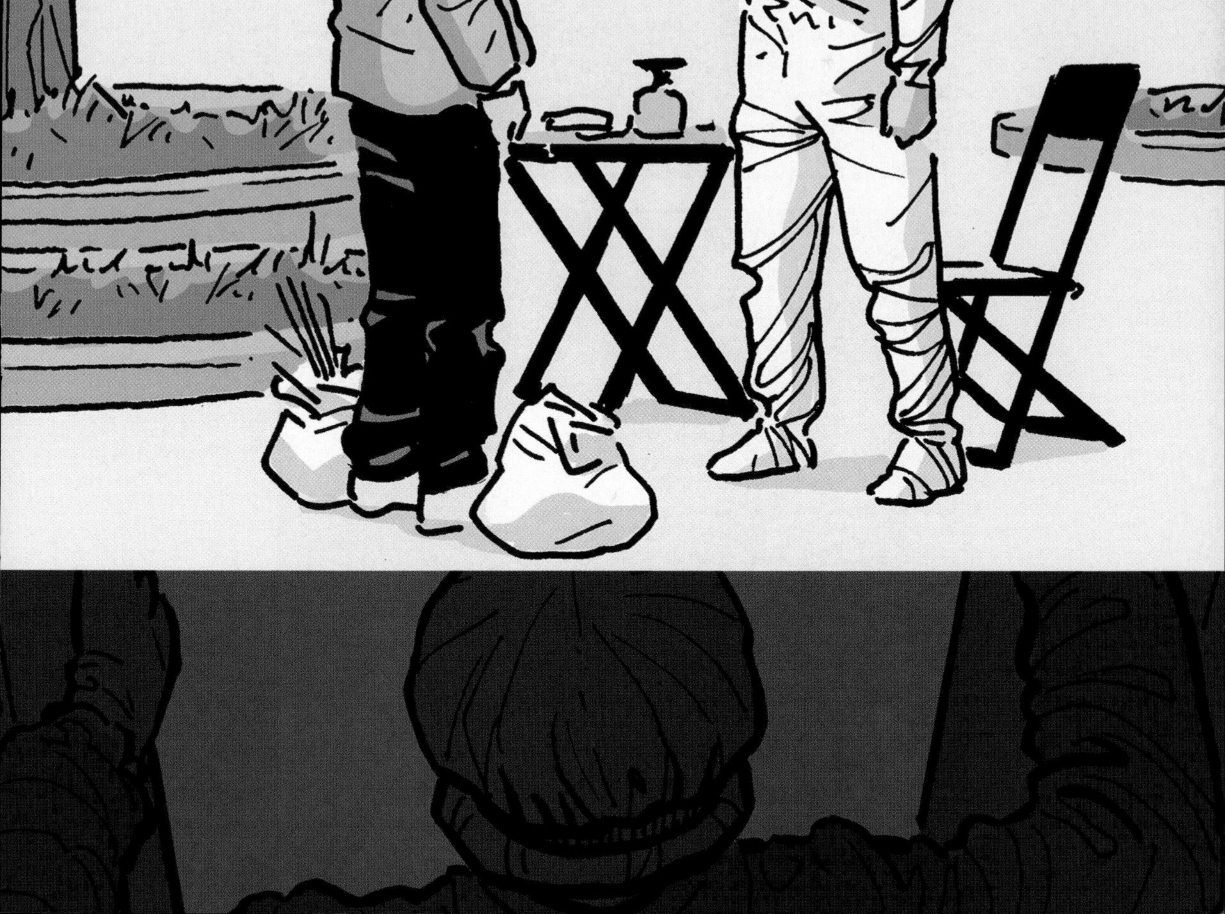

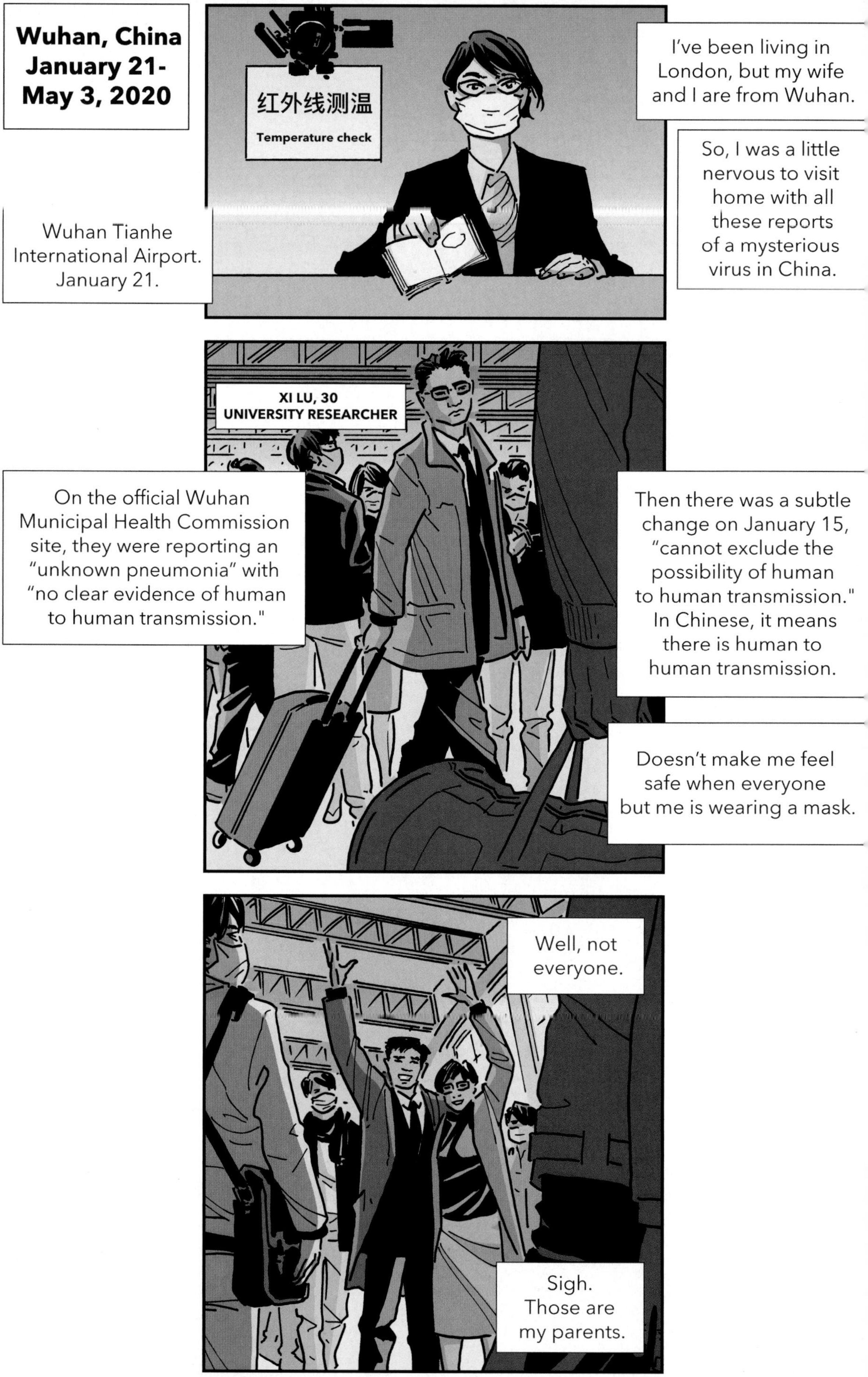
Wuhan, China January 21- May 3, 2020
Wuhan Tianhe International Airport. January 21.
红外线测温
Temperature check
I've been living in London, but my wife and I are from Wuhan.
So, I was a little nervous to visit home with all these reports of a mysterious virus in China.
XI LU, 30 UNIVERSITY RESEARCHER
On the official Wuhan Municipal Health Commission site, they were reporting an "unknown pneumonia" with "no clear evidence of human to human transmission."
Then there was a subtle change on January 15, "cannot exclude the possibility of human to human transmission." In Chinese, it means there is human to human transmission.
Doesn't make me feel safe when everyone but me is wearing a mask.
Well, not everyone.
Sigh. Those are my parents.

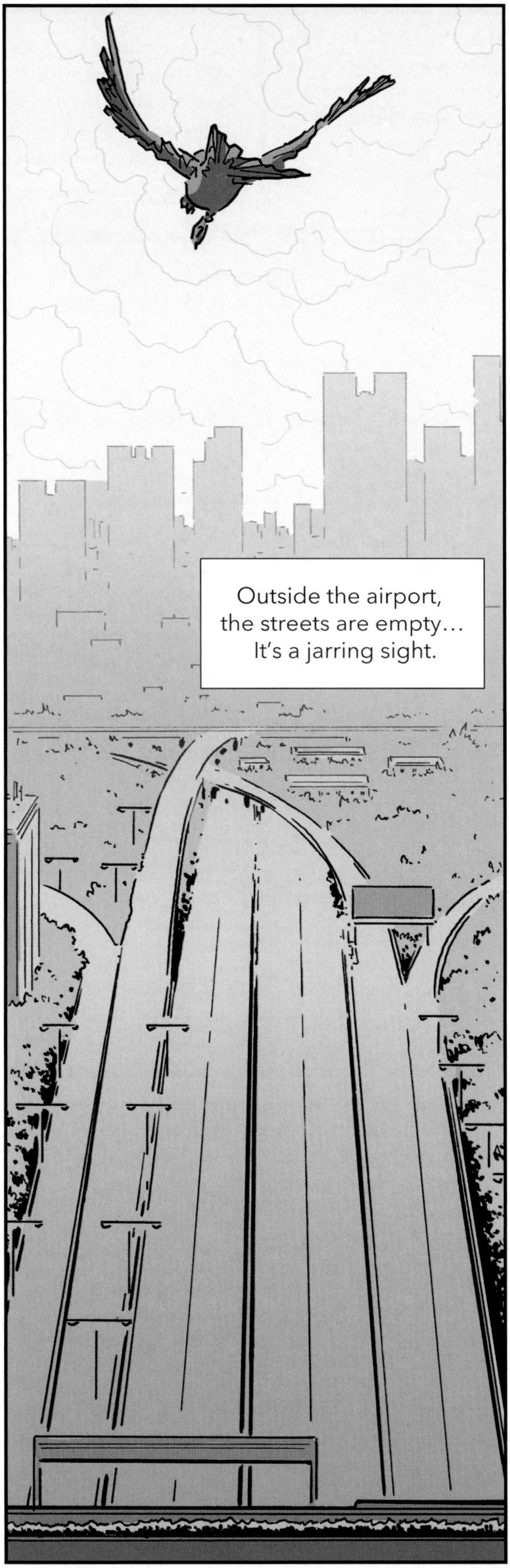
Outside the airport,
the streets are empty…
It's a jarring sight.

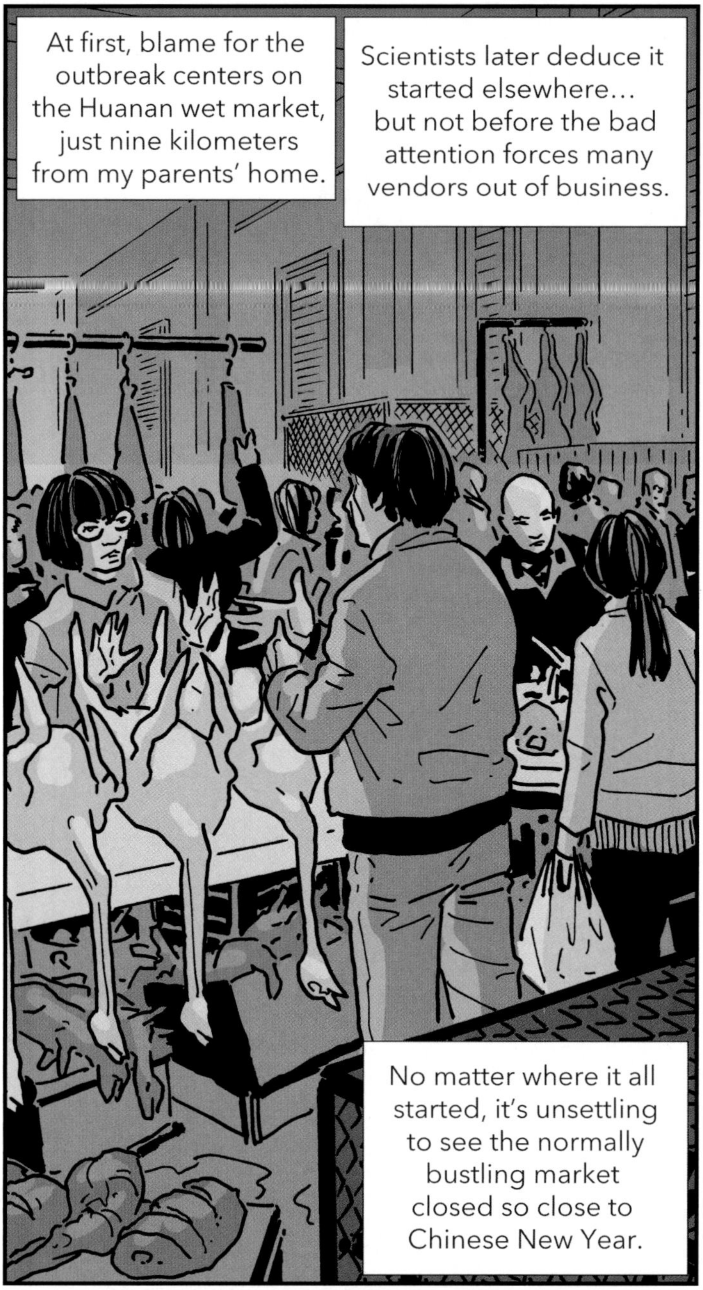
At first, blame for the outbreak centers on the Huanan wet market, just nine kilometers from my parents' home.
Scientists later deduce it started elsewhere… but not before the bad attention forces many vendors out of business.
No matter where it all started, it's unsettling to see the normally bustling market closed so close to Chinese New Year.

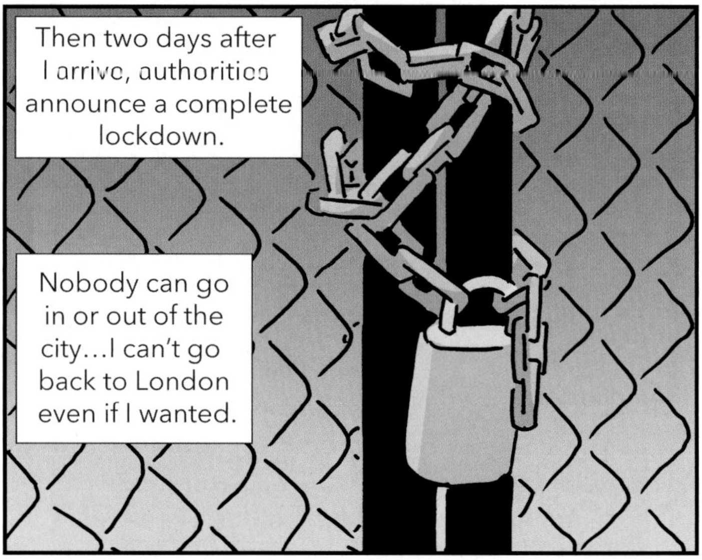
Then two days after I arrive, authorities announce a complete lockdown.
Nobody can go in or out of the city…I can't go back to London even if I wanted.

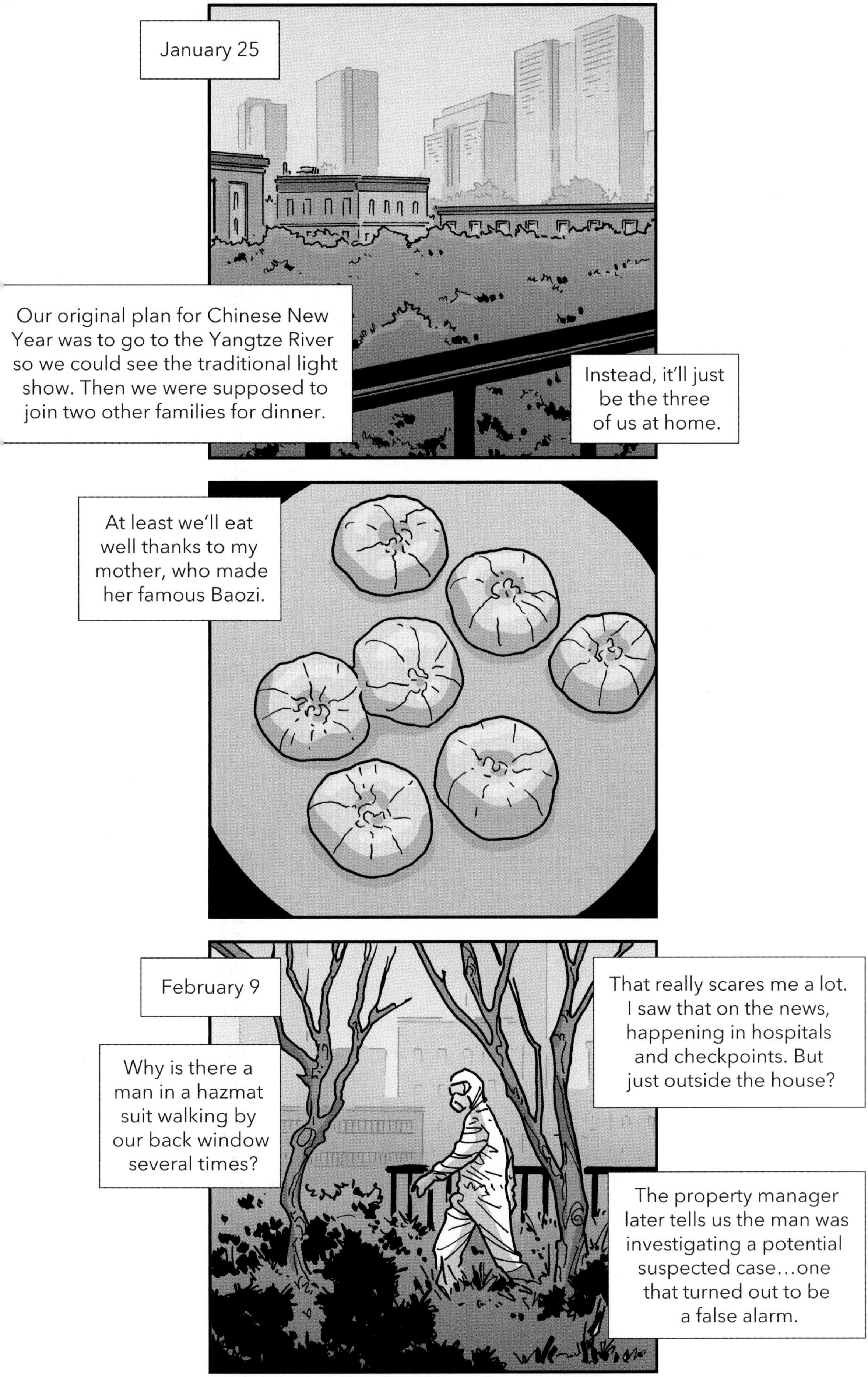
January 25
Our original plan for Chinese New Year was to go to the Yangtze River so we could see the traditional light show. Then we were supposed to join two other families for dinner.
Instead, it'll just be the three of us at home.
At least we'll eat well thanks to my mother, who made her famous Baozi.
February 9
Why is there a man in a hazmat suit walking by our back window several times?
That really scares me a lot. I saw that on the news, happening in hospitals and checkpoints. But just outside the house?
The property manager later tells us the man was investigating a potential suspected case…one that turned out to be a false alarm.

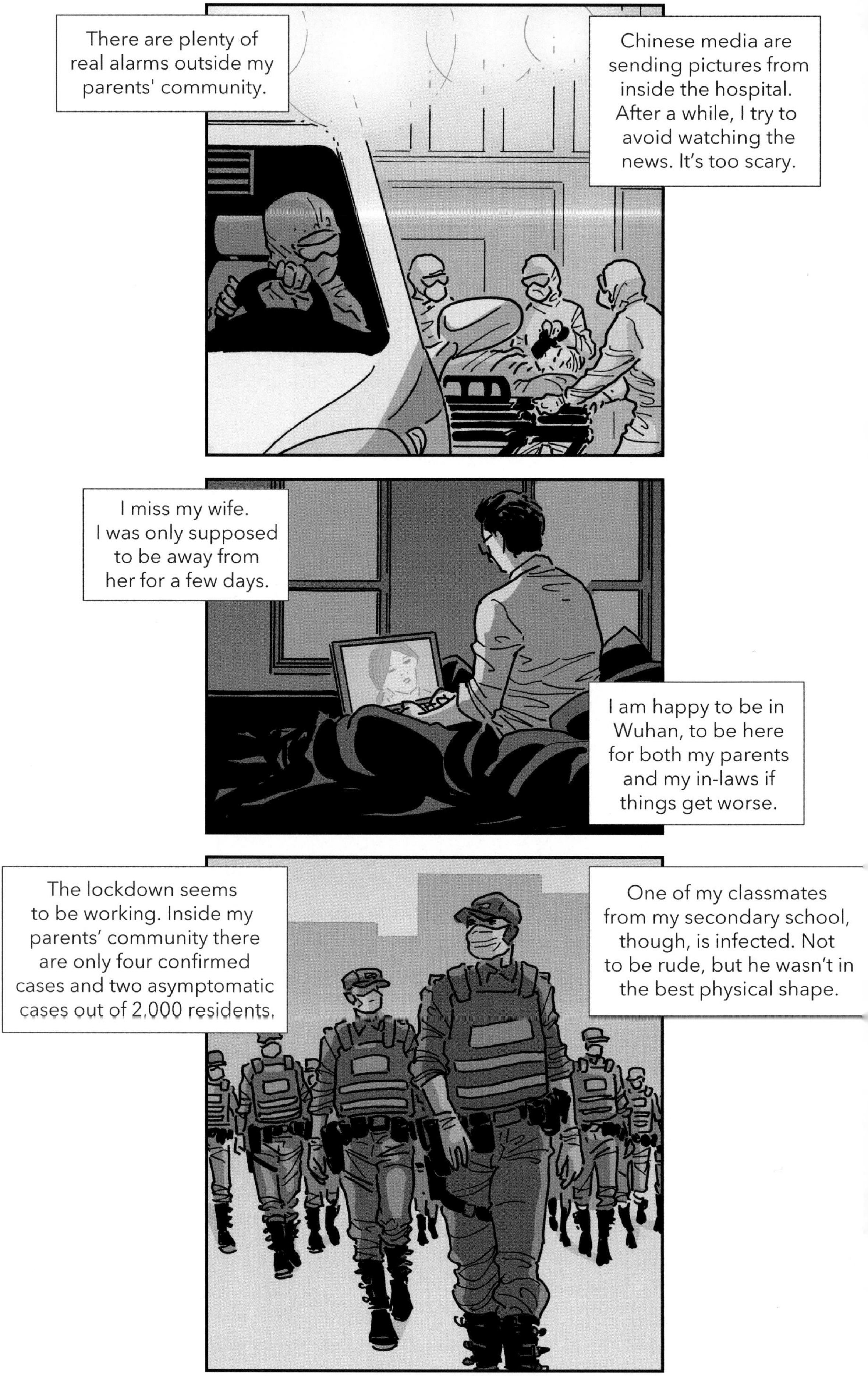
There are plenty of real alarms outside my parents' community.
Chinese media are sending pictures from inside the hospital. After a while, I try to avoid watching the news. It's too scary.
I miss my wife. I was only supposed to be away from her for a few days.
I am happy to be in Wuhan, to be here for both my parents and my in-laws if things get worse.
The lockdown seems to be working. Inside my parents' community there are only four confirmed cases and two asymptomatic cases out of 2,000 residents.
One of my classmates from my secondary school, though, is infected. Not to be rude, but he wasn't in the best physical shape.

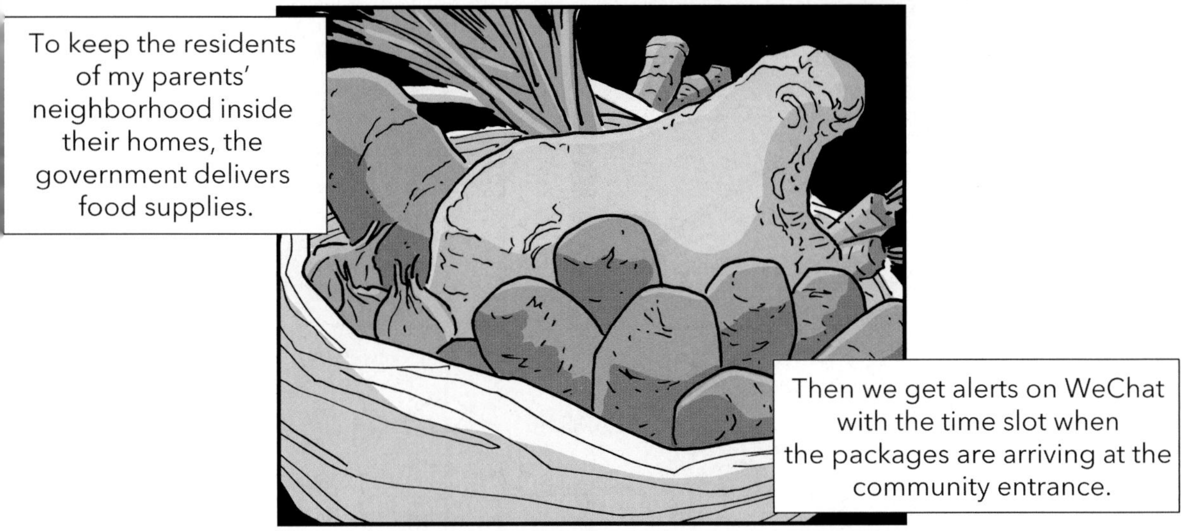
To keep the residents of my parents' neighborhood inside their homes, the government delivers food supplies.
Then we get alerts on WeChat with the time slot when the packages are arriving at the community entrance.

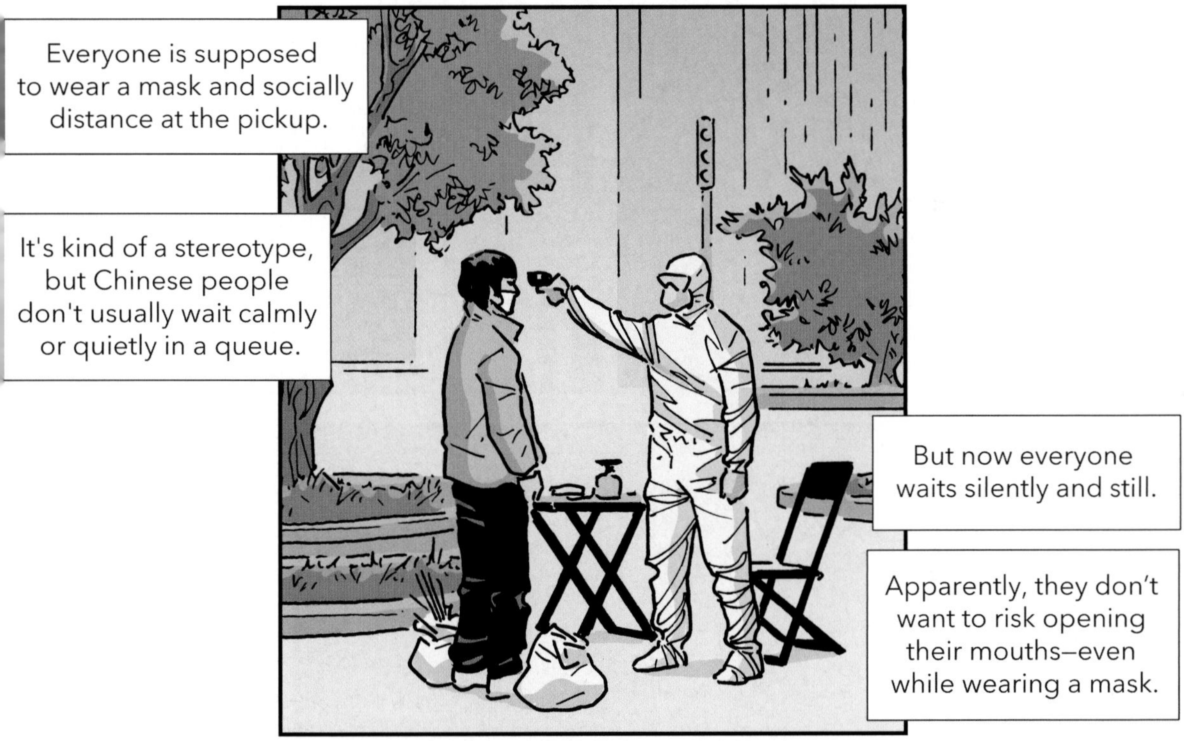
Everyone is supposed to wear a mask and socially distance at the pickup.
It's kind of a stereotype, but Chinese people don't usually wait calmly or quietly in a queue.
But now everyone waits silently and still.
Apparently, they don't want to risk opening their mouths–even while wearing a mask.

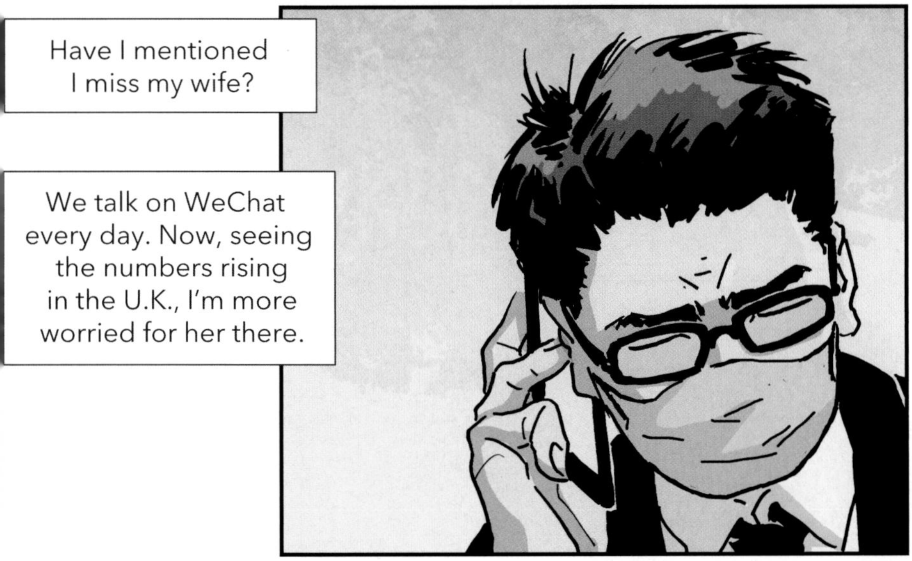
Have I mentioned I miss my wife?
We talk on WeChat every day. Now, seeing the numbers rising in the U.K., I'm more worried for her there.

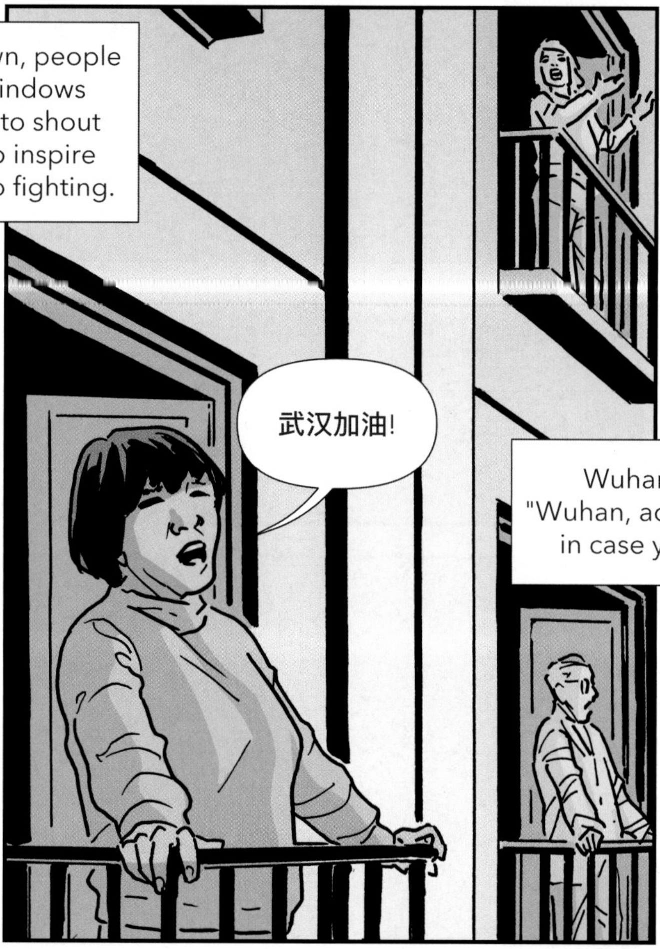
During lockdown, people go to their windows and balconies to shout out slogans to inspire my city to keep fighting.
武汉加油!
Wuhan jiayou means "Wuhan, add oil" or "carry on!" in case you're wondering.

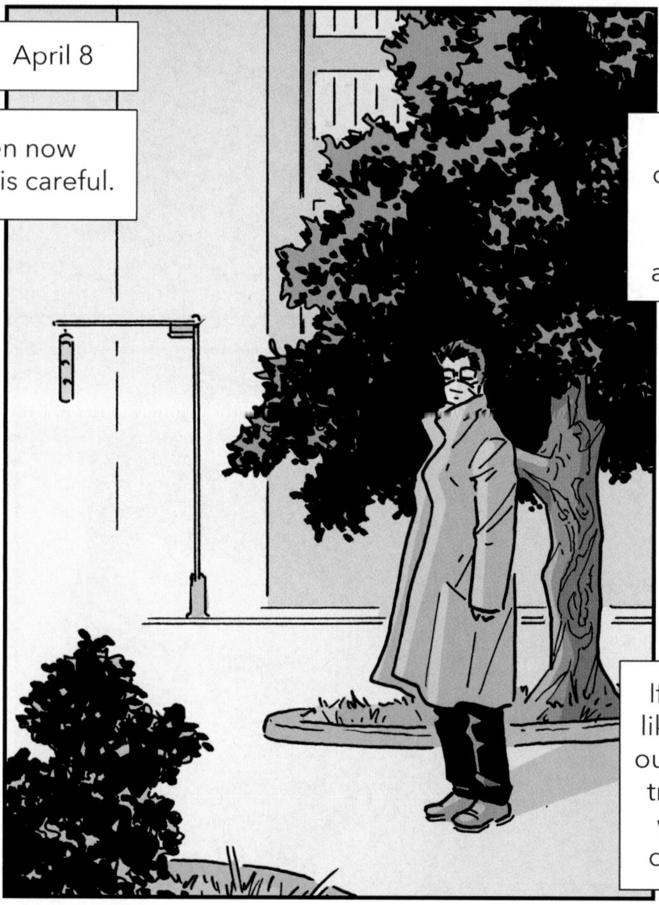
April 8
But even now everyone is careful.
The government officially ended the lockdown, so I can finally move around more freely.
If we treat the virus like SARS, it will turn out to be the flu. If we treat it like the flu, it will turn out to be deadlier, like SARS.

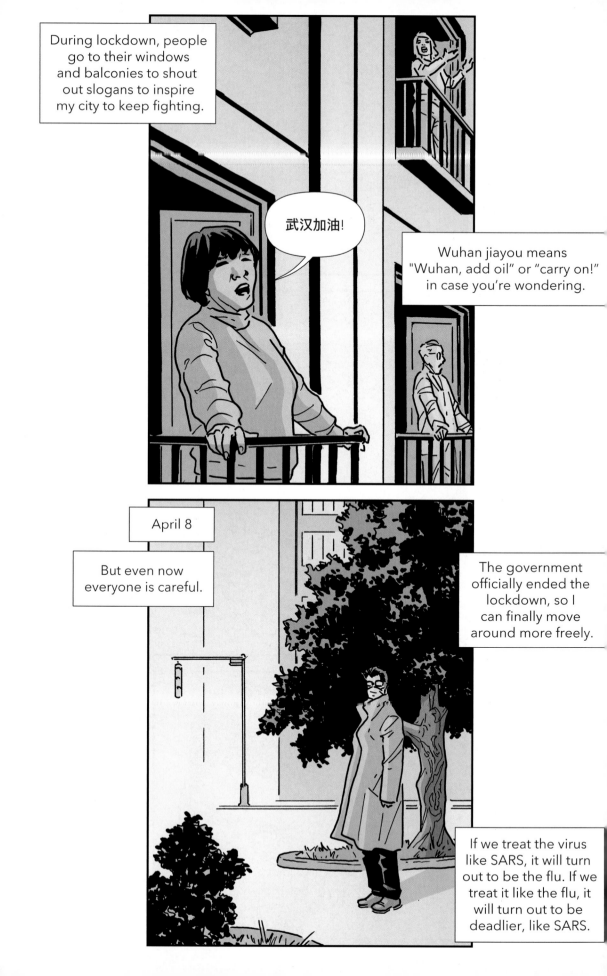

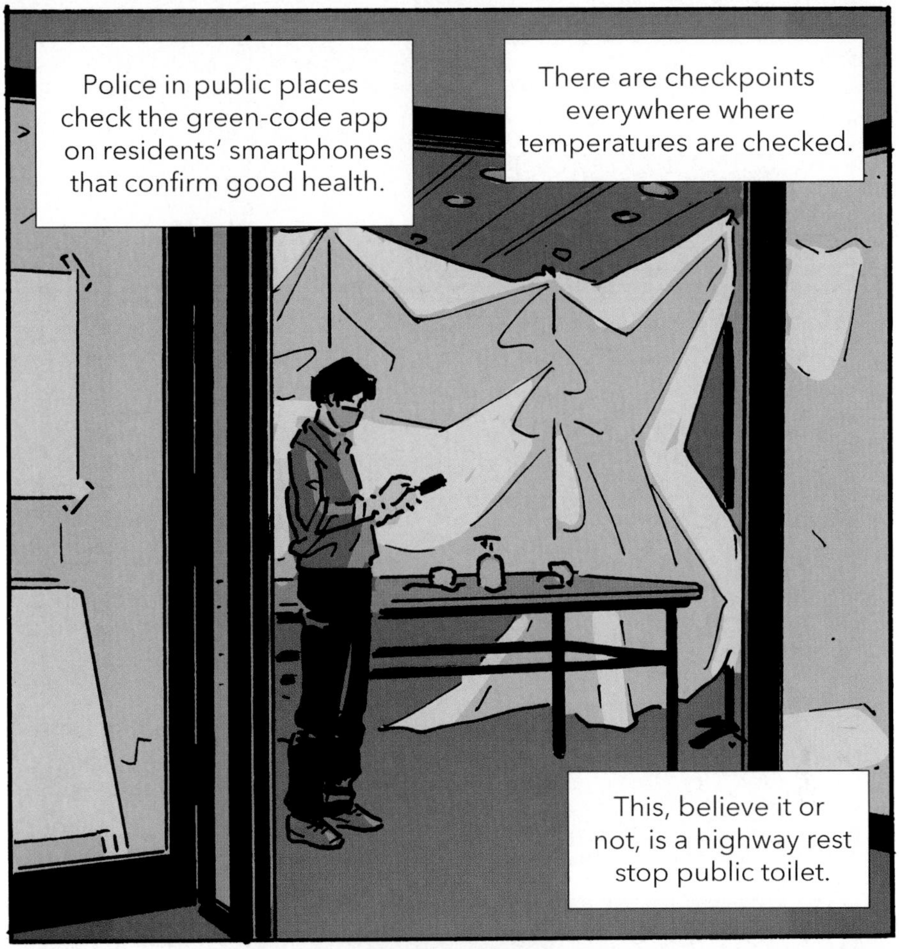
Police in public places check the green-code app on residents' smartphones that confirm good health.
There are checkpoints everywhere where temperatures are checked.
This, believe it or not, is a highway rest stop public toilet.

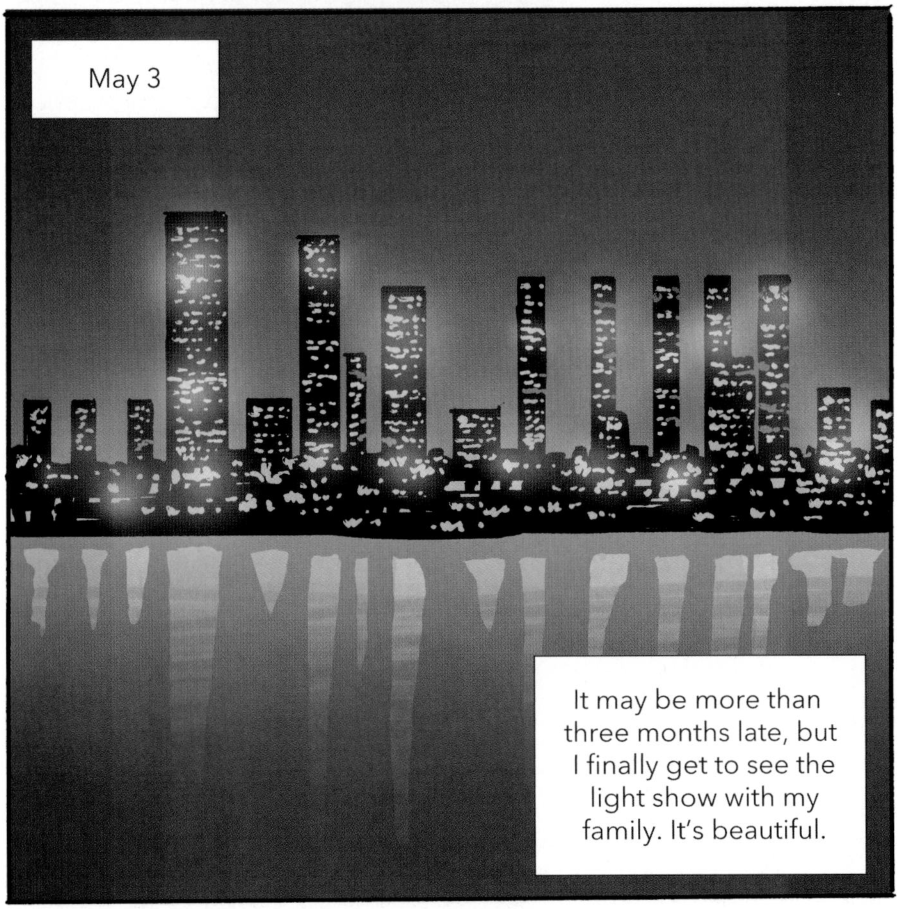
May 3
It may be more than three months late, but I finally get to see the light show with my family. It's beautiful.

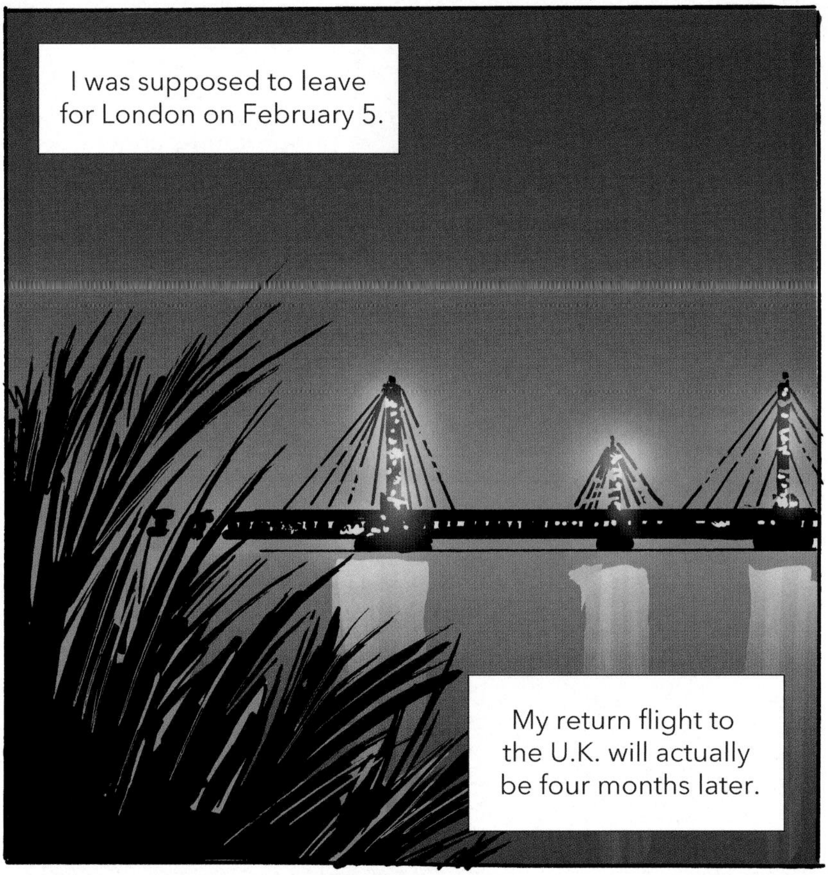
I was supposed to leave for London on February 5.
My return flight to the U.K. will actually be four months later.

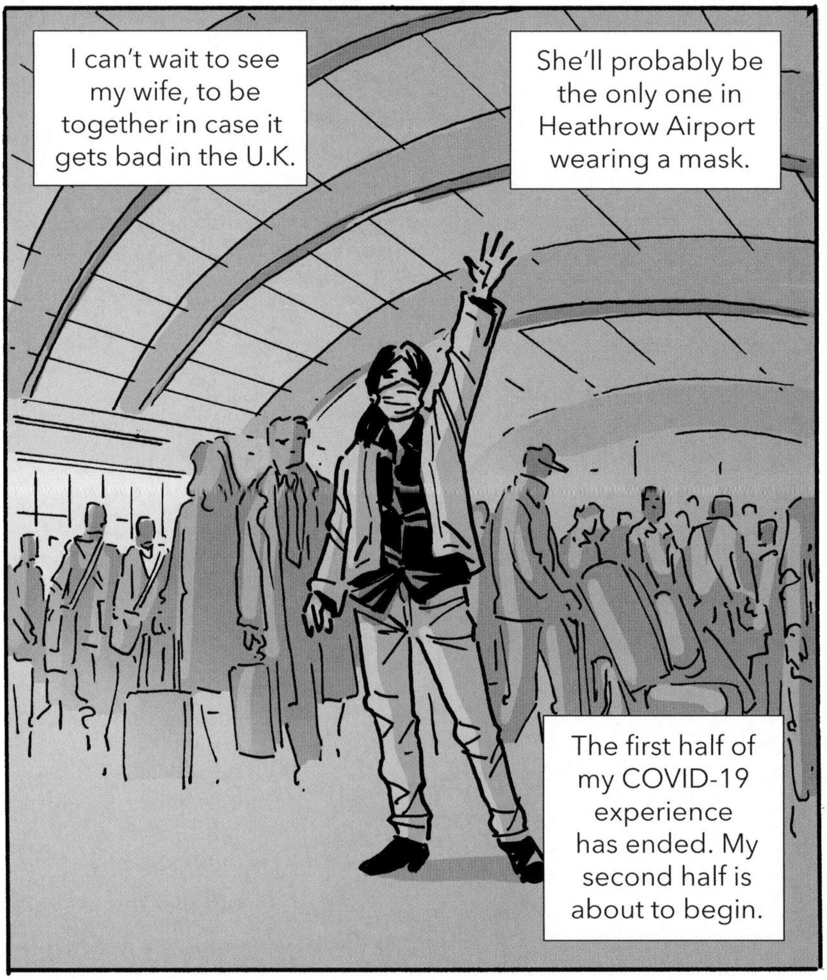
I can't wait to see my wife, to be together in case it gets bad in the U.K.
She'll probably be the only one in Heathrow Airport wearing a mask.
The first half of my COVID-19 experience has ended. My second half is about to begin.

CHAPTER 6

VIRUS TESTING BECOMES A TEST OF CHARACTER

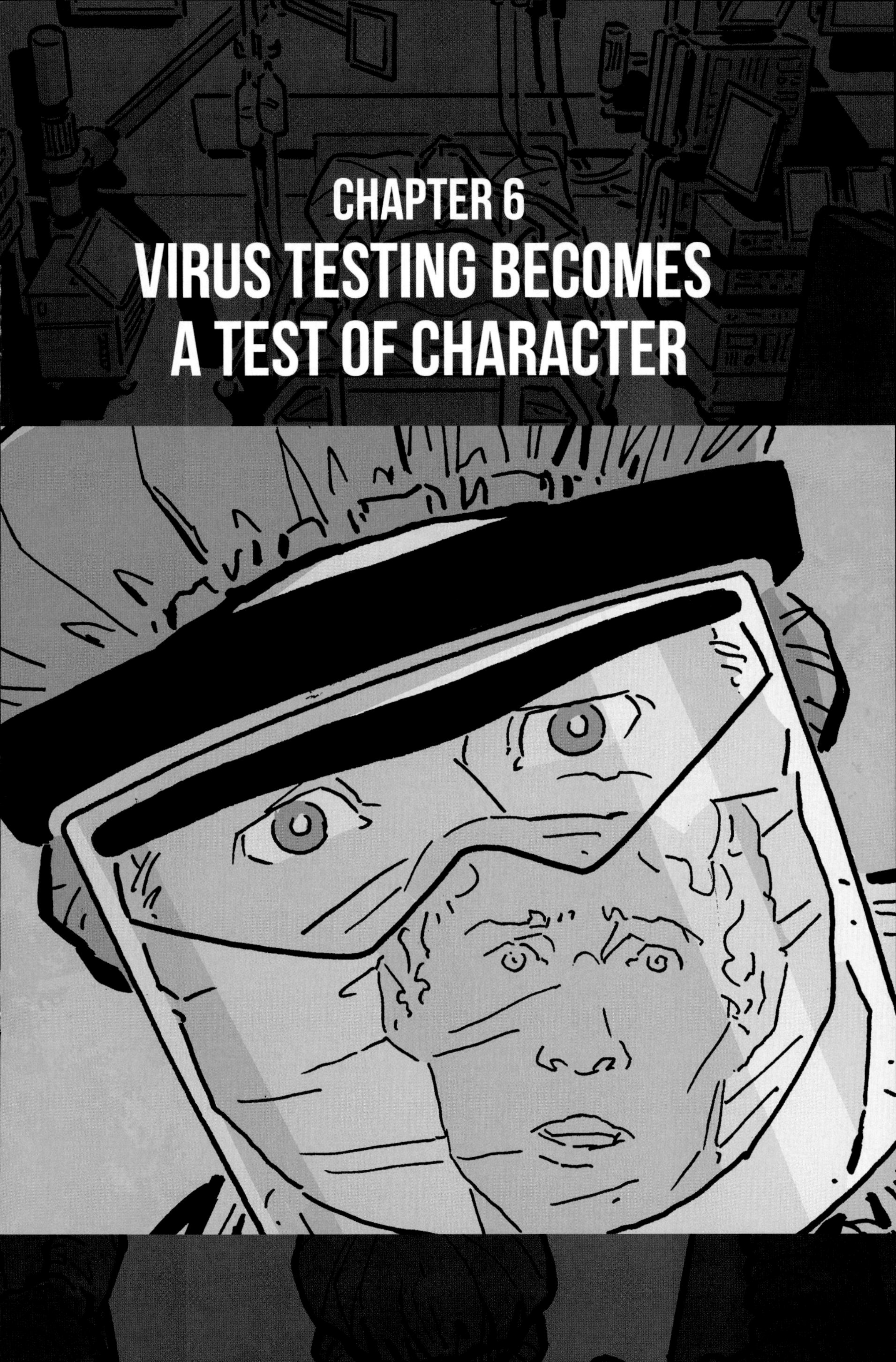

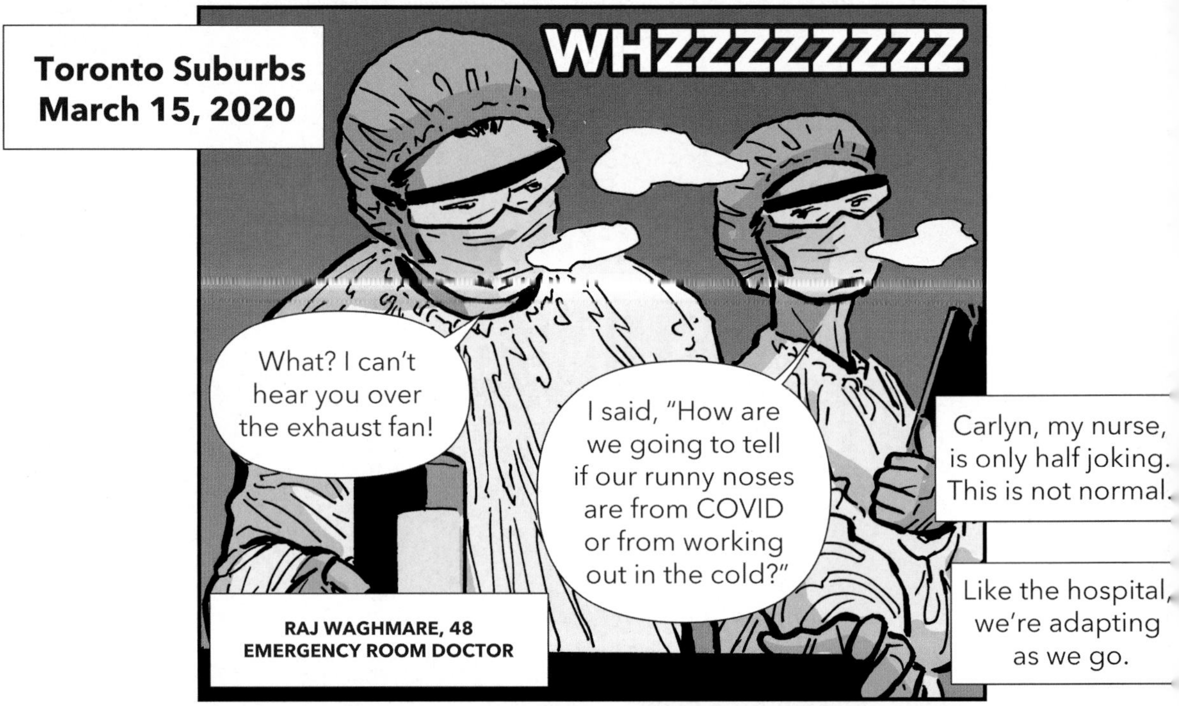
Toronto Suburbs
March 15, 2020
WHZZZZZZZZZ
RAJ WAGHMARE, 48
EMERGENCY ROOM DOCTOR
What? I can't hear you over the exhaust fan!
I said, "How are we going to tell if our runny noses are from COVID or from working out in the cold?"
Carlyn, my nurse, is only half joking. This is not normal.
Like the hospital, we're adapting as we go.

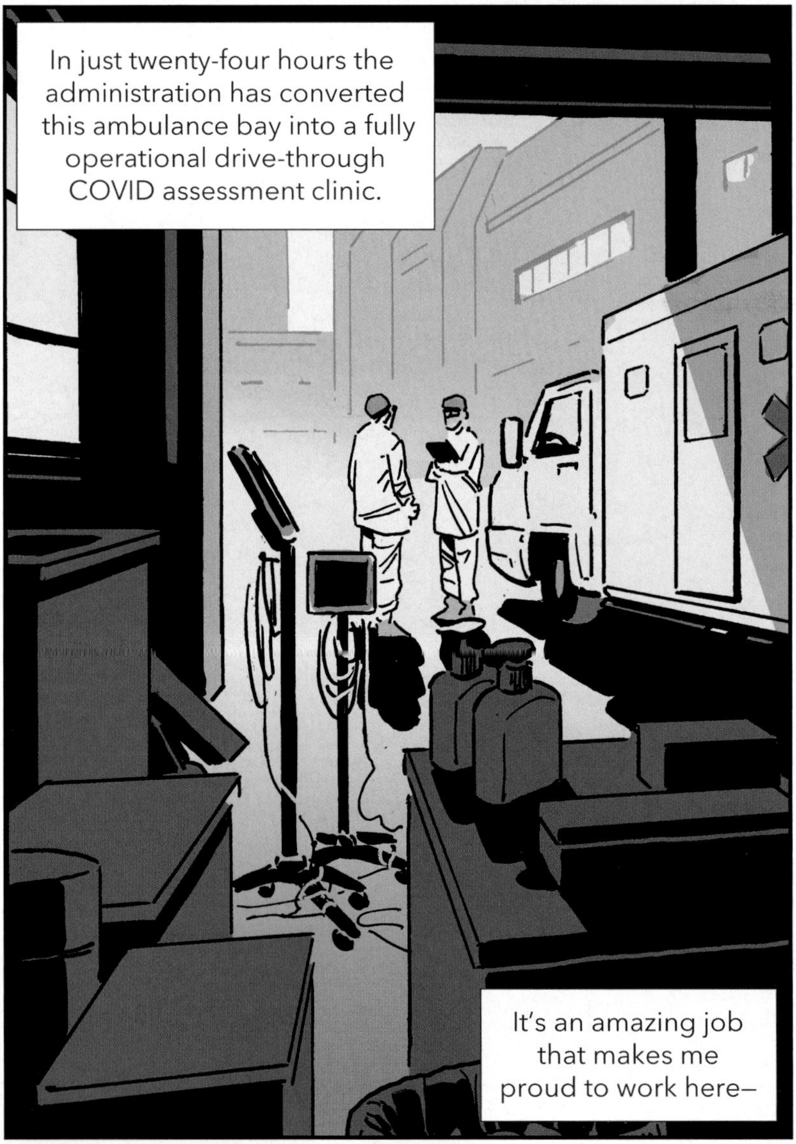
In just twenty-four hours the administration has converted this ambulance bay into a fully operational drive-through COVID assessment clinic.
It's an amazing job that makes me proud to work here–

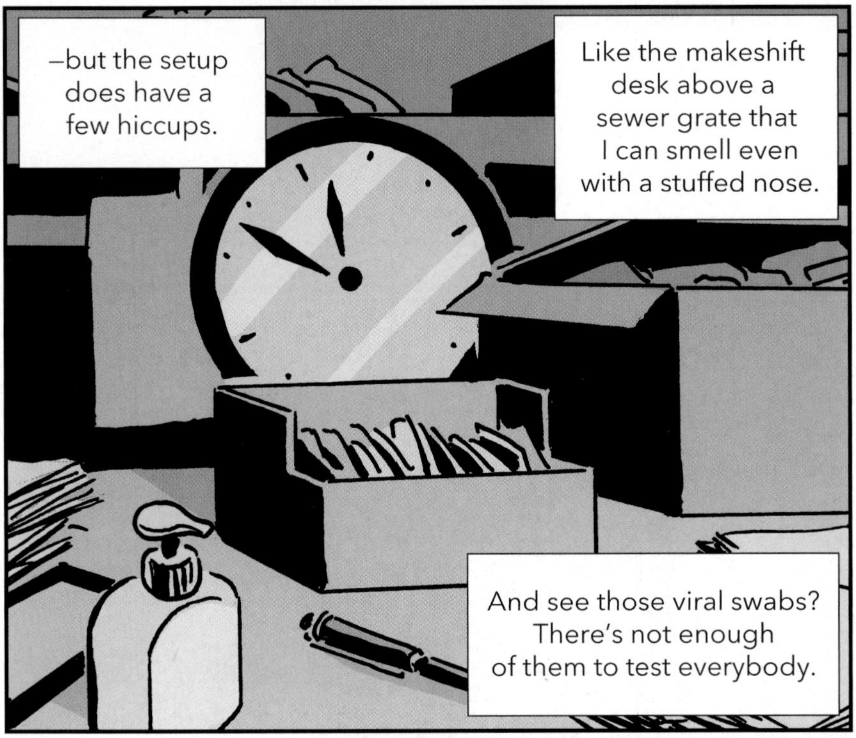
–but the setup does have a few hiccups.
Like the makeshift desk above a sewer grate that I can smell even with a stuffed nose.
And see those viral swabs? There's not enough of them to test everybody.

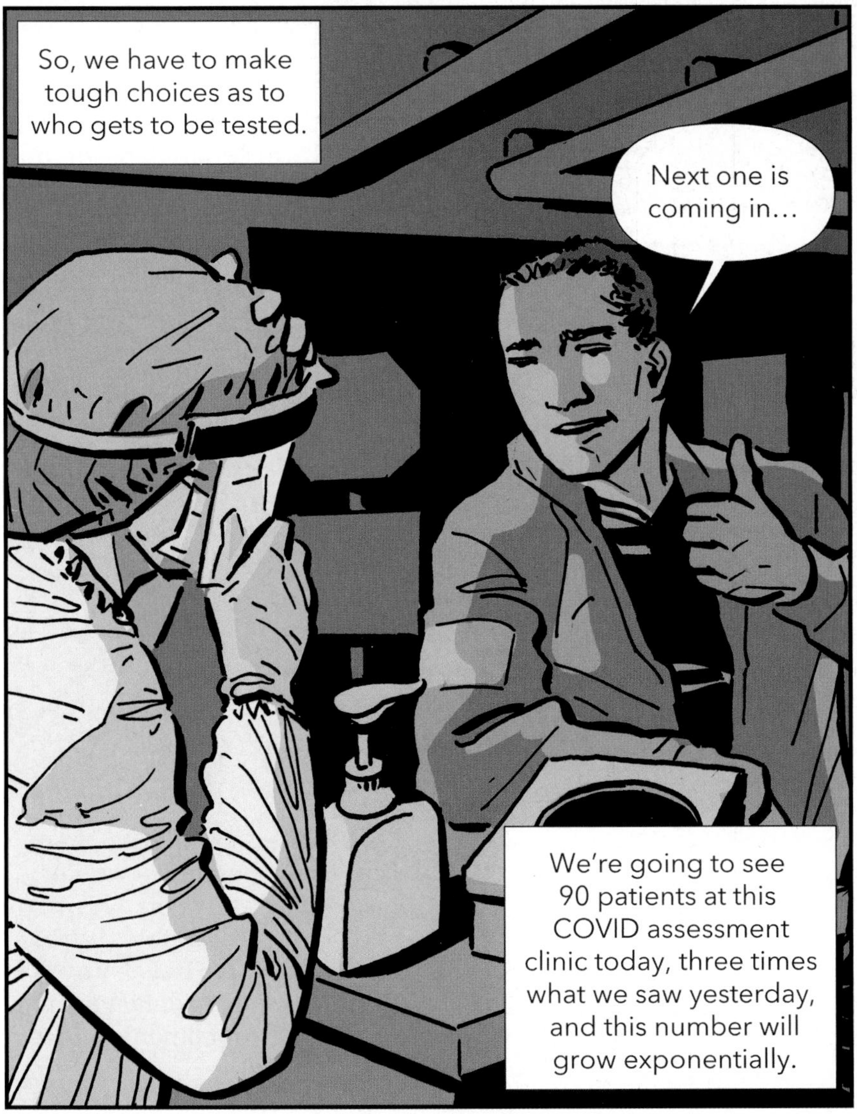
So, we have to make tough choices as to who gets to be tested.
Next one is coming in…
We're going to see 90 patients at this COVID assessment clinic today, three times what we saw yesterday, and this number will grow exponentially.

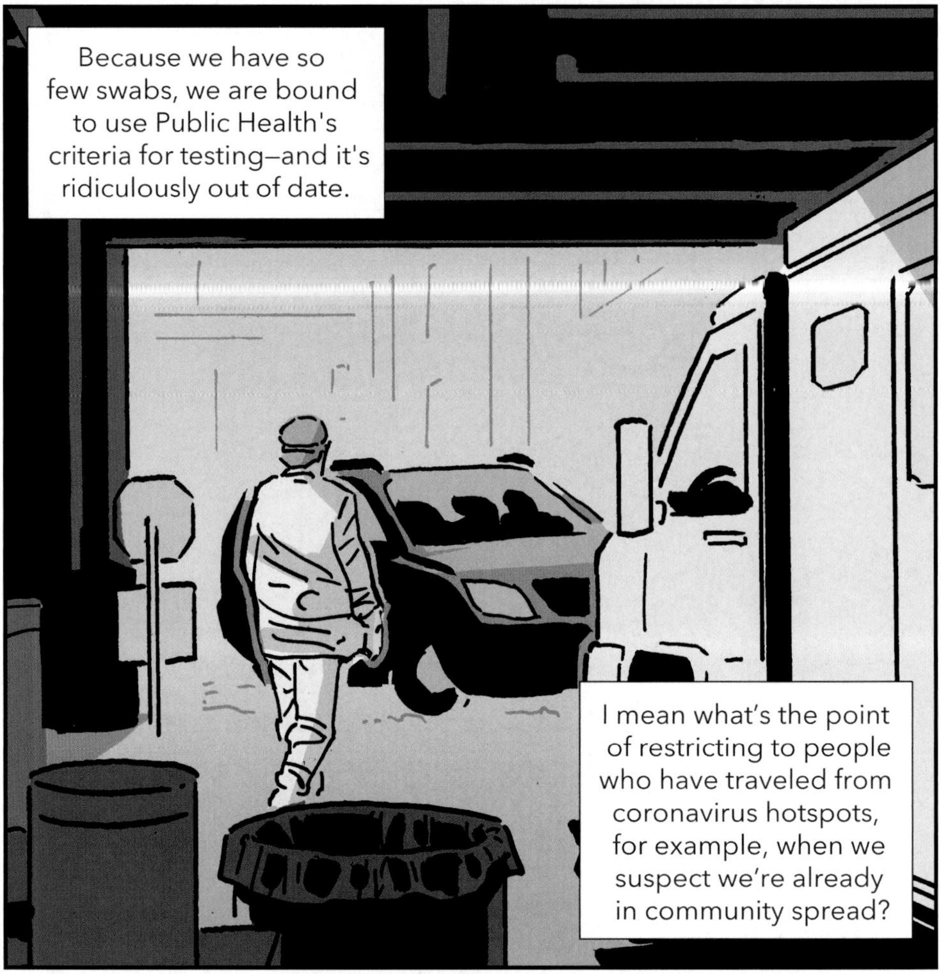
Because we have so few swabs, we are bound to use Public Health's criteria for testing–and it's ridiculously out of date.
I mean what's the point of restricting to people who have traveled from coronavirus hotspots, for example, when we suspect we're already in community spread?

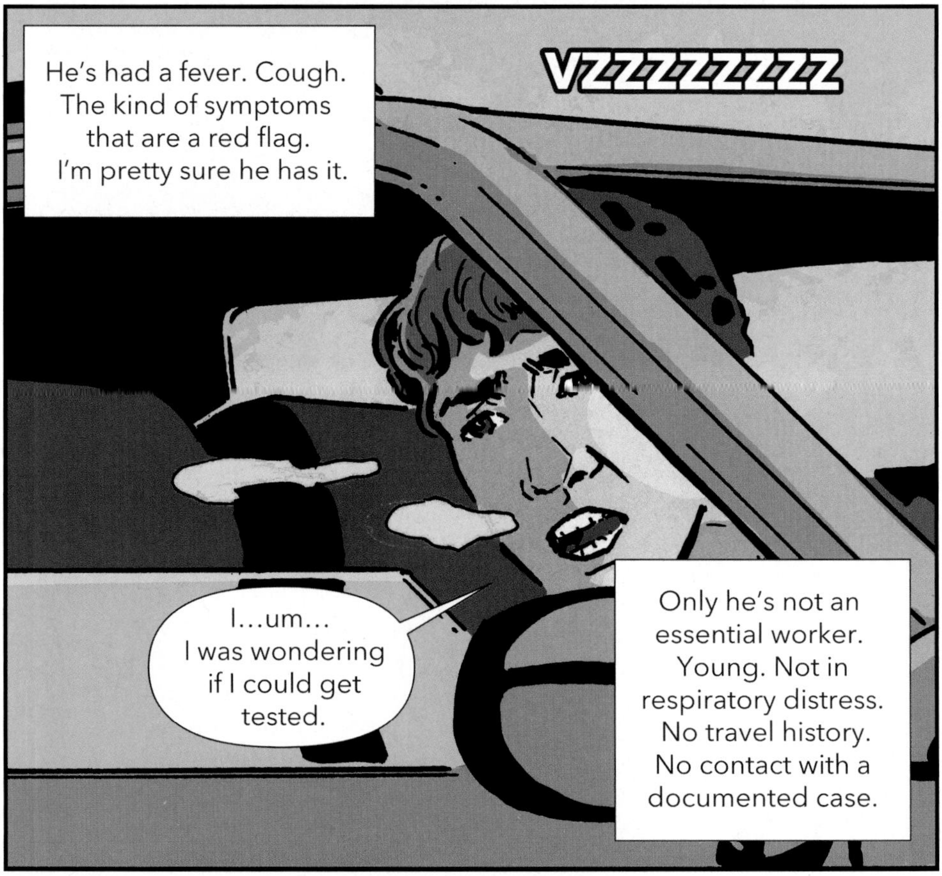
He's had a fever. Cough. The kind of symptoms that are a red flag. I'm pretty sure he has it.
VZZZZZZZZZ
I...um... I was wondering if I could get tested.
Only he's not an essential worker. Young. Not in respiratory distress. No travel history. No contact with a documented case.

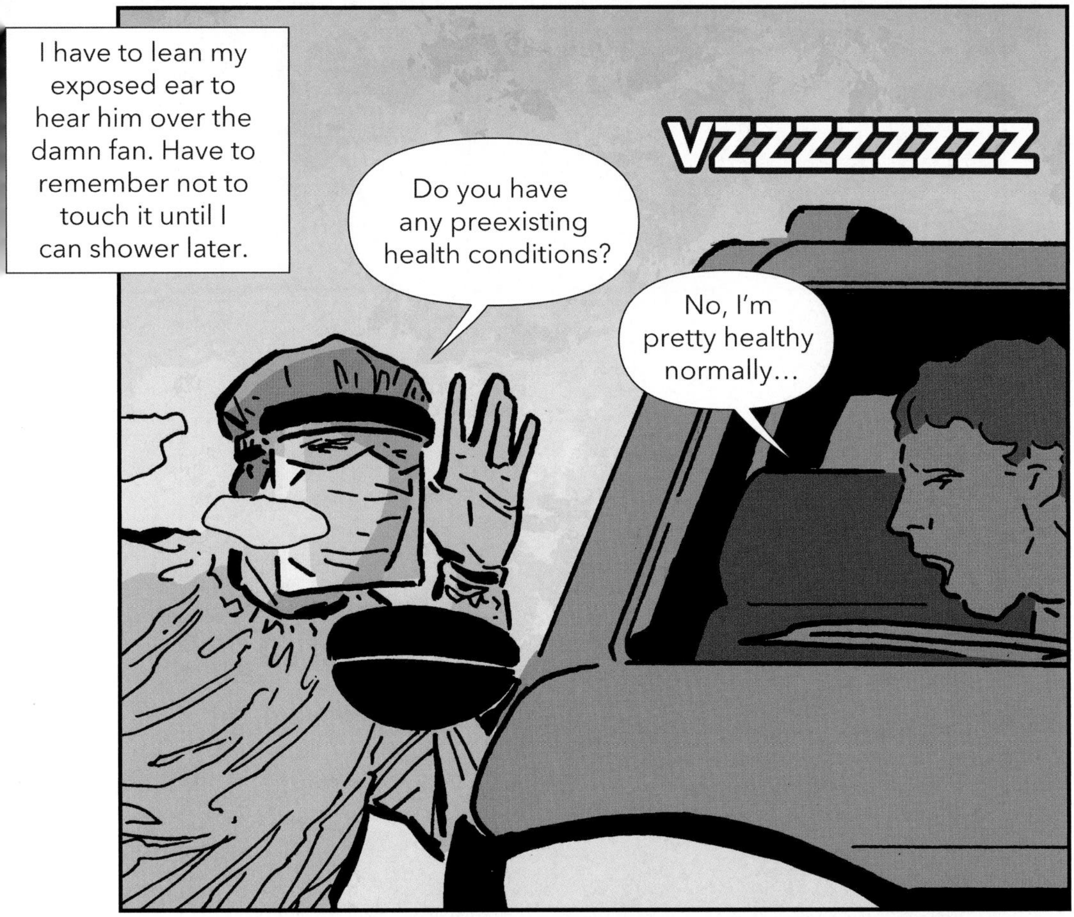
I have to lean my exposed ear to hear him over the damn fan. Have to remember not to touch it until I can shower later.
VZZZZZZZZZZ
Do you have any preexisting health conditions?
No, I'm pretty healthy normally…

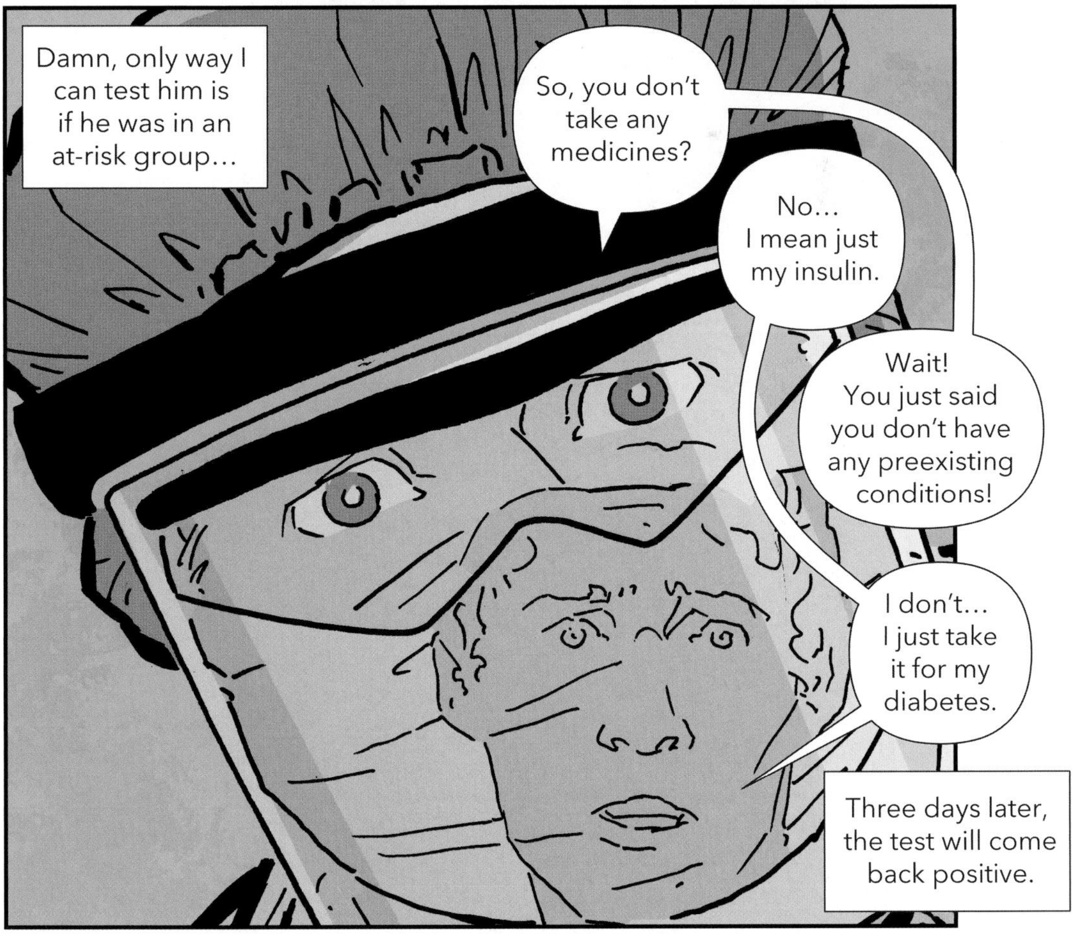
Damn, only way I can test him is if he was in an at-risk group…
So, you don't take any medicines?
No… I mean just my insulin.
Wait! You just said you don't have any preexisting conditions!
I don't… I just take it for my diabetes.
Three days later, the test will come back positive.

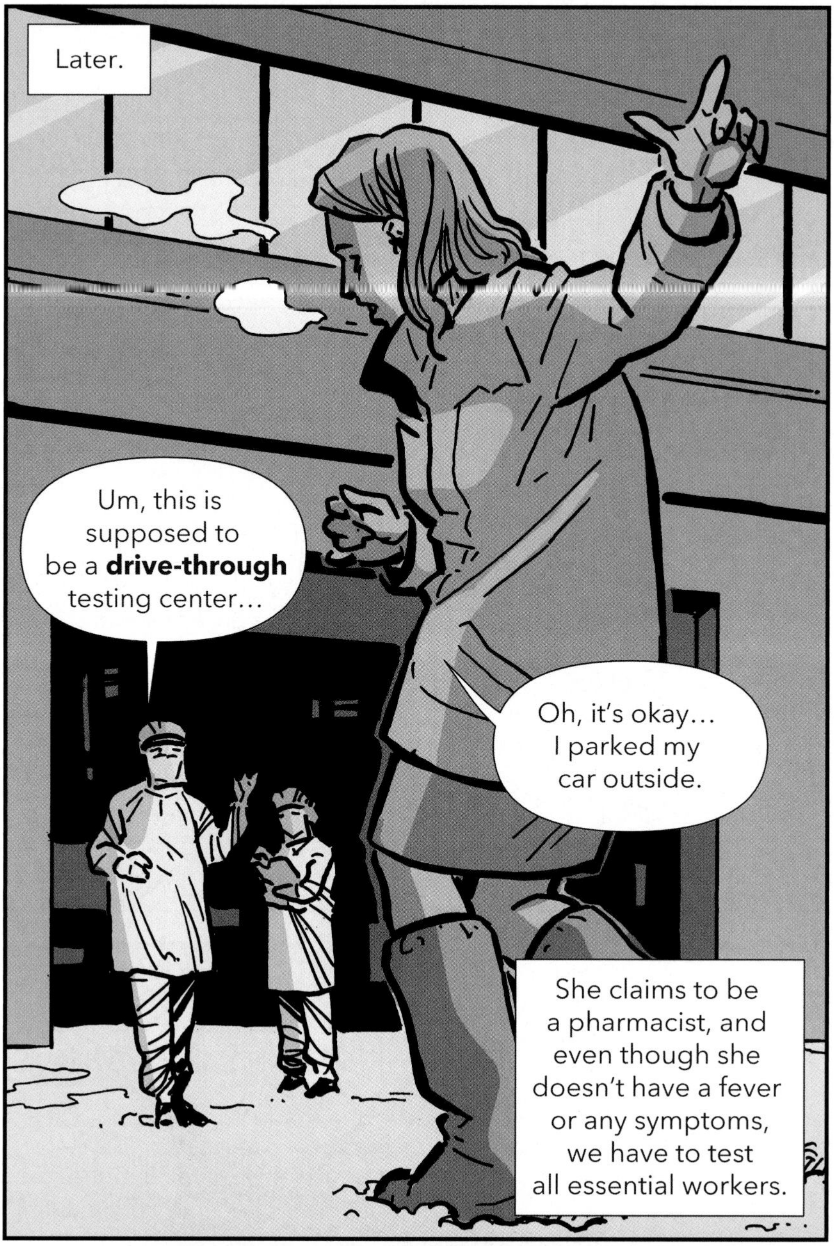
Later.
Um, this is supposed to be a **drive-through** testing center…
Oh, it's okay… I parked my car outside.
She claims to be a pharmacist, and even though she doesn't have a fever or any symptoms, we have to test all essential workers.

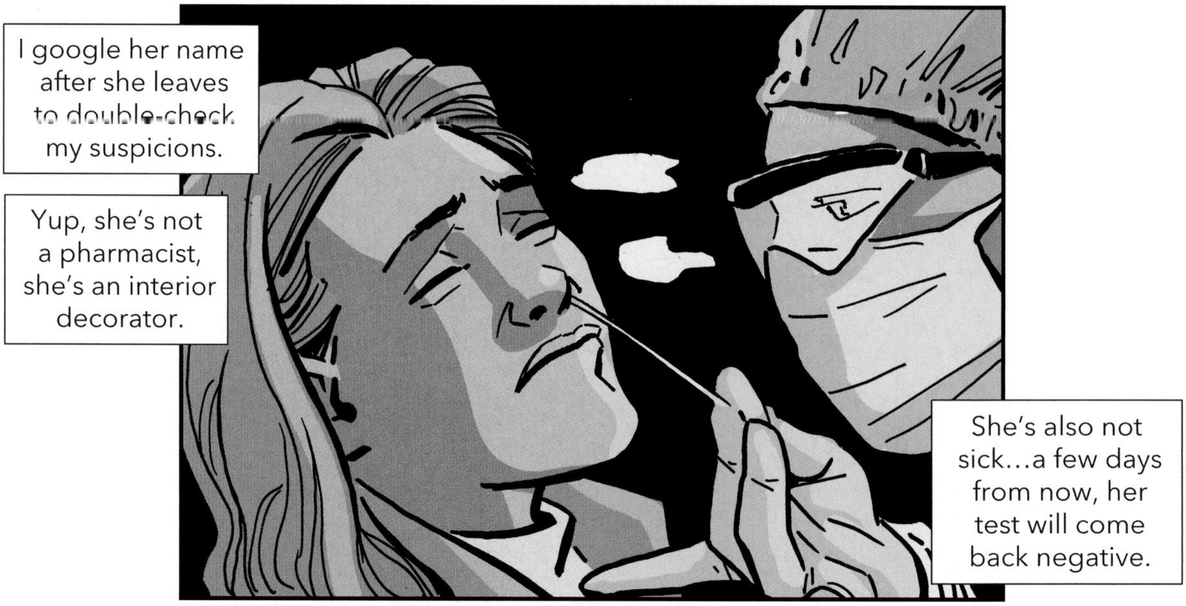
I google her name after she leaves to double-check my suspicions.
Yup, she's not a pharmacist, she's an interior decorator.
She's also not sick…a few days from now, her test will come back negative.

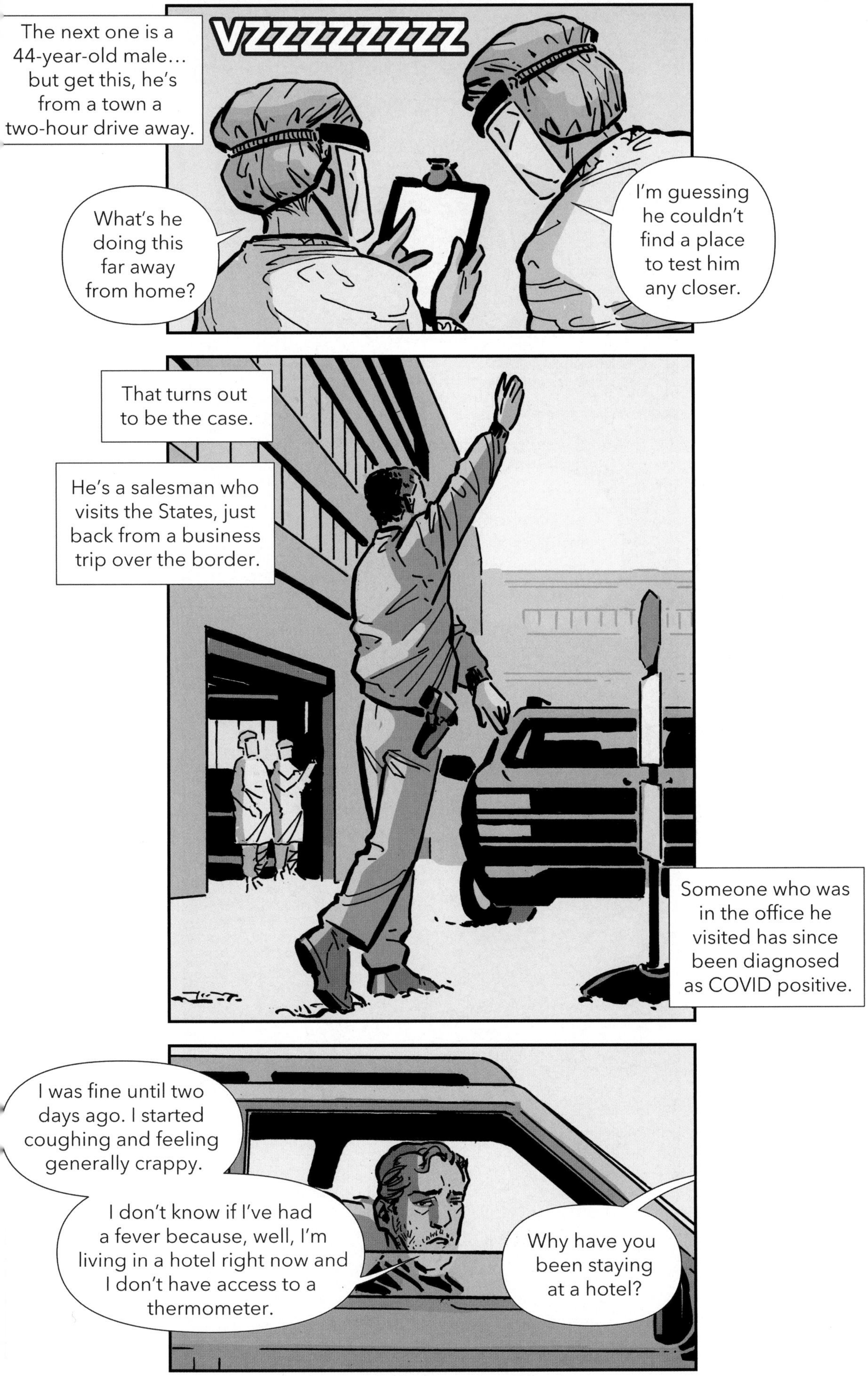
The next one is a 44-year-old male… but get this, he's from a town a two-hour drive away.
VZZZZZZZZZ
What's he doing this far away from home?
I'm guessing he couldn't find a place to test him any closer.
That turns out to be the case.
He's a salesman who visits the States, just back from a business trip over the border.
Someone who was in the office he visited has since been diagnosed as COVID positive.
I was fine until two days ago. I started coughing and feeling generally crappy.
I don't know if I've had a fever because, well, I'm living in a hotel right now and I don't have access to a thermometer.
Why have you been staying at a hotel?

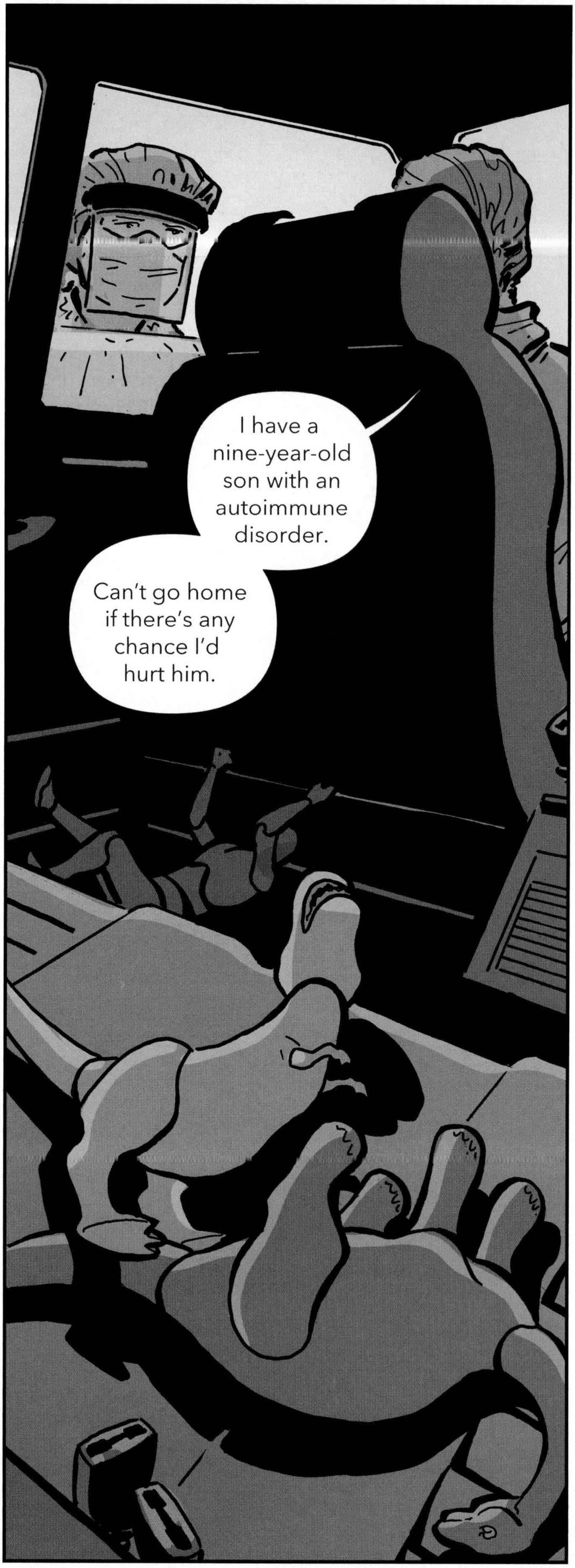
I have a nine-year-old son with an autoimmune disorder.
Can't go home if there's any chance I'd hurt him.

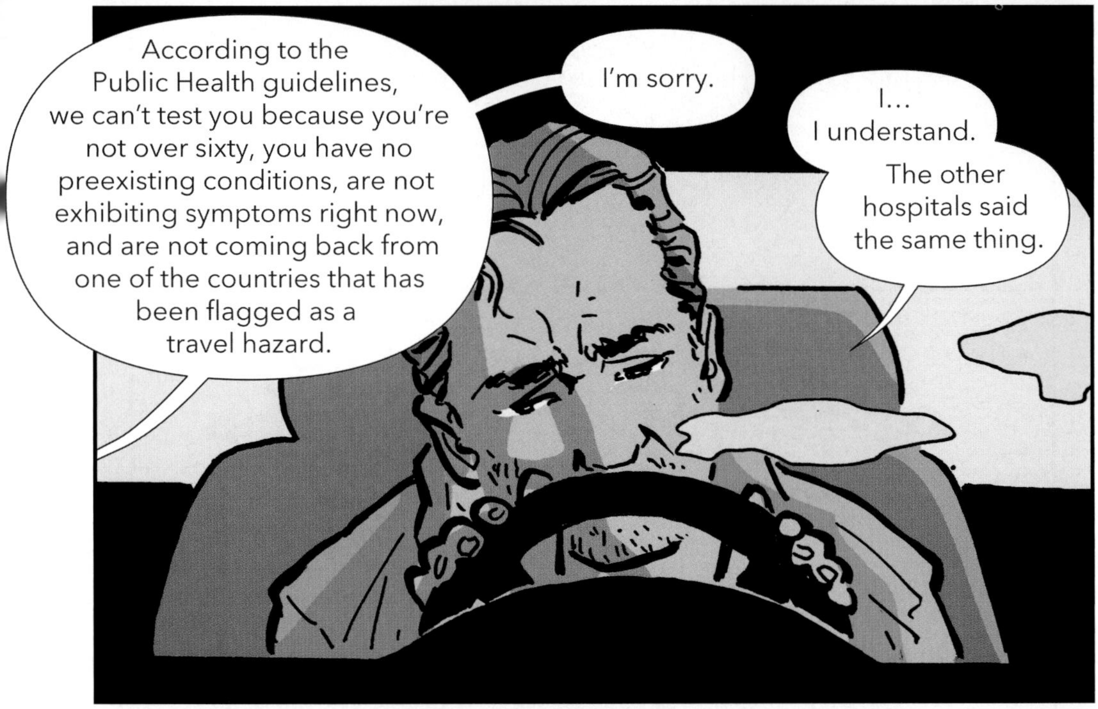
According to the Public Health guidelines, we can't test you because you're not over sixty, you have no preexisting conditions, are not exhibiting symptoms right now, and are not coming back from one of the countries that has been flagged as a travel hazard.
I'm sorry.
I... I understand.
The other hospitals said the same thing.

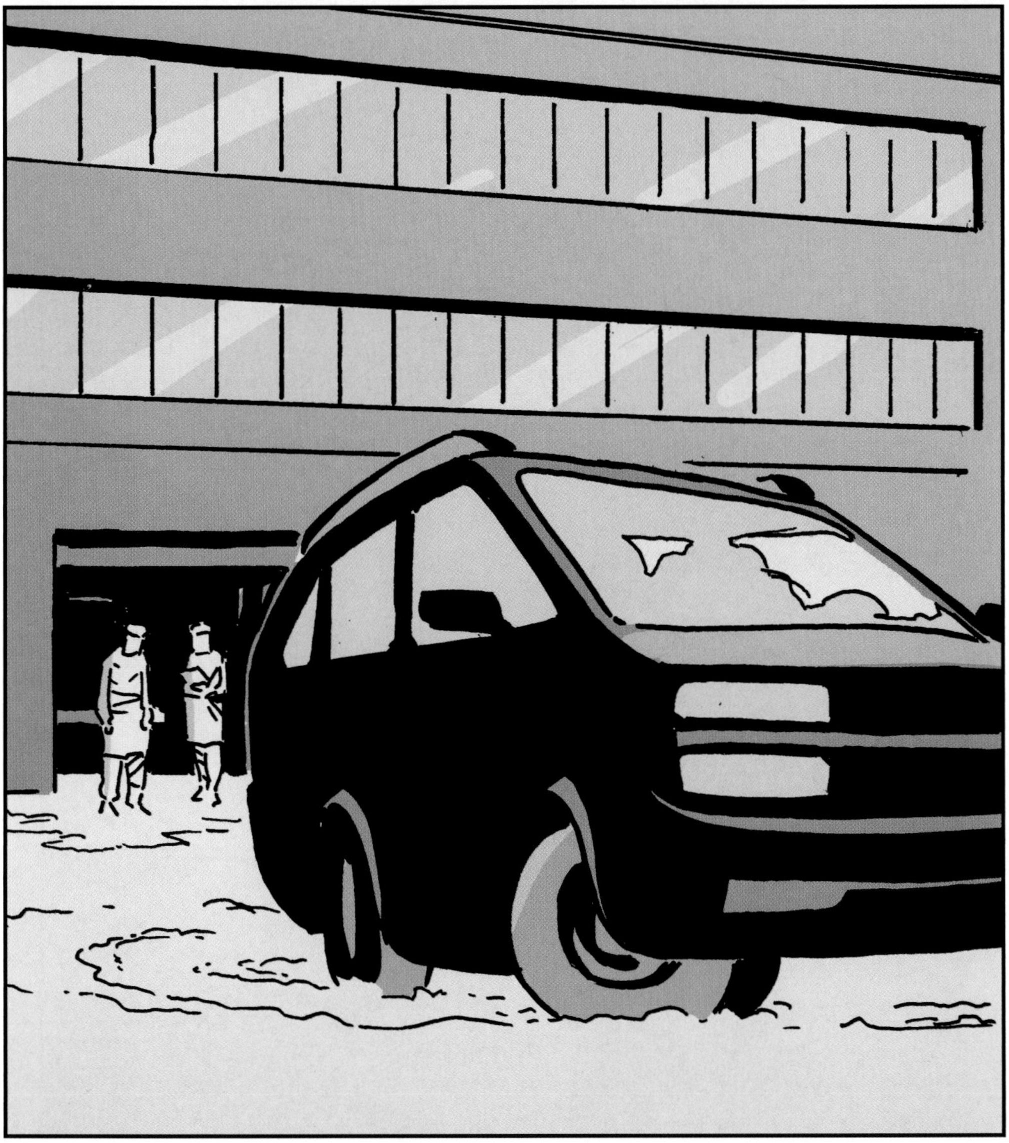

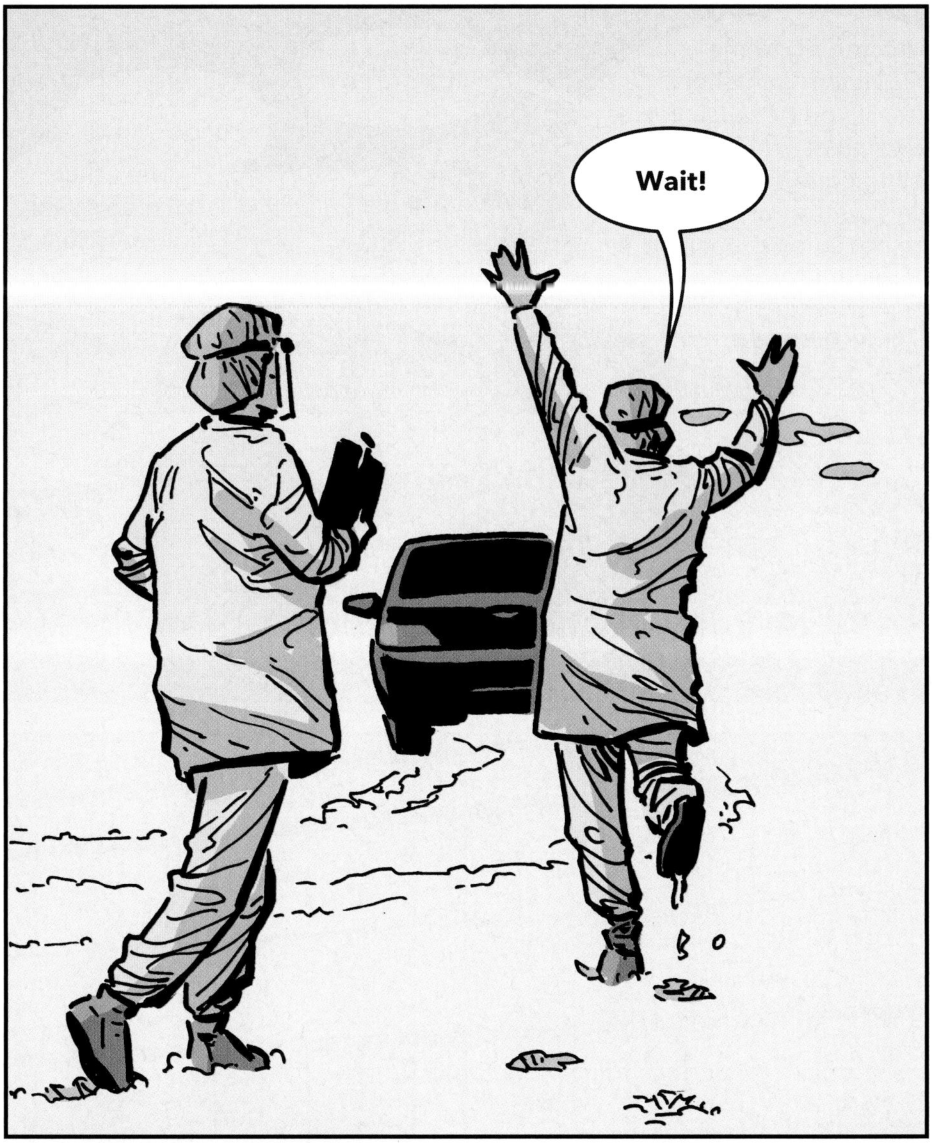
Wait!

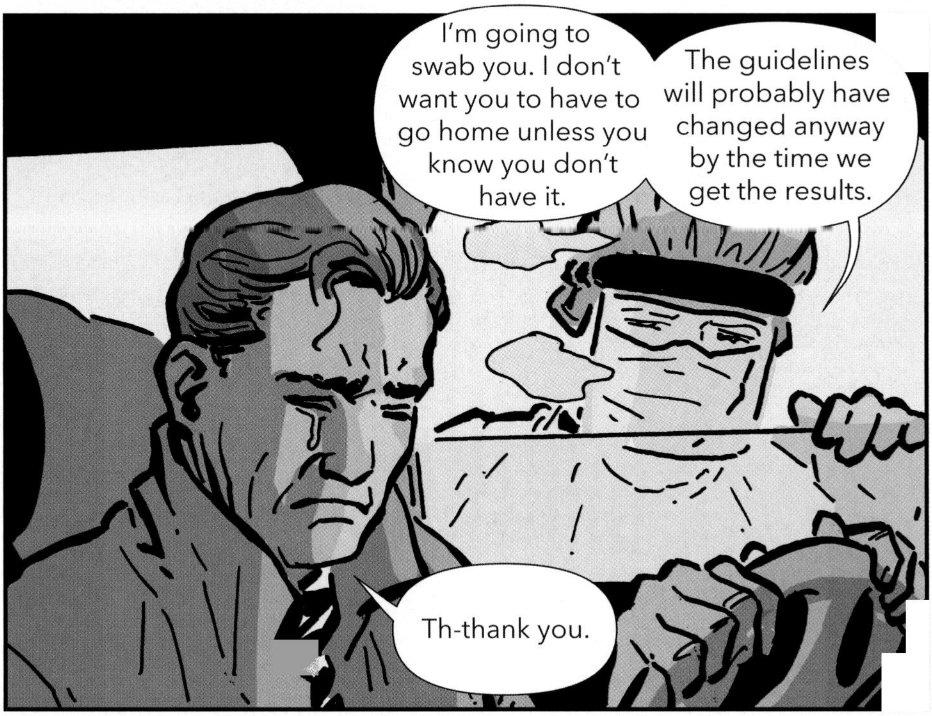
I'm going to swab you. I don't want you to have to go home unless you know you don't have it.
The guidelines will probably have changed anyway by the time we get the results.
Th-thank you.

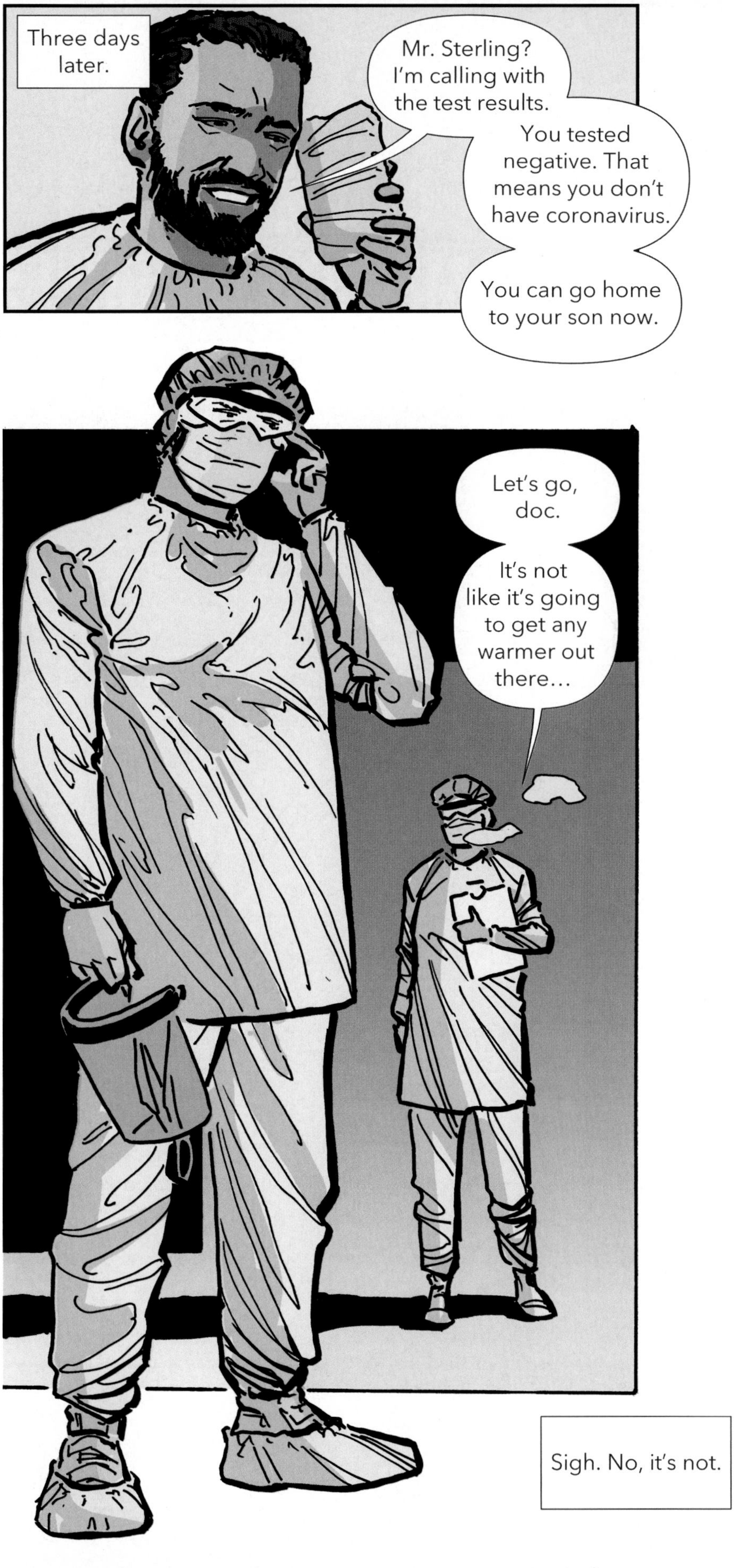
Three days later.
Mr. Sterling? I'm calling with the test results.
You tested negative. That means you don't have coronavirus.
You can go home to your son now.
Let's go, doc.
It's not like it's going to get any warmer out there...
Sigh. No, it's not.

CHAPTER 7

A STREET MEDIC STRUGGLES TO KEEP PROTESTERS SAFE

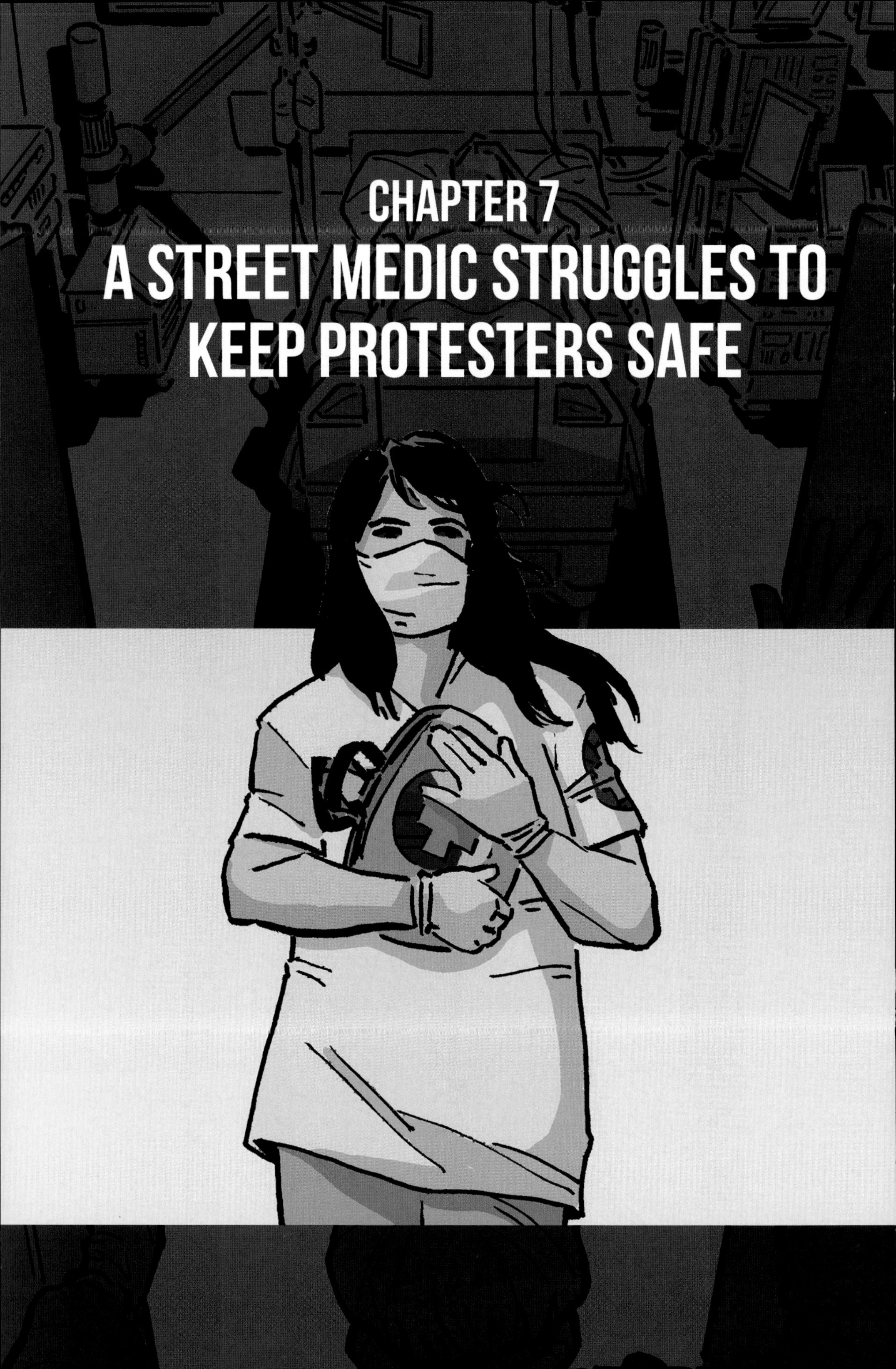

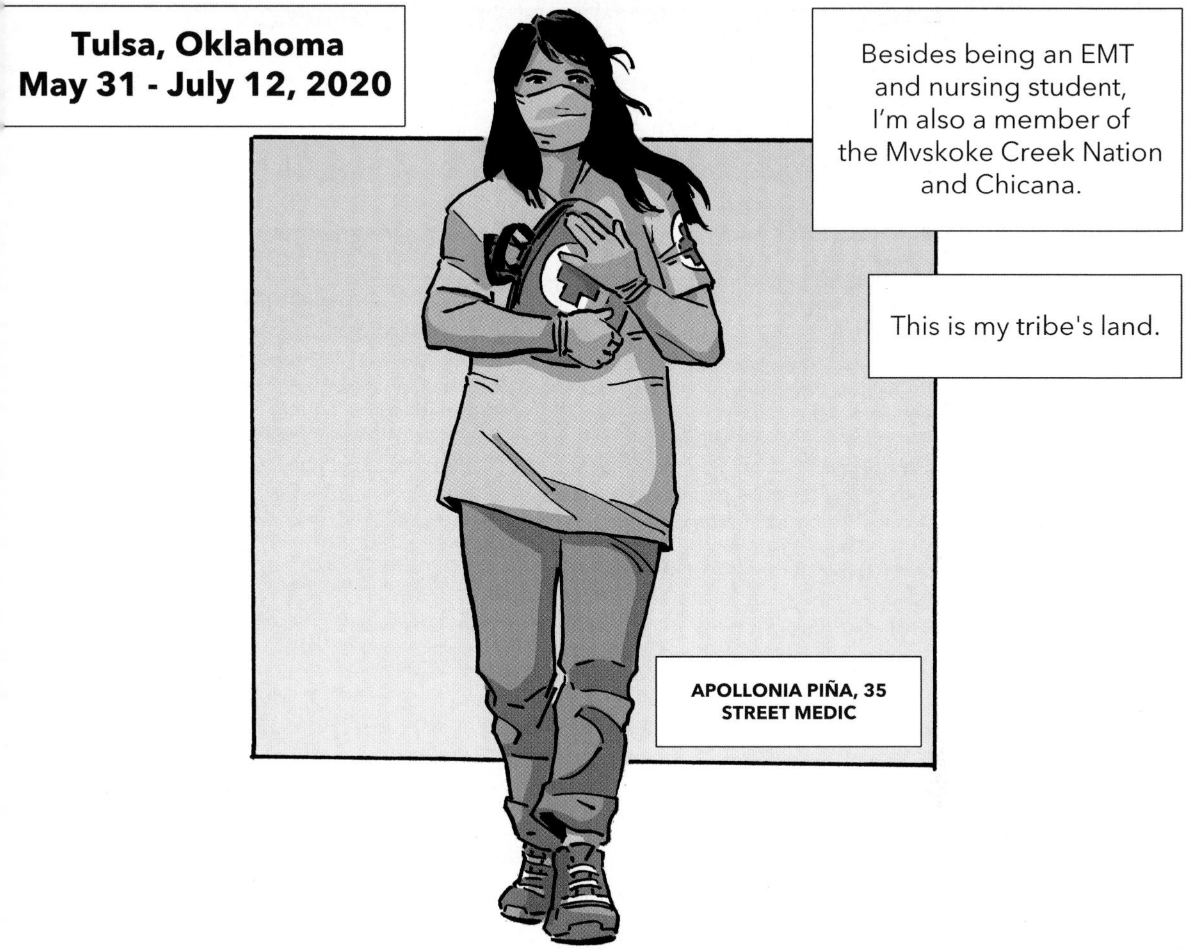
Tulsa, Oklahoma
May 31 - July 12, 2020
Besides being an EMT and nursing student, I'm also a member of the Mvskoke Creek Nation and Chicana.
This is my tribe's land.
APOLLONIA PIÑA, 35
STREET MEDIC

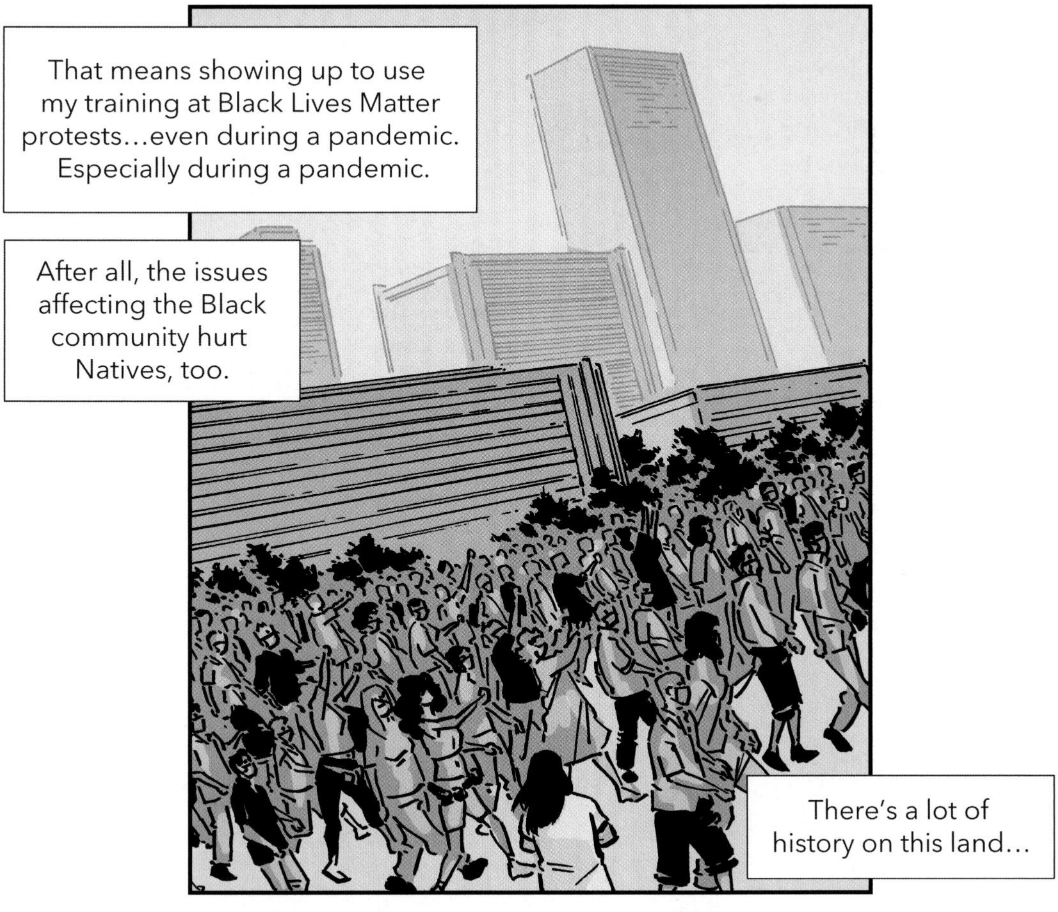
That means showing up to use my training at Black Lives Matter protests…even during a pandemic. Especially during a pandemic.
After all, the issues affecting the Black community hurt Natives, too.
There's a lot of history on this land…

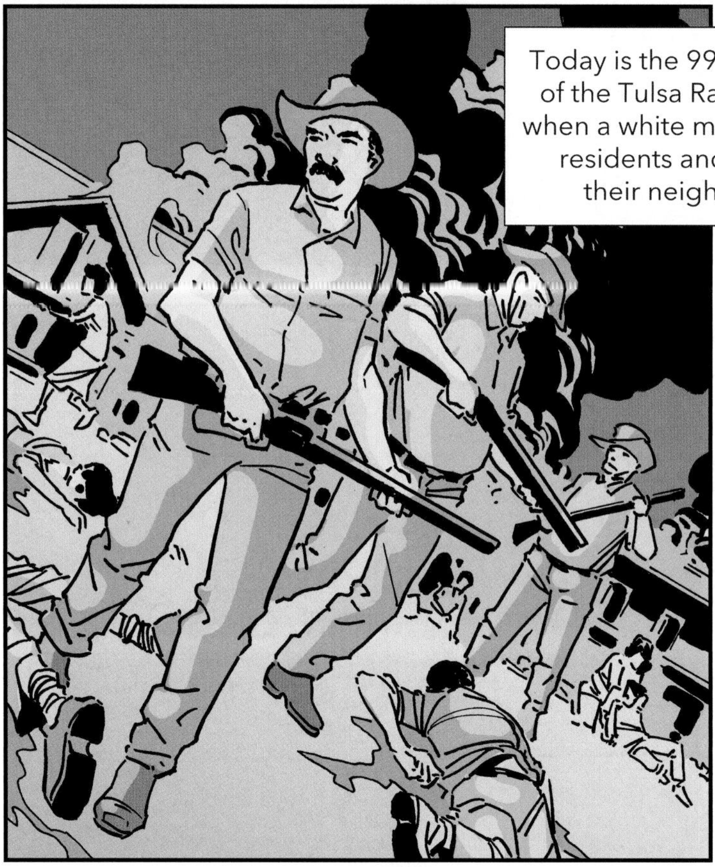
…a lot of it really bad.
Today is the 99th anniversary of the Tulsa Race Massacre, when a white mob killed Black residents and destroyed their neighborhood.

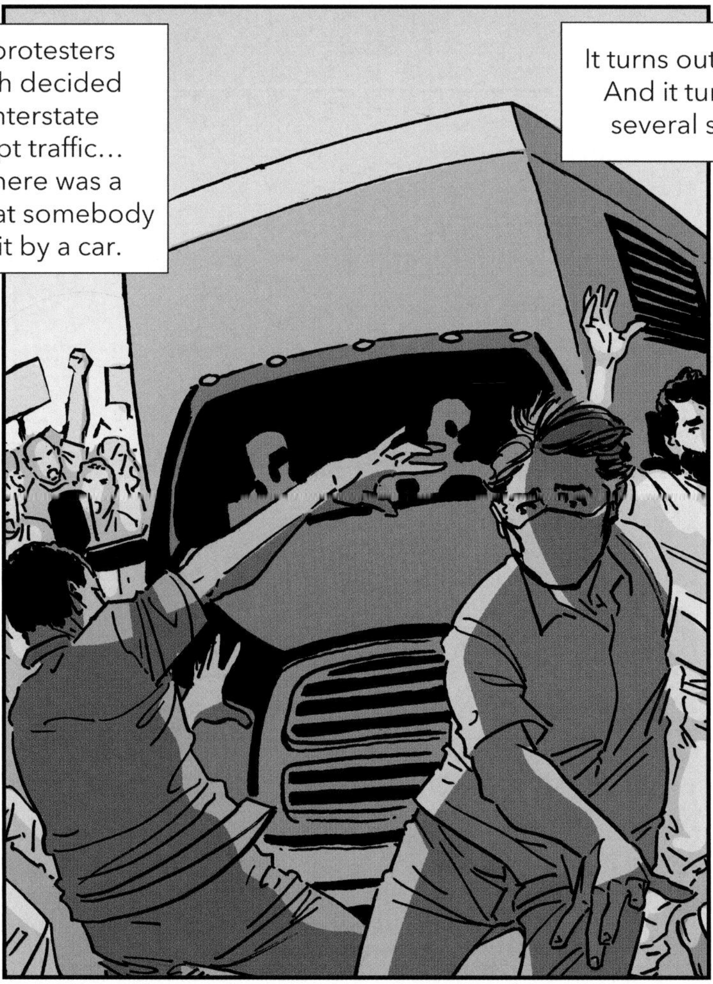
A group of protesters on the march decided to go on Interstate 244 to disrupt traffic… I knew that there was a high chance that somebody would get hit by a car.
It turns out to be a truck. And it turns out to be several somebodies.

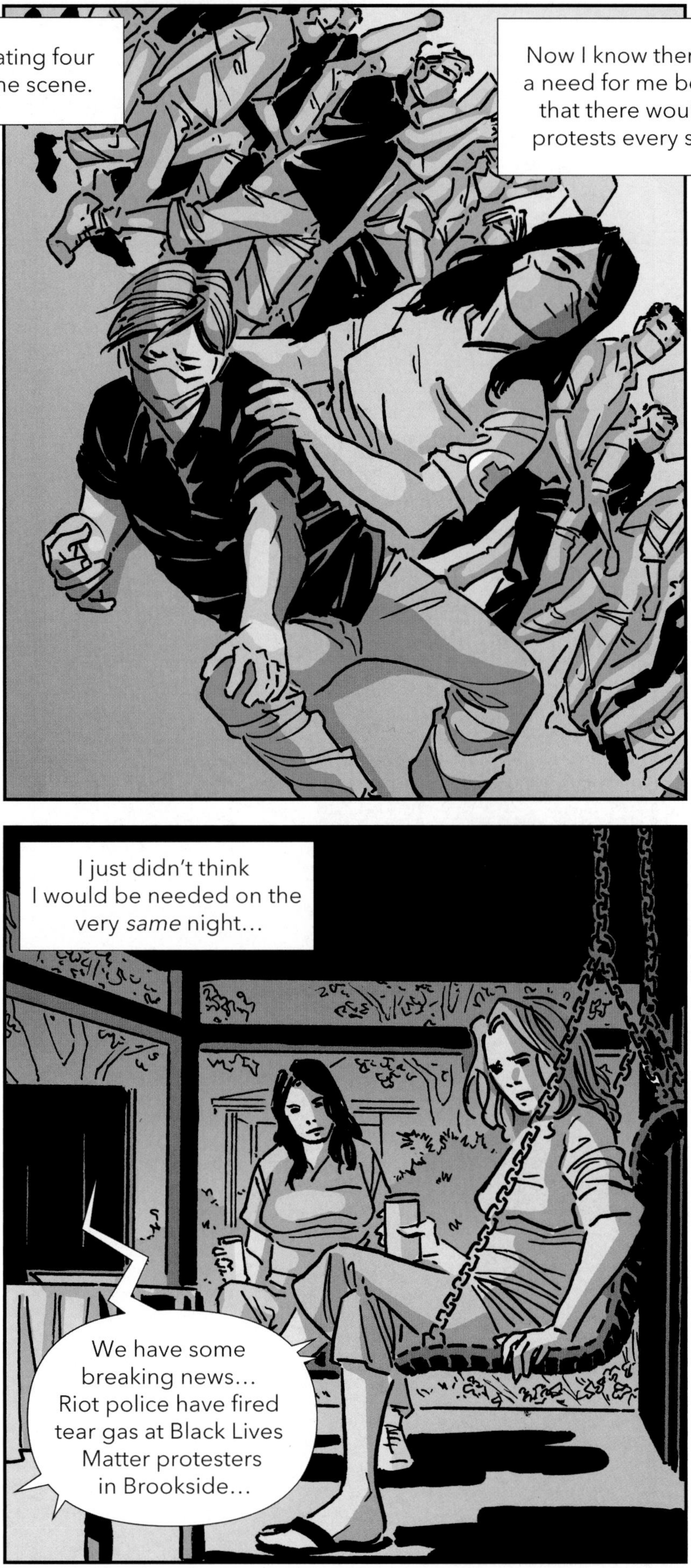
I end up treating four people at the scene.
Now I know there could be a need for me because after that there would be more protests every single night.
I just didn't think I would be needed on the very *same* night...
We have some breaking news... Riot police have fired tear gas at Black Lives Matter protesters in Brookside...

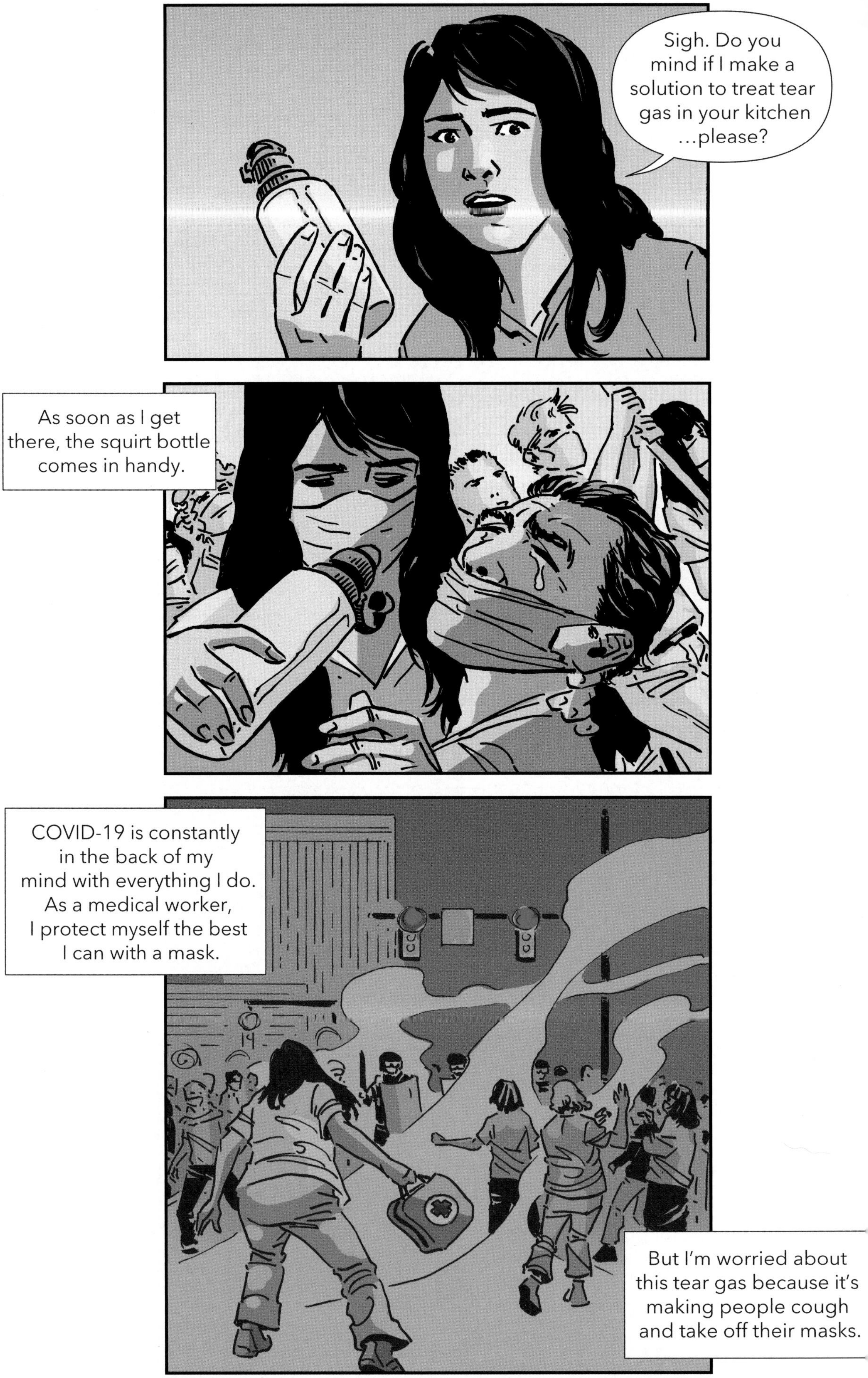
Sigh. Do you mind if I make a solution to treat tear gas in your kitchen …please?
As soon as I get there, the squirt bottle comes in handy.
COVID-19 is constantly in the back of my mind with everything I do. As a medical worker, I protect myself the best I can with a mask.
But I'm worried about this tear gas because it's making people cough and take off their masks.

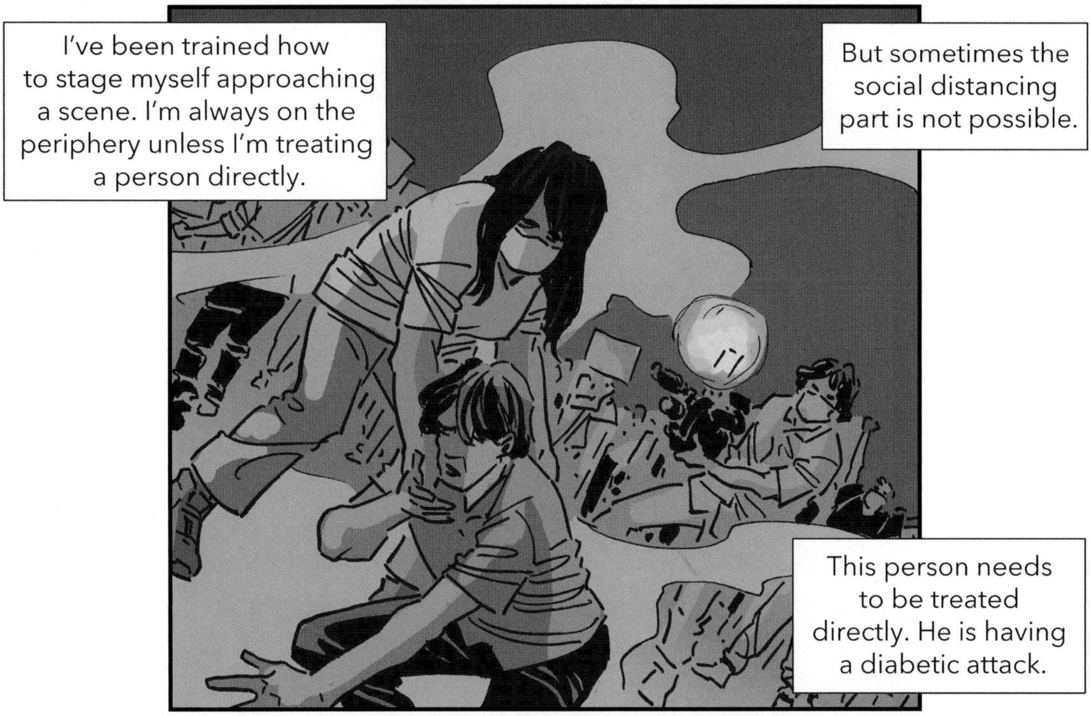
I've been trained how to stage myself approaching a scene. I'm always on the periphery unless I'm treating a person directly.
But sometimes the social distancing part is not possible.
This person needs to be treated directly. He is having a diabetic attack.

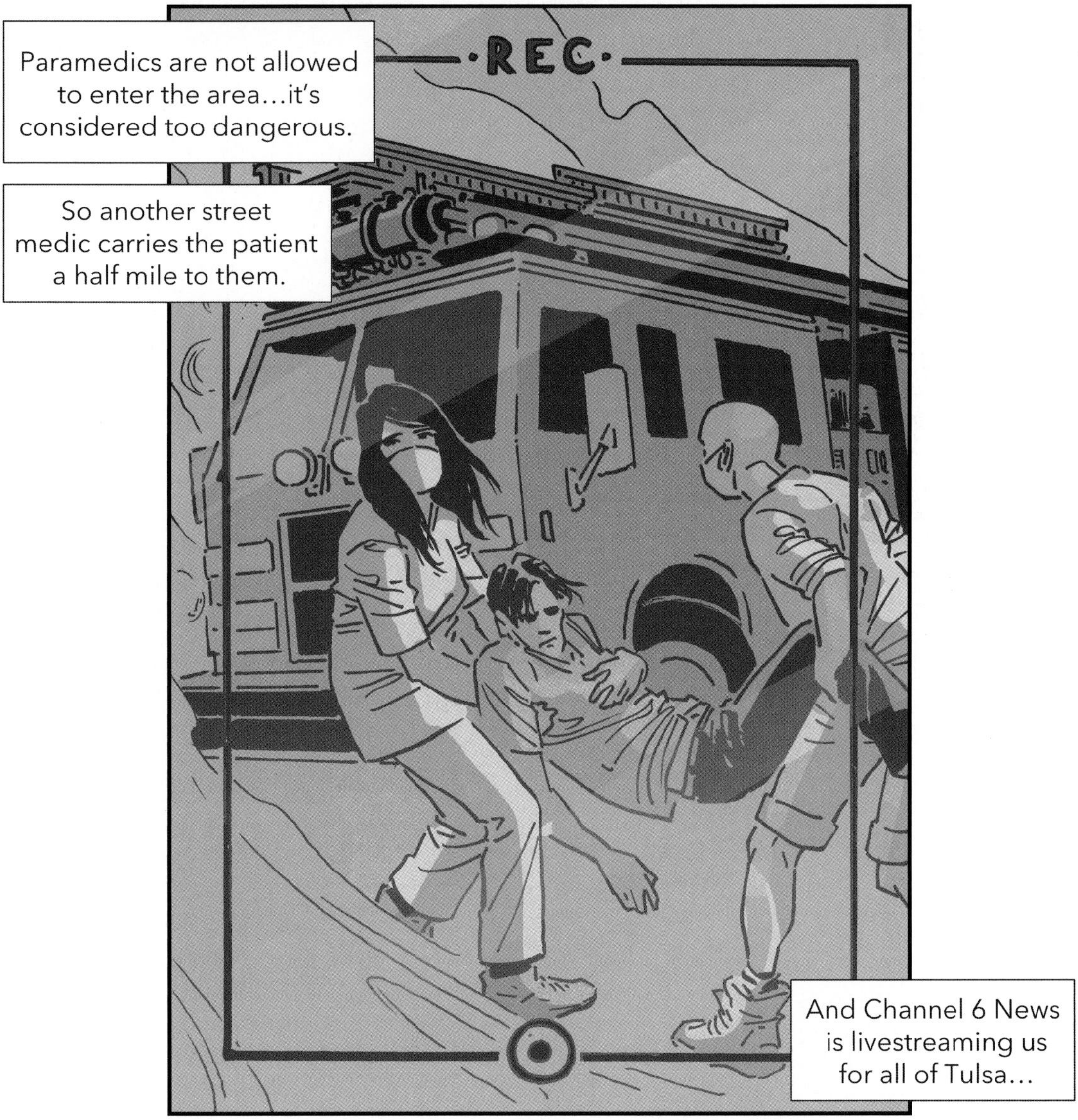
Paramedics are not allowed to enter the area…it's considered too dangerous.
So another street medic carries the patient a half mile to them.
•REC•
And Channel 6 News is livestreaming us for all of Tulsa…

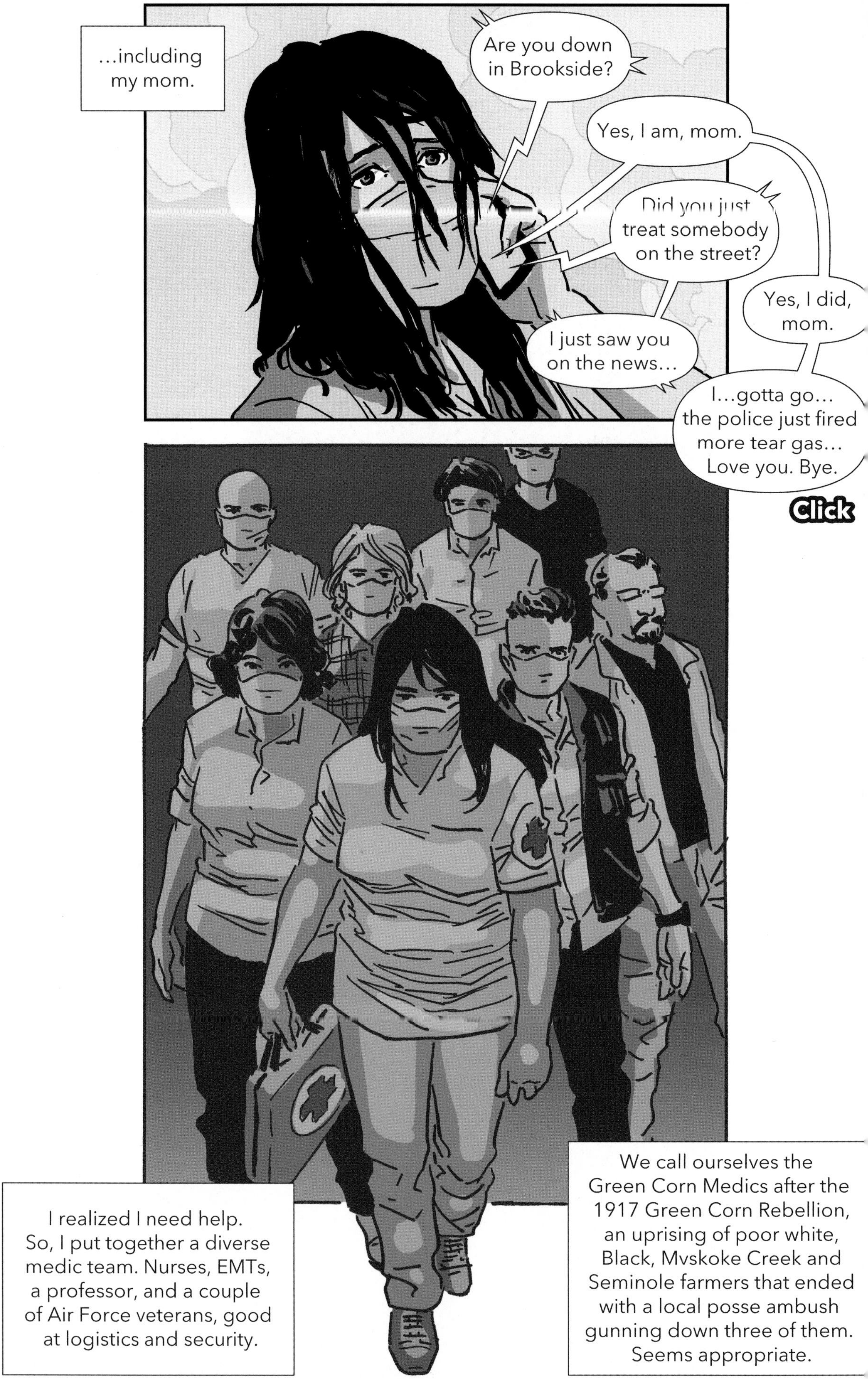
...including my mom.
Are you down in Brookside?
Yes, I am, mom.
Did you just treat somebody on the street?
I just saw you on the news...
Yes, I did, mom.
I...gotta go... the police just fired more tear gas... Love you. Bye.
Click
I realized I need help. So, I put together a diverse medic team. Nurses, EMTs, a professor, and a couple of Air Force veterans, good at logistics and security.
We call ourselves the Green Corn Medics after the 1917 Green Corn Rebellion, an uprising of poor white, Black, Mvskoke Creek and Seminole farmers that ended with a local posse ambush gunning down three of them. Seems appropriate.

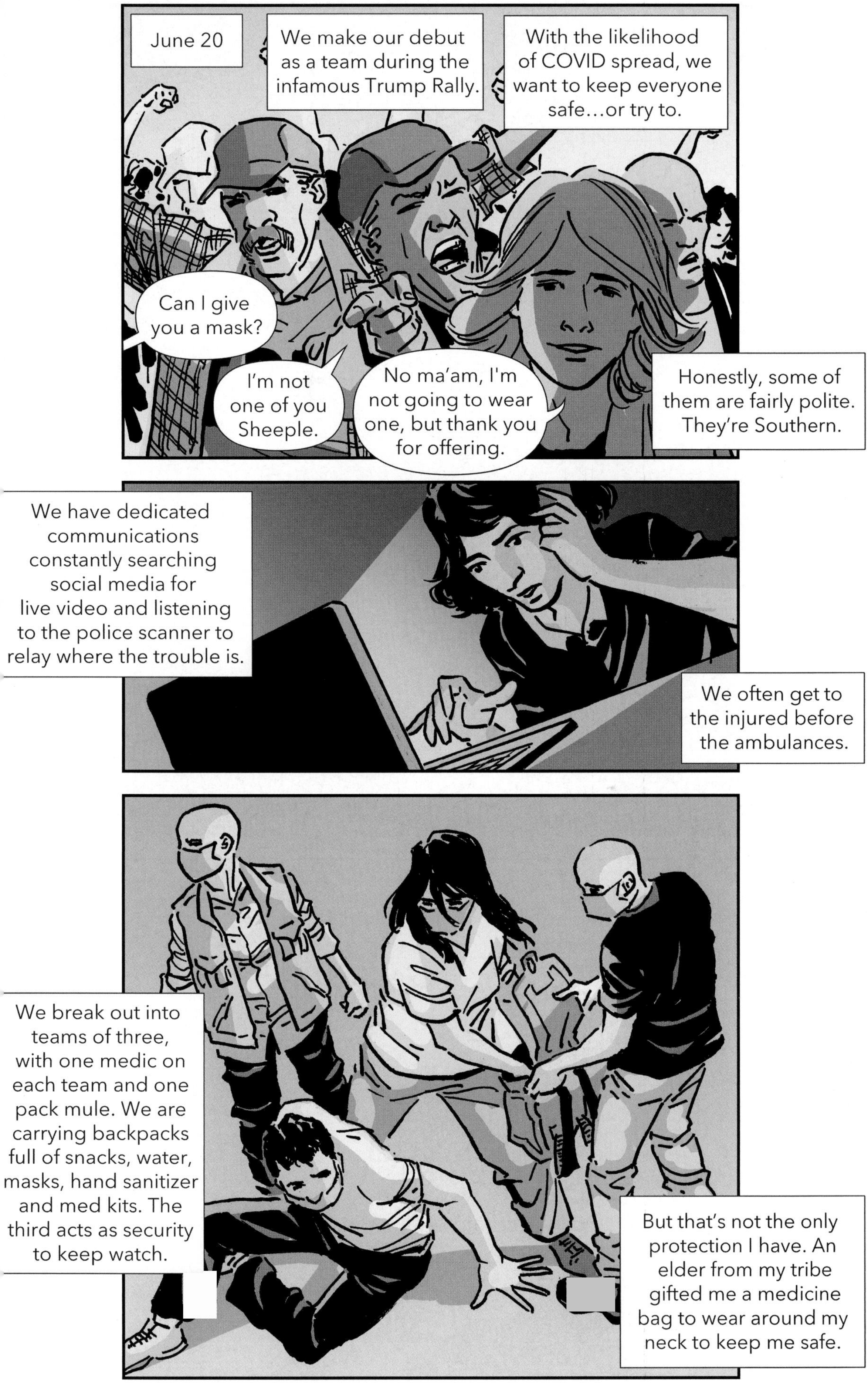
June 20
We make our debut as a team during the infamous Trump Rally.
With the likelihood of COVID spread, we want to keep everyone safe…or try to.
Can I give you a mask?
I'm not one of you Sheeple.
No ma'am, I'm not going to wear one, but thank you for offering.
Honestly, some of them are fairly polite. They're Southern.
We have dedicated communications constantly searching social media for live video and listening to the police scanner to relay where the trouble is.
We often get to the injured before the ambulances.
We break out into teams of three, with one medic on each team and one pack mule. We are carrying backpacks full of snacks, water, masks, hand sanitizer and med kits. The third acts as security to keep watch.
But that's not the only protection I have. An elder from my tribe gifted me a medicine bag to wear around my neck to keep me safe.

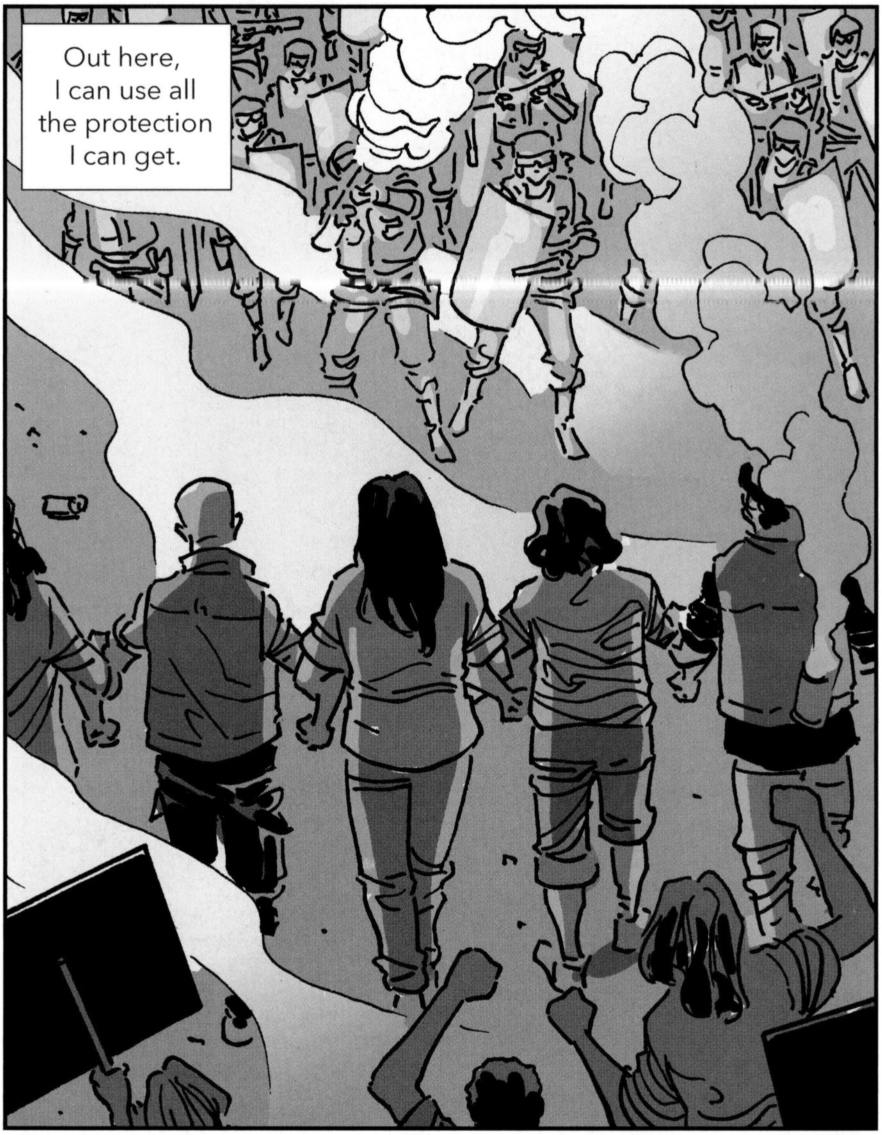
Out here, I can use all the protection I can get.

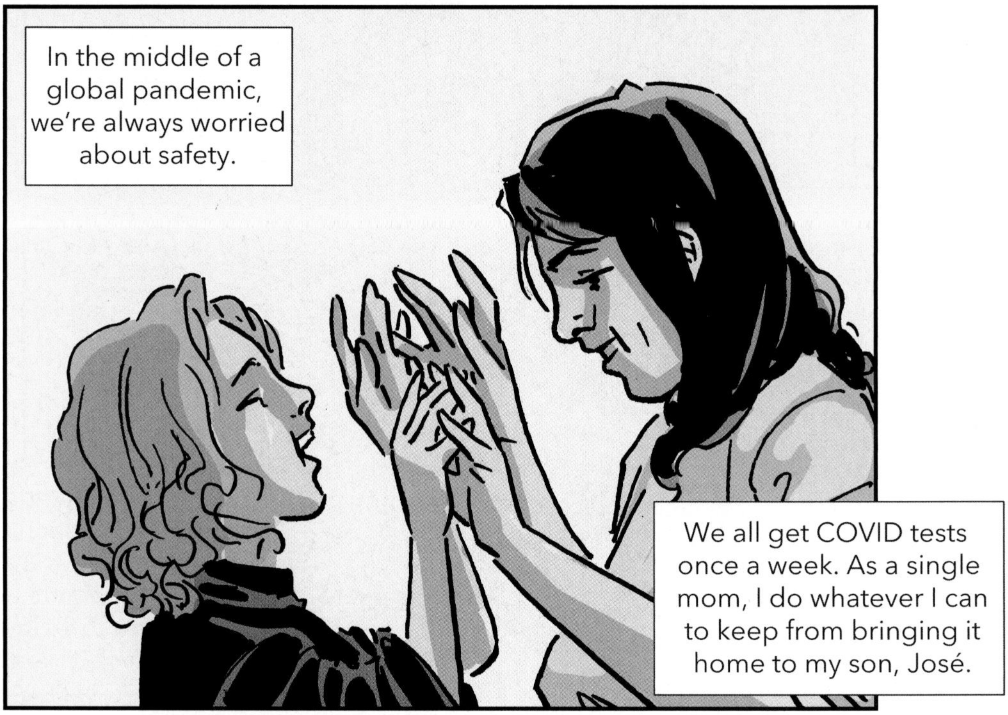
In the middle of a global pandemic, we're always worried about safety.
We all get COVID tests once a week. As a single mom, I do whatever I can to keep from bringing it home to my son, José.

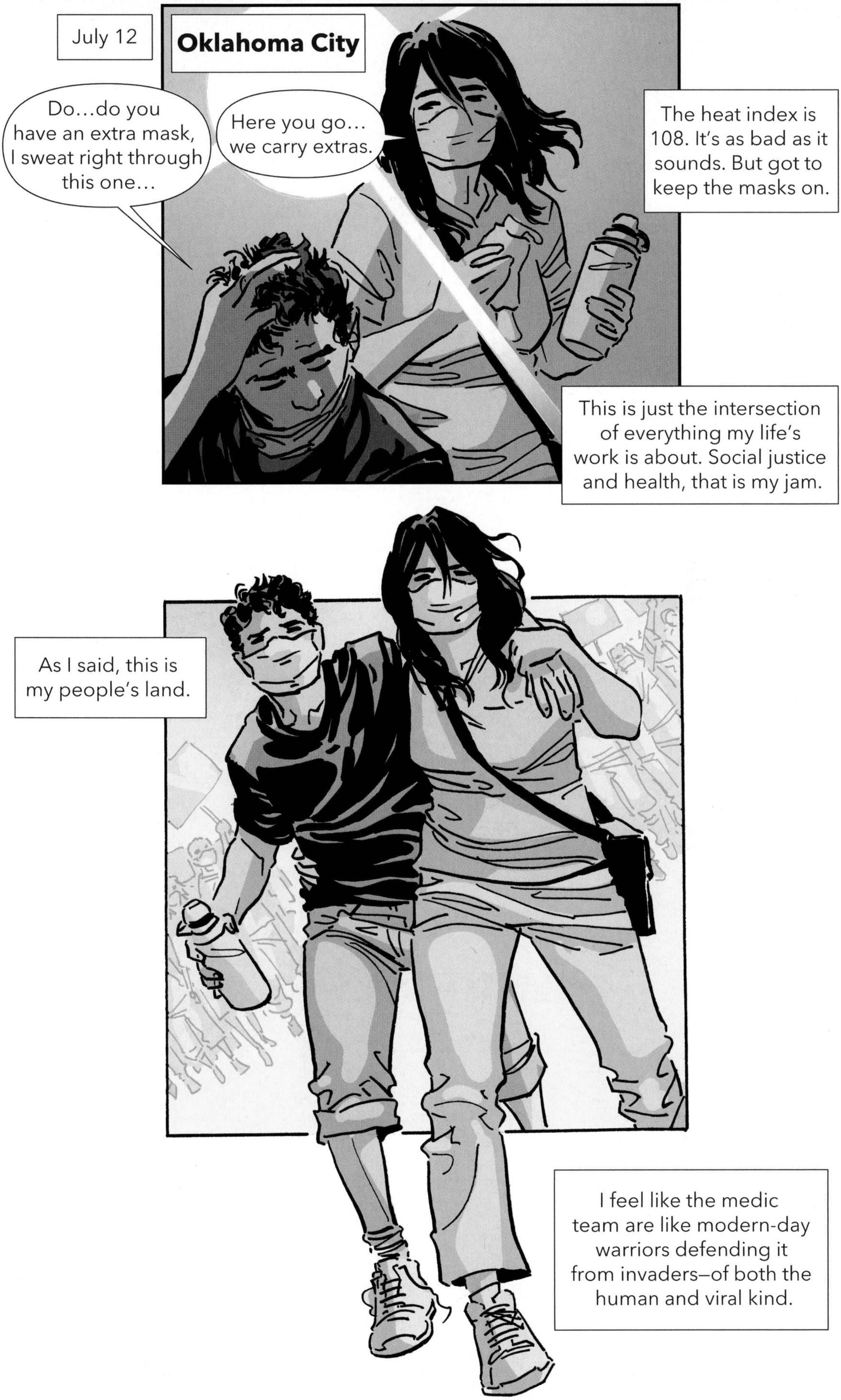
July 12
Oklahoma City
Do…do you have an extra mask, I sweat right through this one…
Here you go… we carry extras.
The heat index is 108. It's as bad as it sounds. But got to keep the masks on.
This is just the intersection of everything my life's work is about. Social justice and health, that is my jam.
As I said, this is my people's land.
I feel like the medic team are like modern-day warriors defending it from invaders—of both the human and viral kind.

CHAPTER 8

FROM FIGHTING TO SAVE PATIENTS TO FIGHTING TO SAVE HIMSELF

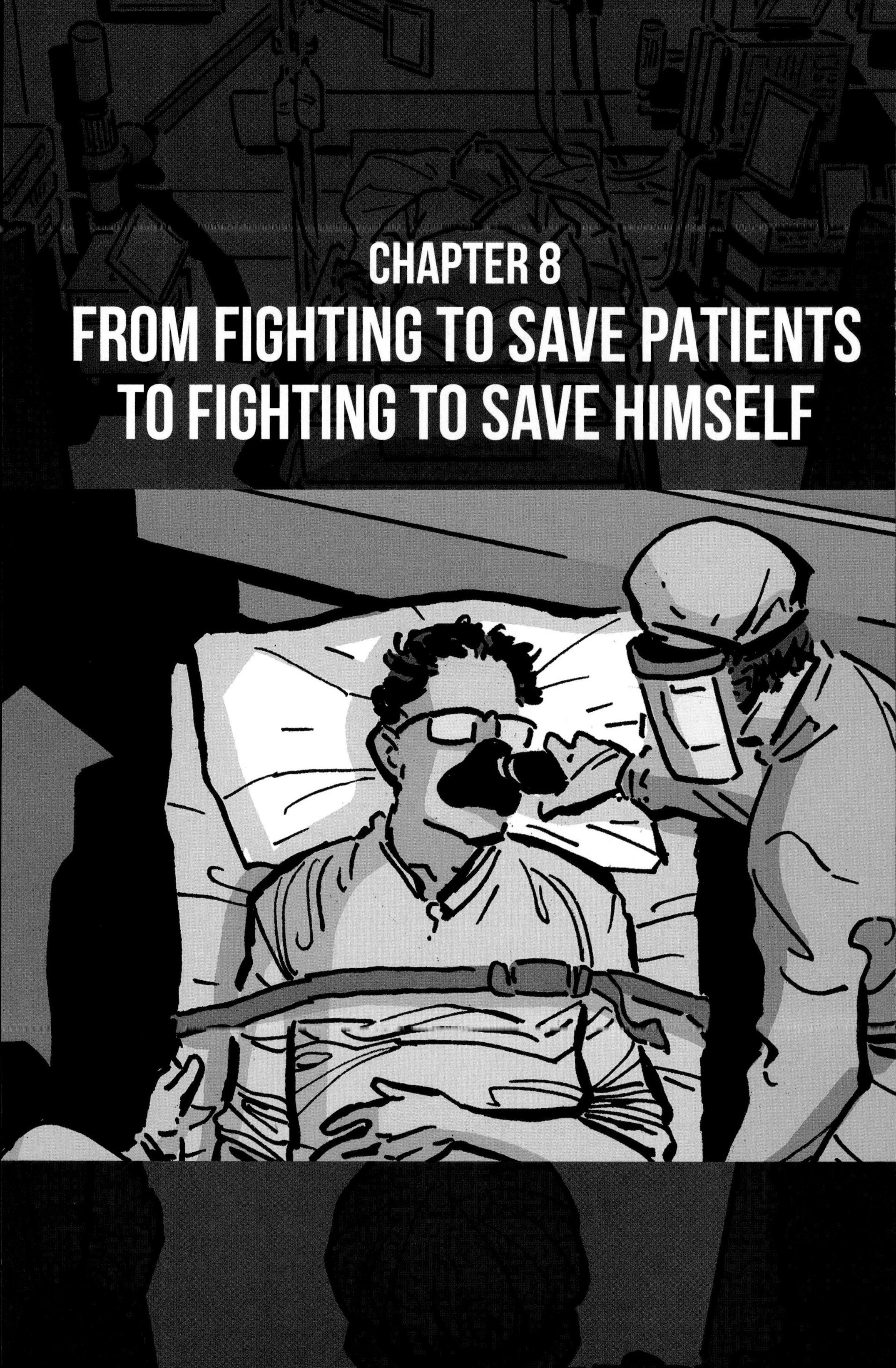

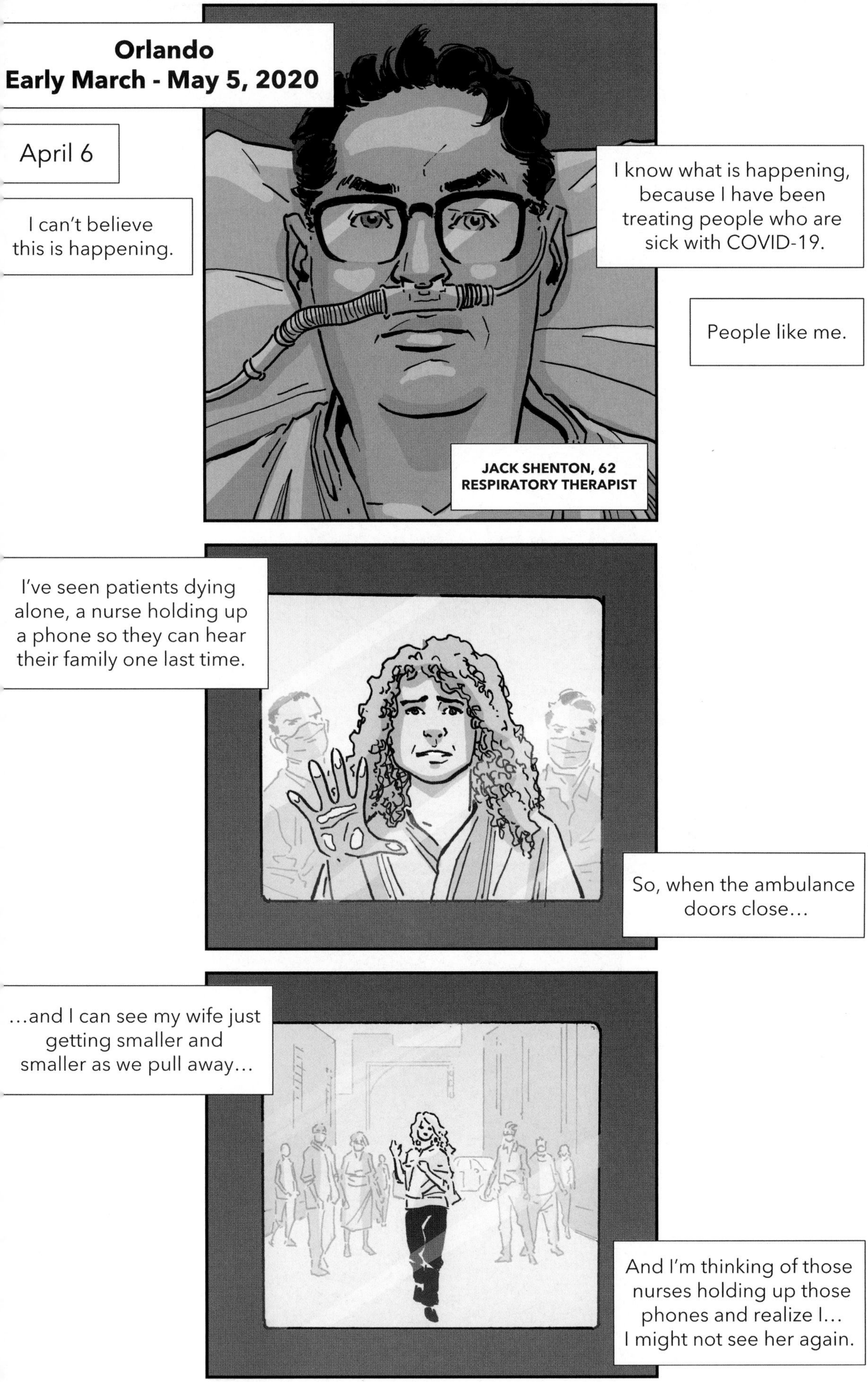
Orlando
Early March - May 5, 2020
April 6
I can't believe this is happening.
I know what is happening, because I have been treating people who are sick with COVID-19.
People like me.
JACK SHENTON, 62
RESPIRATORY THERAPIST
I've seen patients dying alone, a nurse holding up a phone so they can hear their family one last time.
So, when the ambulance doors close...
...and I can see my wife just getting smaller and smaller as we pull away...
And I'm thinking of those nurses holding up those phones and realize I... I might not see her again.

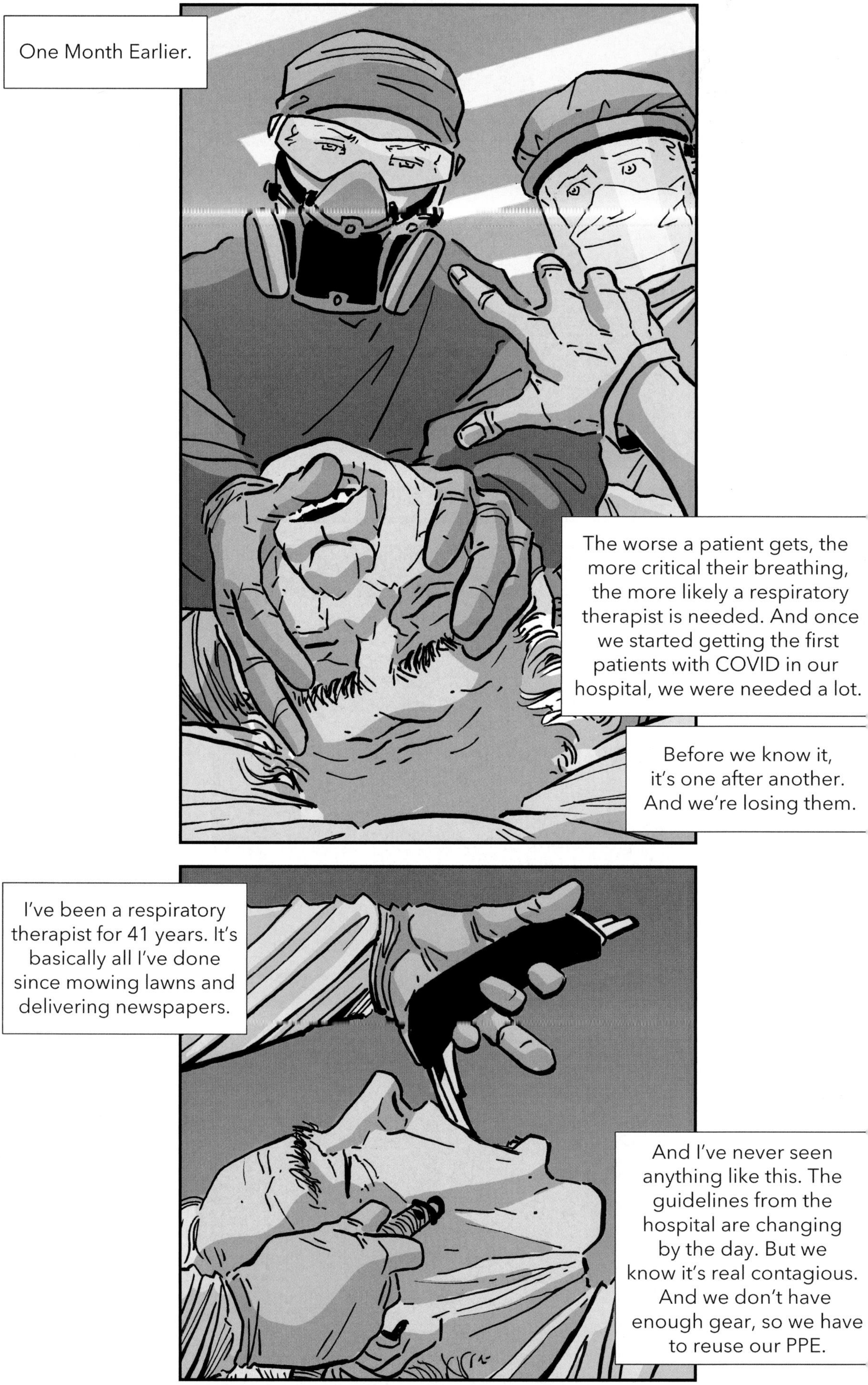

One Month Earlier.

The worse a patient gets, the more critical their breathing, the more likely a respiratory therapist is needed. And once we started getting the first patients with COVID in our hospital, we were needed a lot.

Before we know it, it's one after another. And we're losing them.

I've been a respiratory therapist for 41 years. It's basically all I've done since mowing lawns and delivering newspapers.

And I've never seen anything like this. The guidelines from the hospital are changing by the day. But we know it's real contagious. And we don't have enough gear, so we have to reuse our PPE.

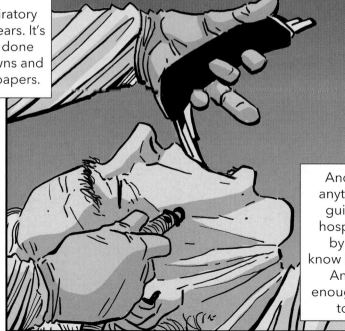

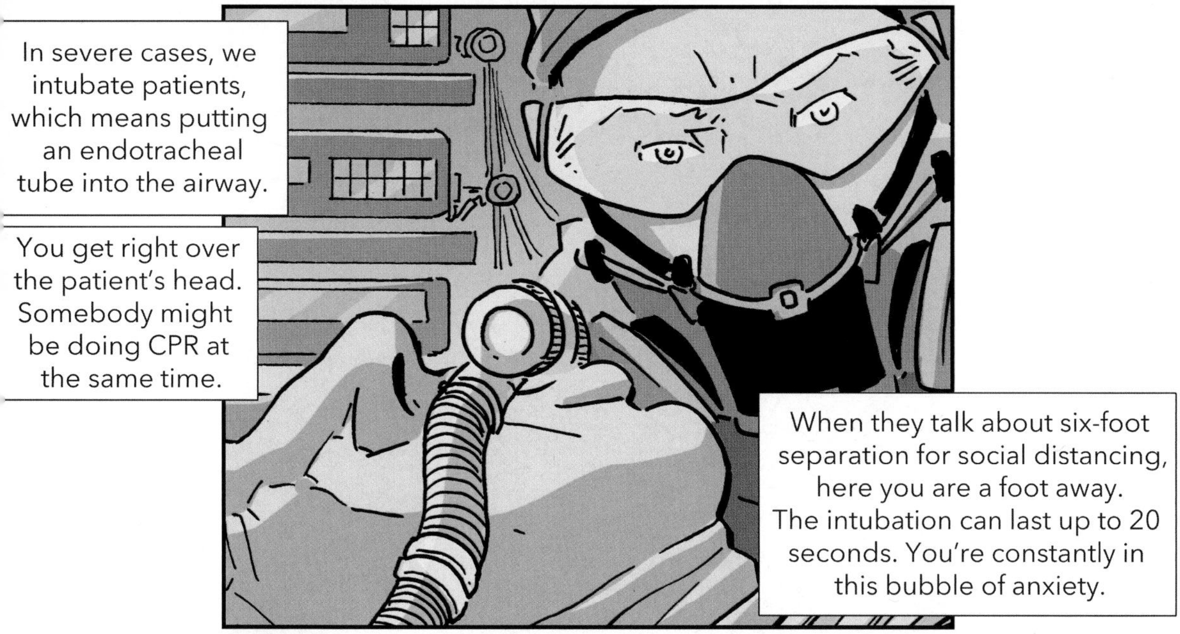
In severe cases, we intubate patients, which means putting an endotracheal tube into the airway.
You get right over the patient's head. Somebody might be doing CPR at the same time.
When they talk about six-foot separation for social distancing, here you are a foot away. The intubation can last up to 20 seconds. You're constantly in this bubble of anxiety.

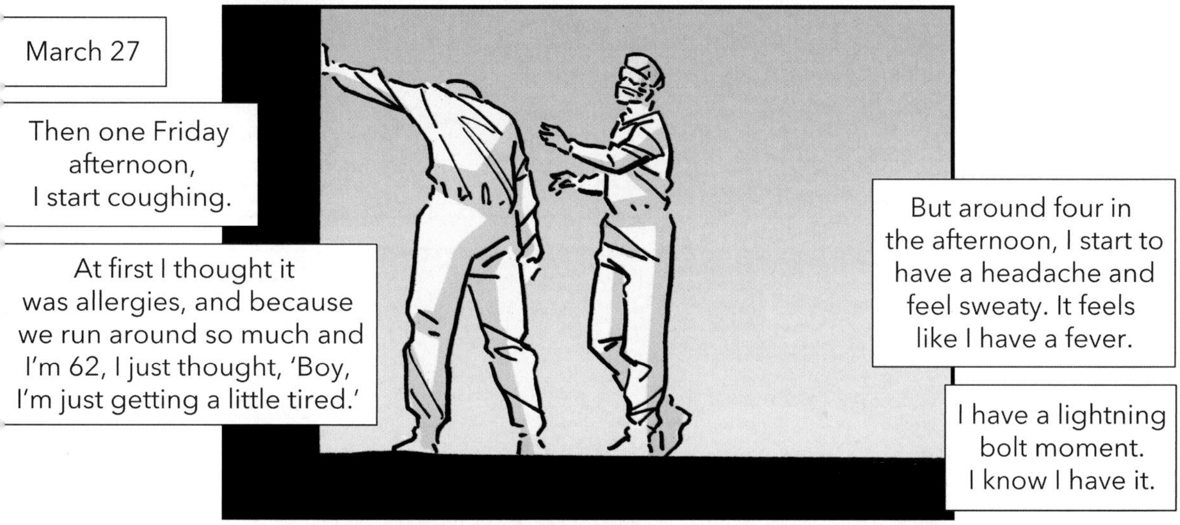
March 27
Then one Friday afternoon, I start coughing.
At first I thought it was allergies, and because we run around so much and I'm 62, I just thought, 'Boy, I'm just getting a little tired.'
But around four in the afternoon, I start to have a headache and feel sweaty. It feels like I have a fever.
I have a lightning bolt moment. I know I have it.

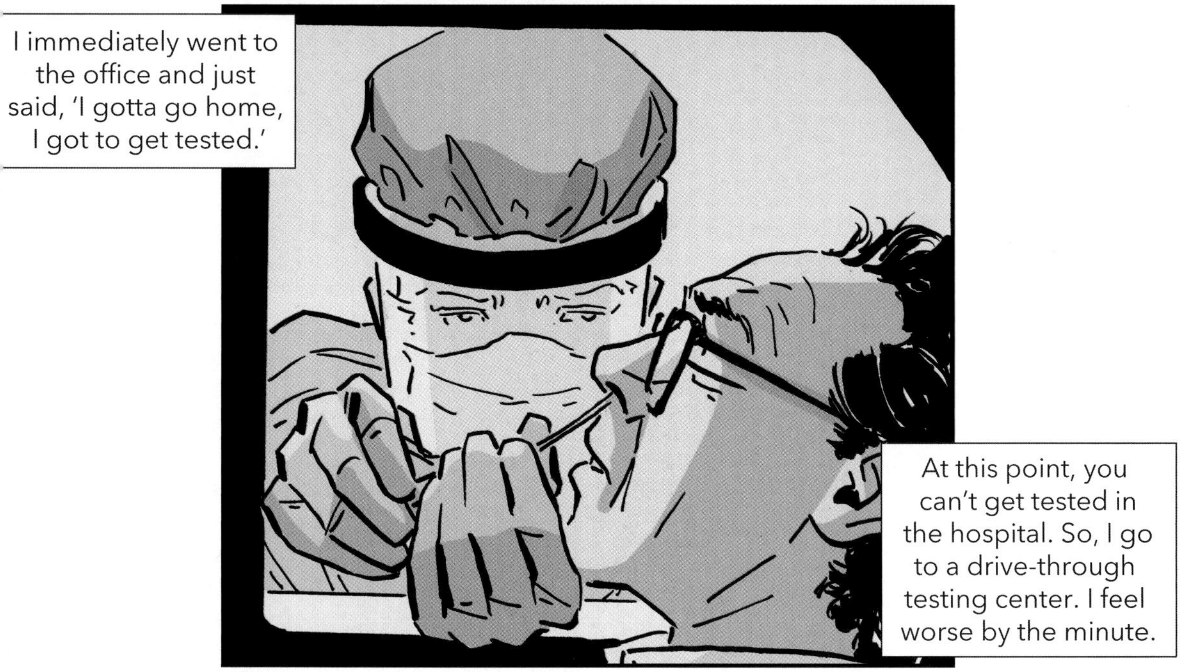
I immediately went to the office and just said, 'I gotta go home, I got to get tested.'
At this point, you can't get tested in the hospital. So, I go to a drive-through testing center. I feel worse by the minute.

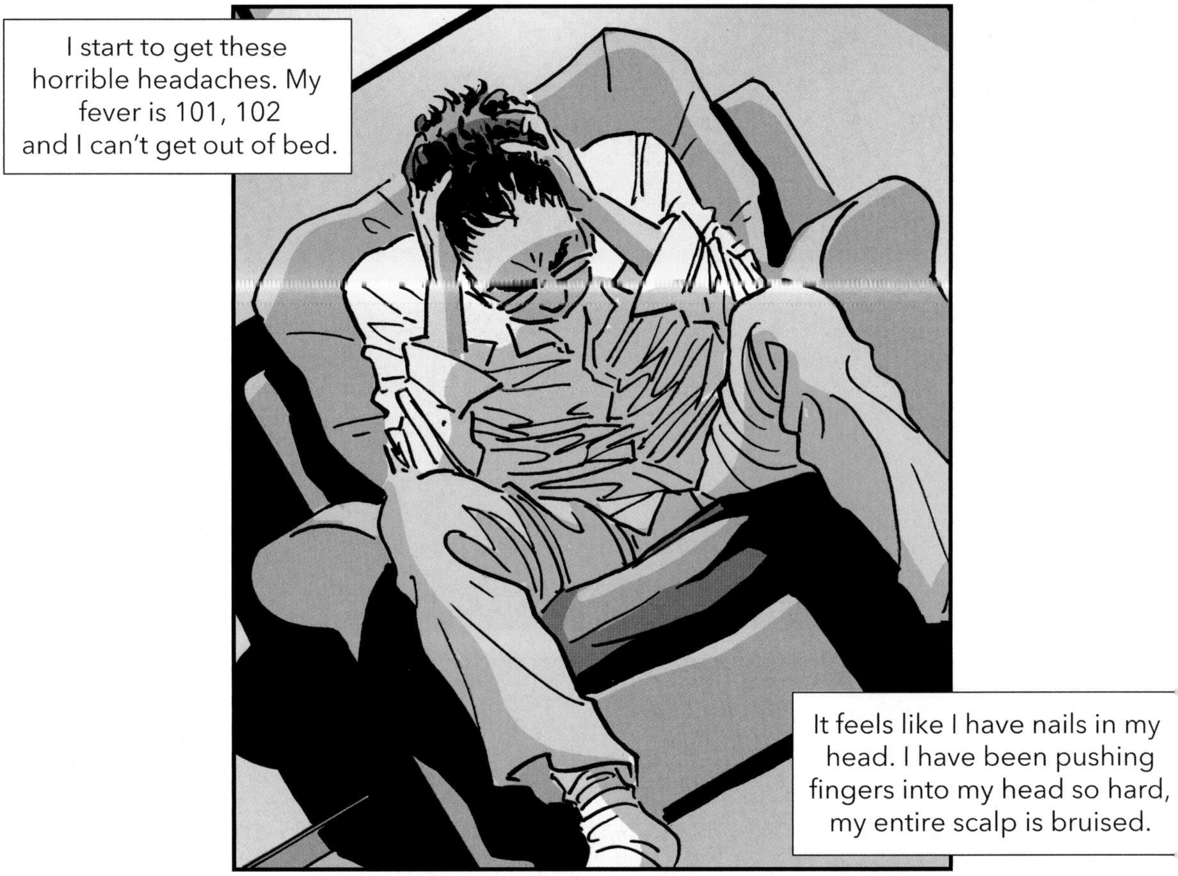
I start to get these horrible headaches. My fever is 101, 102 and I can't get out of bed.
It feels like I have nails in my head. I have been pushing fingers into my head so hard, my entire scalp is bruised.

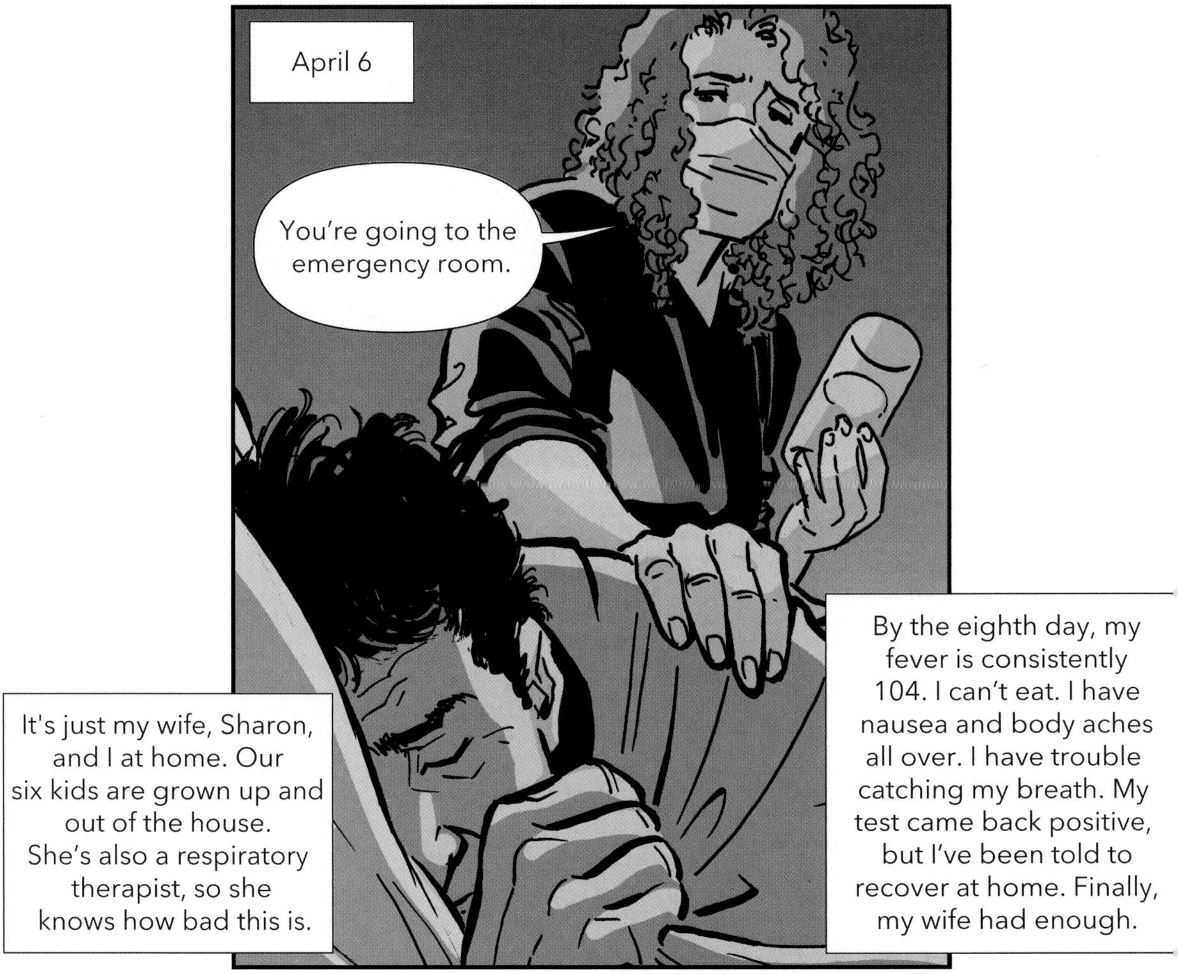
April 6
You're going to the emergency room.
It's just my wife, Sharon, and I at home. Our six kids are grown up and out of the house. She's also a respiratory therapist, so she knows how bad this is.
By the eighth day, my fever is consistently 104. I can't eat. I have nausea and body aches all over. I have trouble catching my breath. My test came back positive, but I've been told to recover at home. Finally, my wife had enough.

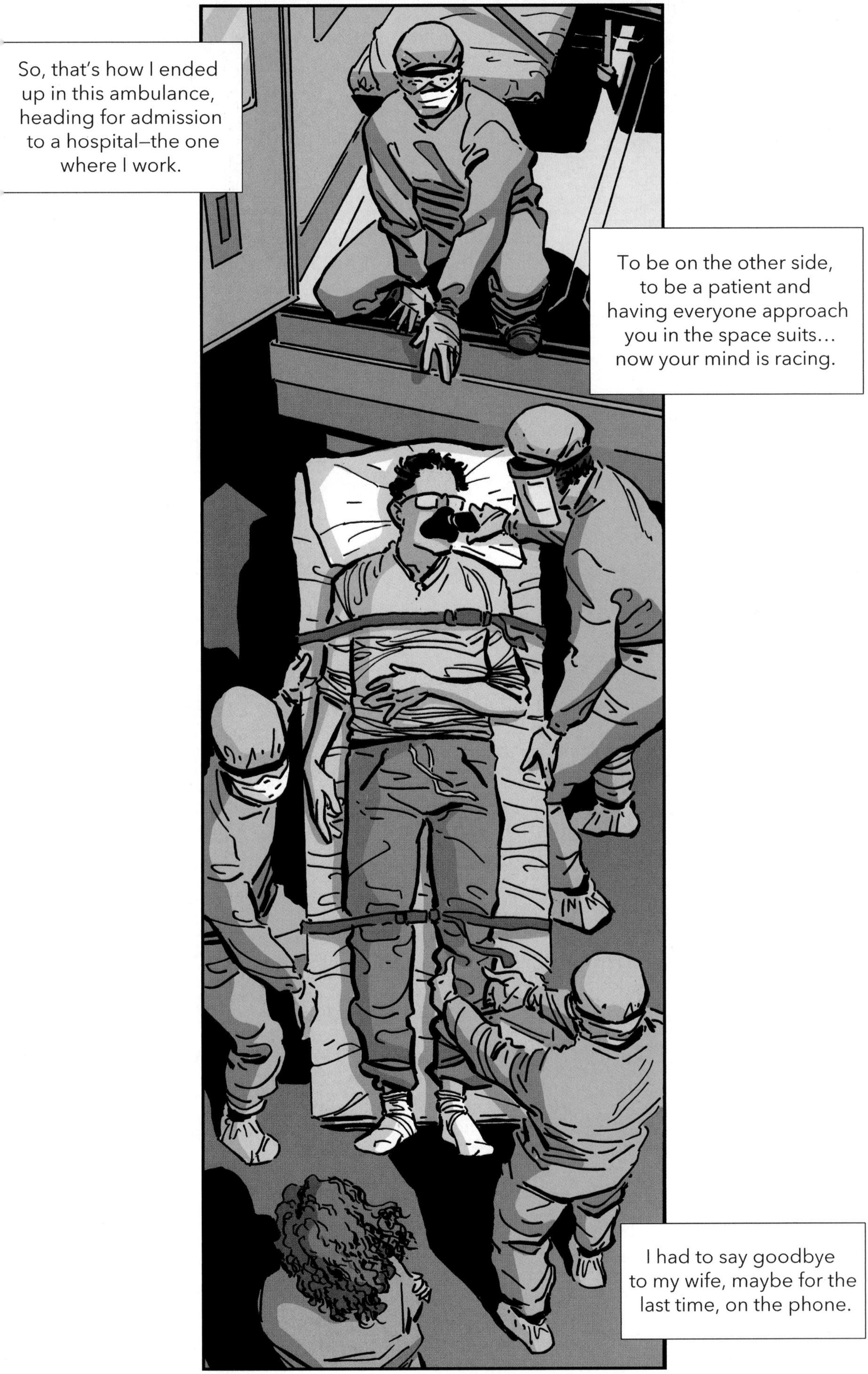
So, that's how I ended up in this ambulance, heading for admission to a hospital—the one where I work.
To be on the other side, to be a patient and having everyone approach you in the space suits… now your mind is racing.
I had to say goodbye to my wife, maybe for the last time, on the phone.

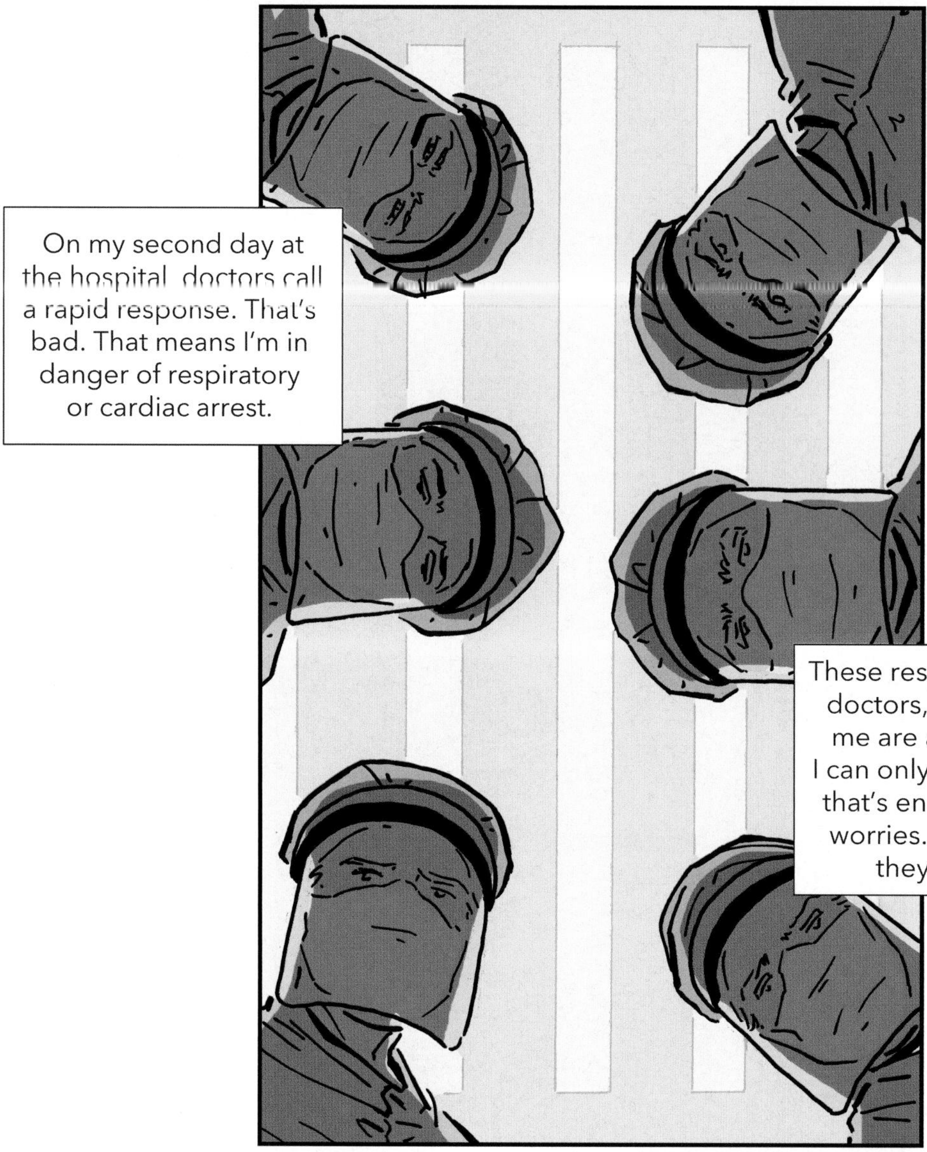
On my second day at the hospital, doctors call a rapid response. That's bad. That means I'm in danger of respiratory or cardiac arrest.
These respiratory therapists, doctors, nurses all around me are all people I know. I can only see their eyes, but that's enough to read their worries. I've stood where they are standing.

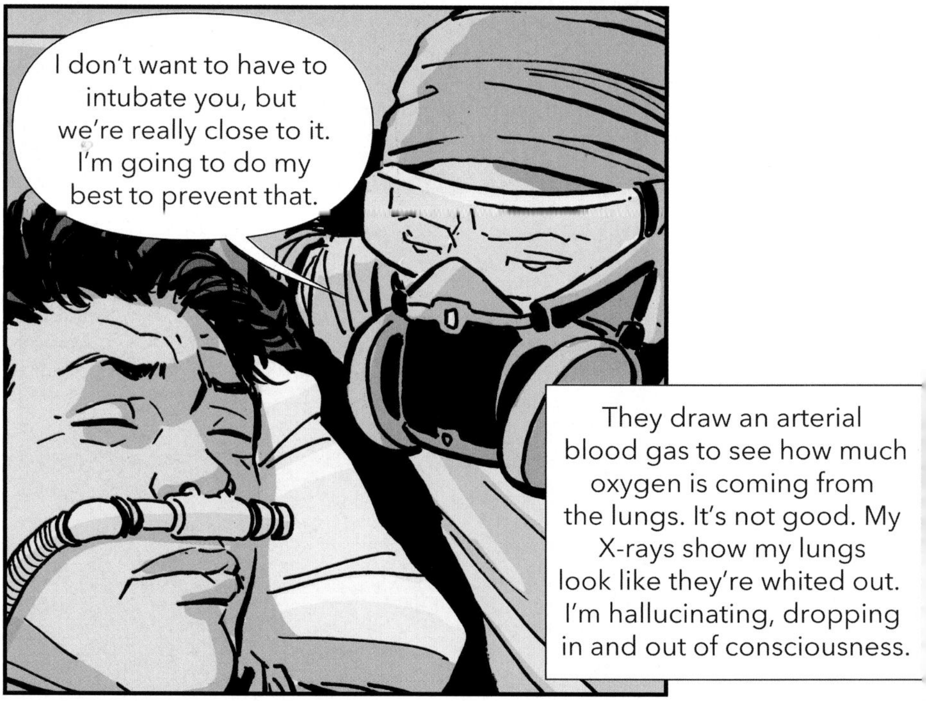
I don't want to have to intubate you, but we're really close to it. I'm going to do my best to prevent that.
They draw an arterial blood gas to see how much oxygen is coming from the lungs. It's not good. My X-rays show my lungs look like they're whited out. I'm hallucinating, dropping in and out of consciousness.

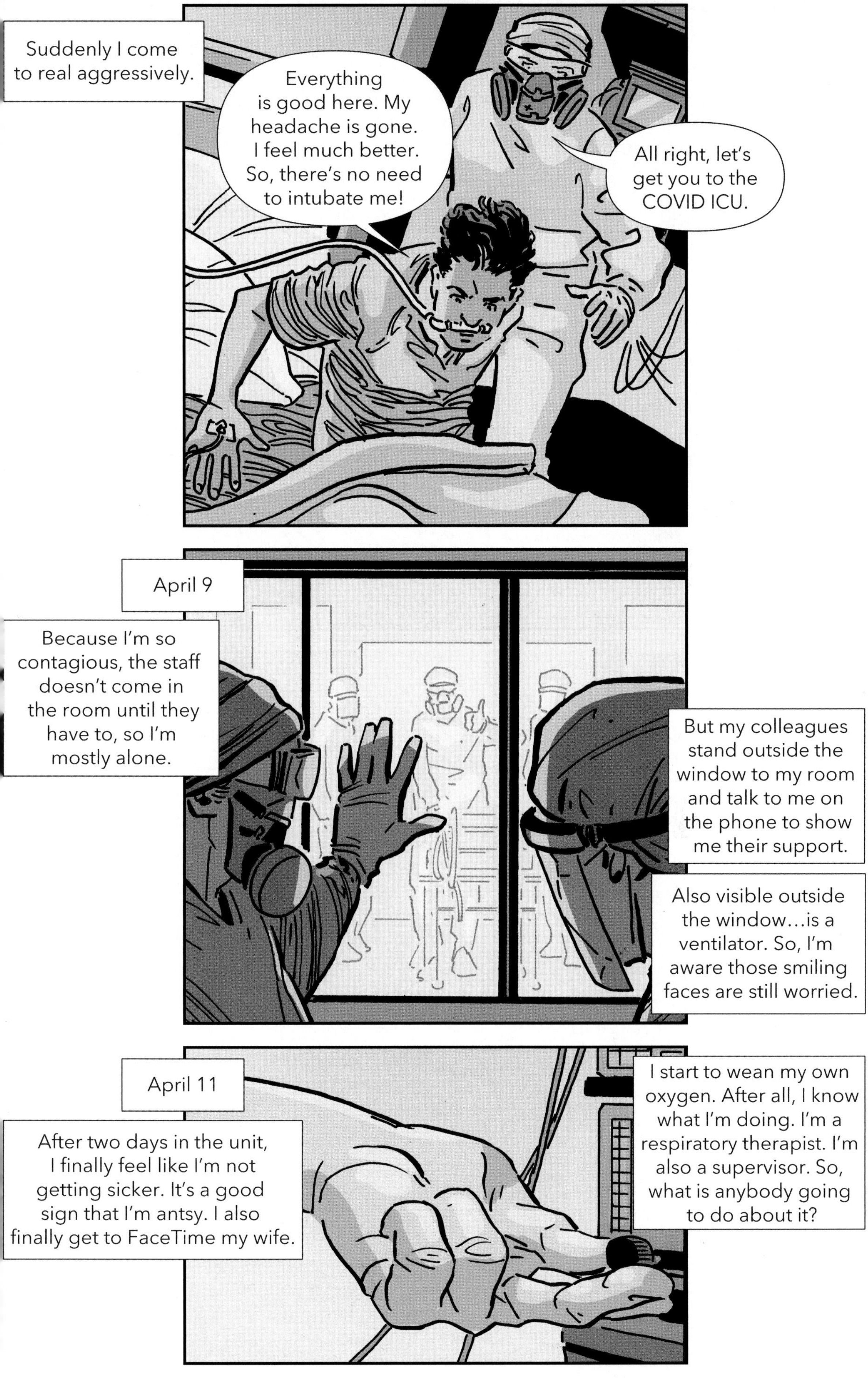
Suddenly I come to real aggressively.
Everything is good here. My headache is gone. I feel much better. So, there's no need to intubate me!
All right, let's get you to the COVID ICU.
April 9
Because I'm so contagious, the staff doesn't come in the room until they have to, so I'm mostly alone.
But my colleagues stand outside the window to my room and talk to me on the phone to show me their support.
Also visible outside the window…is a ventilator. So, I'm aware those smiling faces are still worried.
April 11
After two days in the unit, I finally feel like I'm not getting sicker. It's a good sign that I'm antsy. I also finally get to FaceTime my wife.
I start to wean my own oxygen. After all, I know what I'm doing. I'm a respiratory therapist. I'm also a supervisor. So, what is anybody going to do about it?

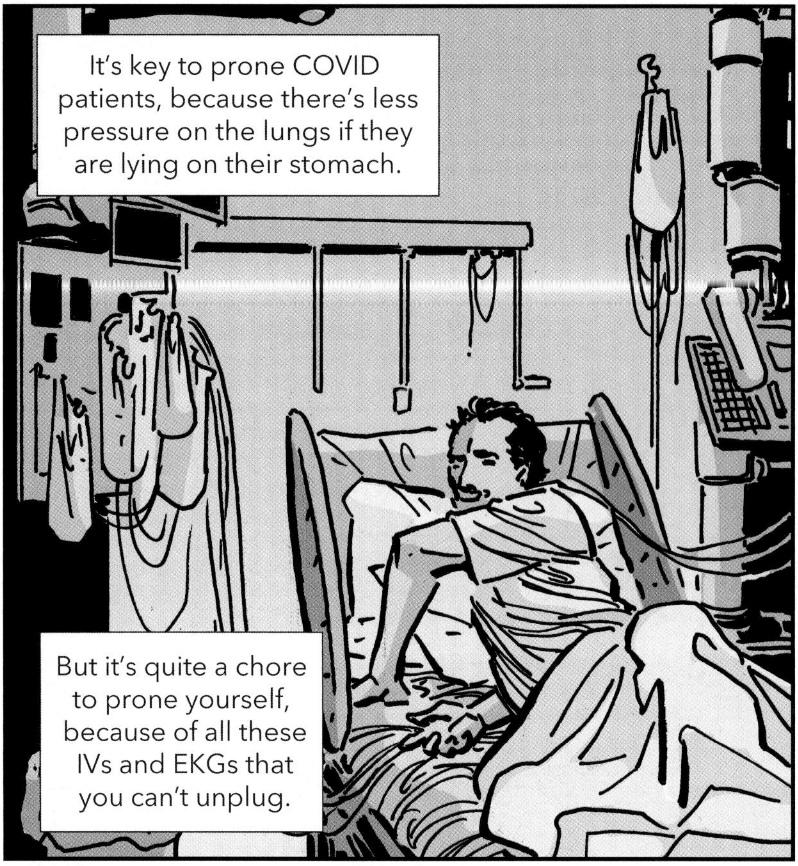
It's key to prone COVID patients, because there's less pressure on the lungs if they are lying on their stomach.
But it's quite a chore to prone yourself, because of all these IVs and EKGs that you can't unplug.

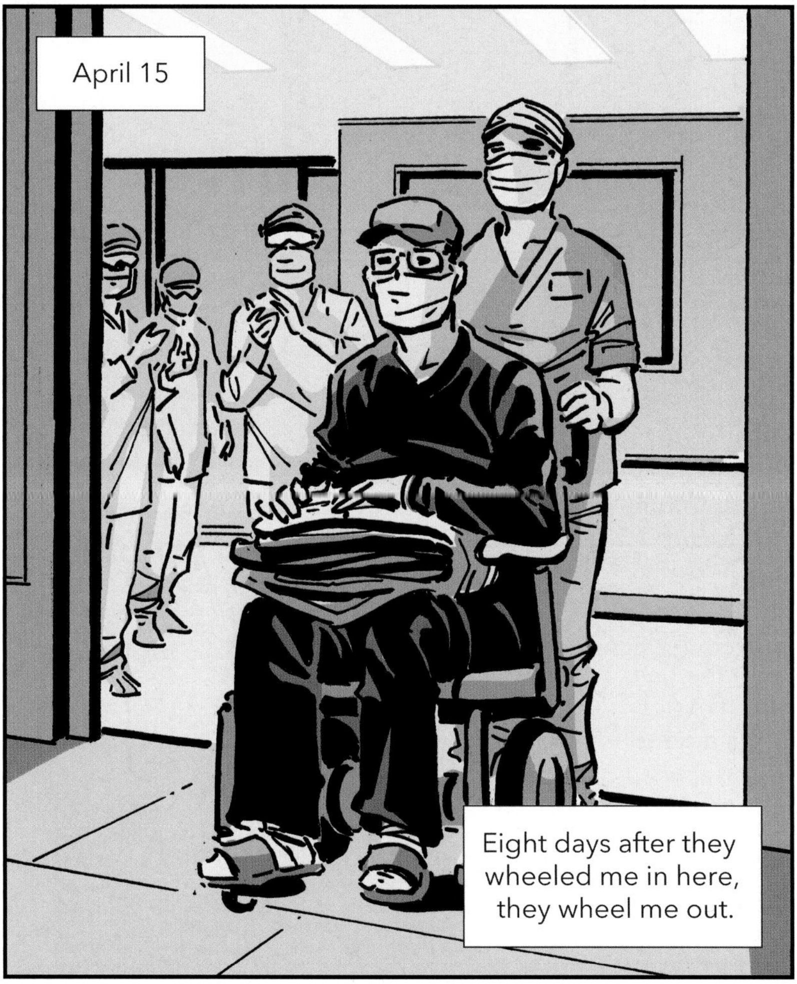
April 15
Eight days after they wheeled me in here, they wheel me out.

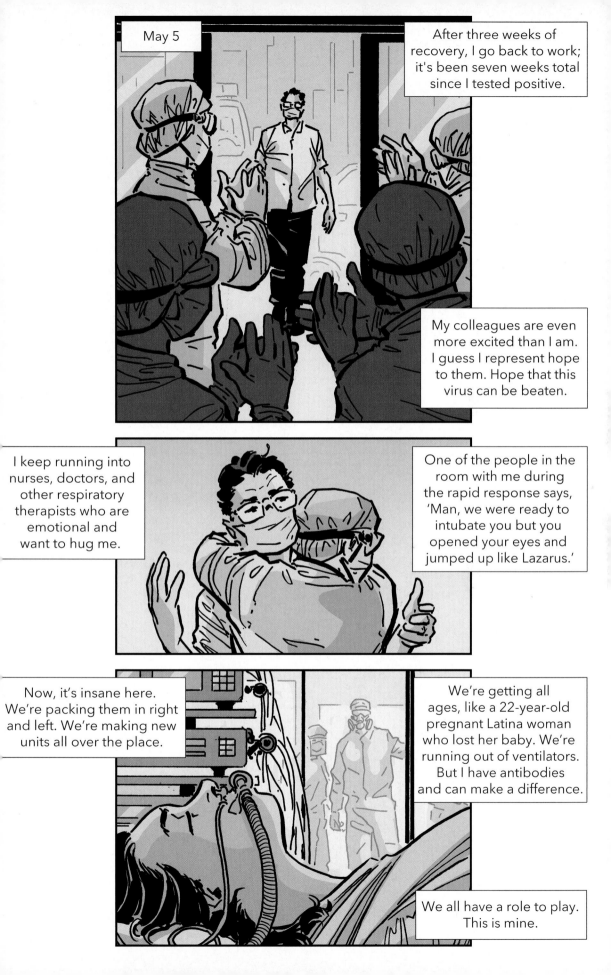

May 5

After three weeks of recovery, I go back to work; it's been seven weeks total since I tested positive.

My colleagues are even more excited than I am. I guess I represent hope to them. Hope that this virus can be beaten.

I keep running into nurses, doctors, and other respiratory therapists who are emotional and want to hug me.

One of the people in the room with me during the rapid response says, 'Man, we were ready to intubate you but you opened your eyes and jumped up like Lazarus.'

Now, it's insane here. We're packing them in right and left. We're making new units all over the place.

We're getting all ages, like a 22-year-old pregnant Latina woman who lost her baby. We're running out of ventilators. But I have antibodies and can make a difference.

We all have a role to play. This is mine.

CHAPTER 9
DOCTORS WITHOUT BORDERS TRAUMA DOC NEEDED CLOSER TO HOME

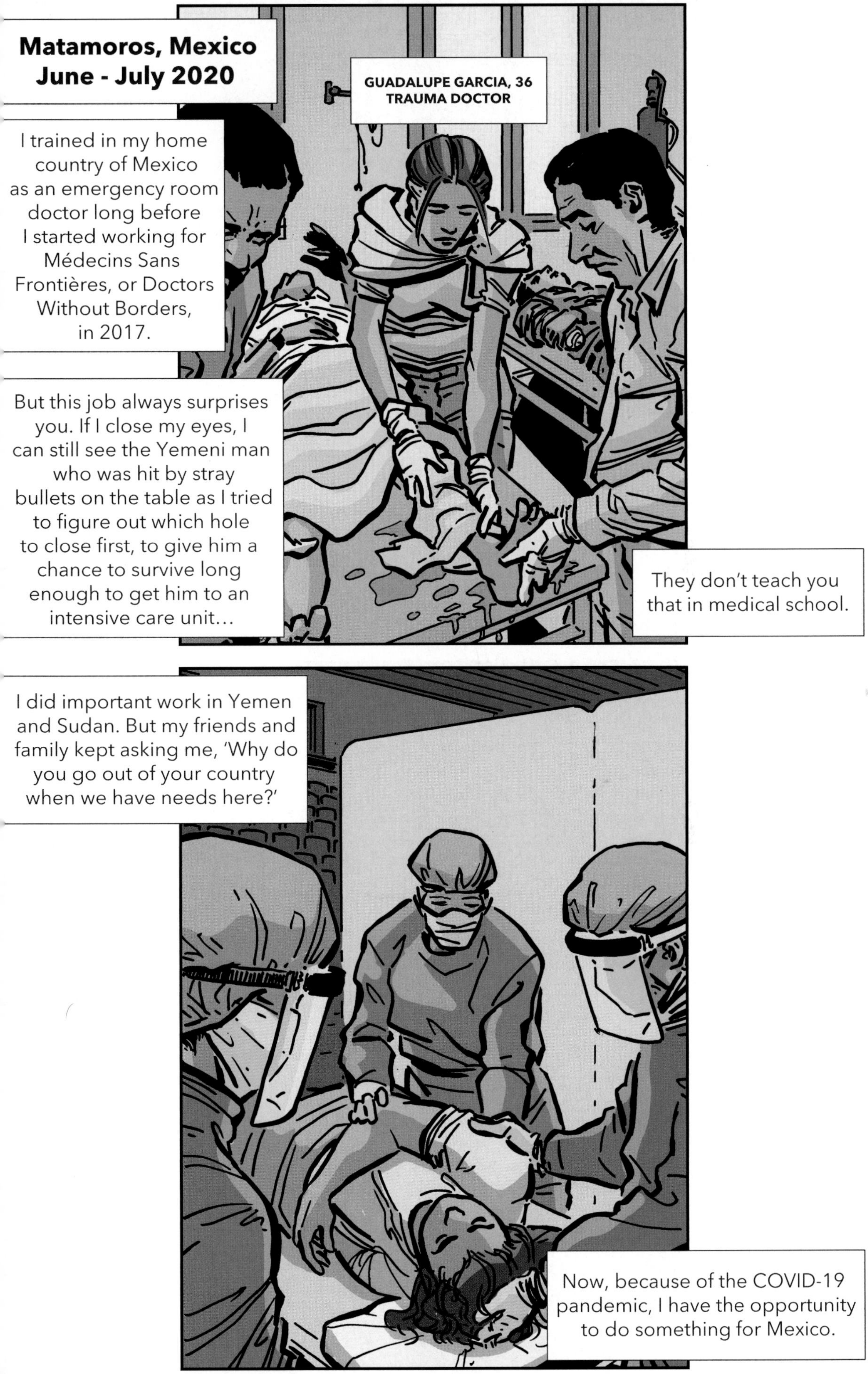
Matamoros, Mexico
June - July 2020
GUADALUPE GARCIA, 36
TRAUMA DOCTOR
I trained in my home country of Mexico as an emergency room doctor long before I started working for Médecins Sans Frontières, or Doctors Without Borders, in 2017.
But this job always surprises you. If I close my eyes, I can still see the Yemeni man who was hit by stray bullets on the table as I tried to figure out which hole to close first, to give him a chance to survive long enough to get him to an intensive care unit...
They don't teach you that in medical school.
I did important work in Yemen and Sudan. But my friends and family kept asking me, 'Why do you go out of your country when we have needs here?'
Now, because of the COVID-19 pandemic, I have the opportunity to do something for Mexico.

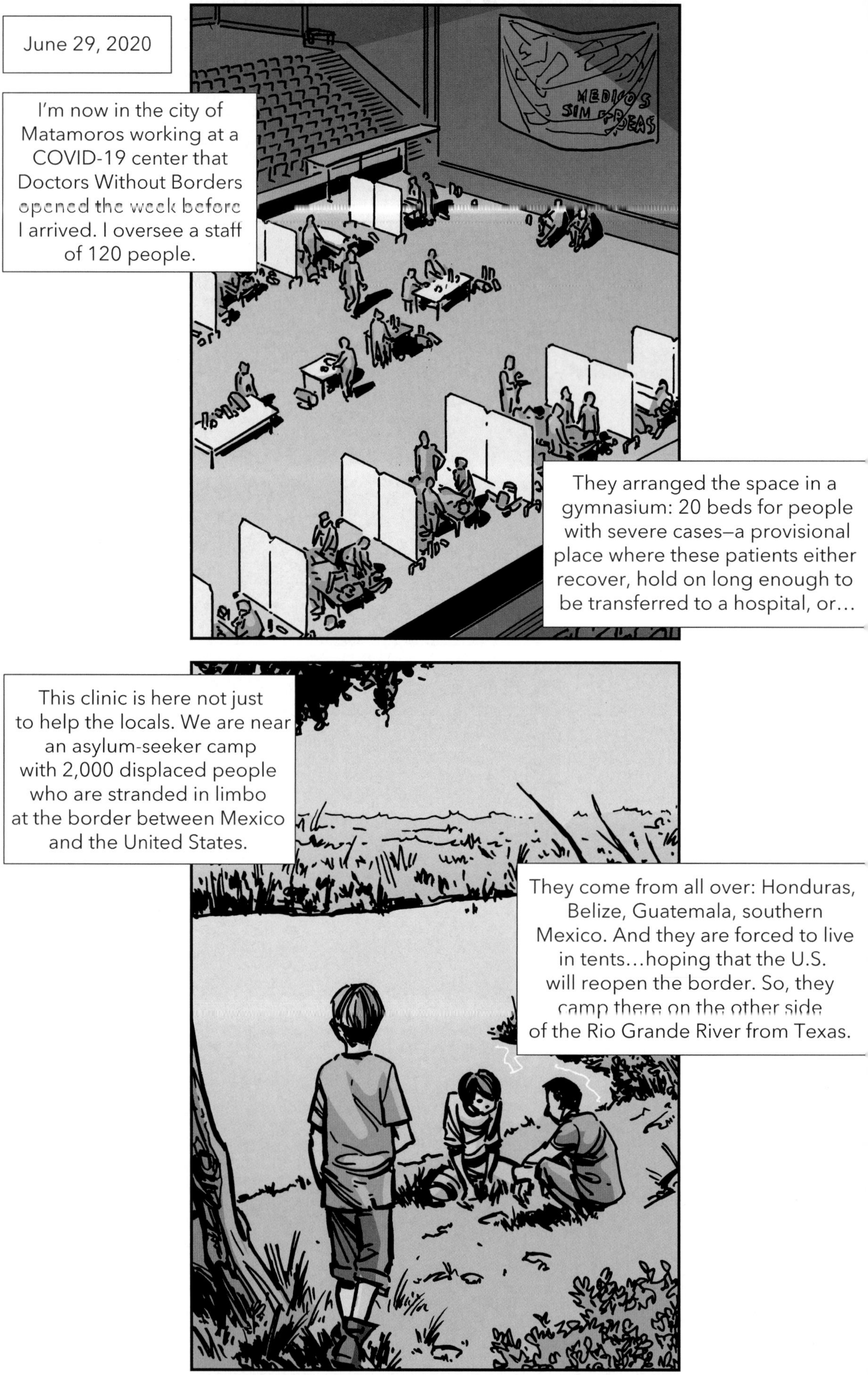
June 29, 2020
I'm now in the city of Matamoros working at a COVID-19 center that Doctors Without Borders opened the week before I arrived. I oversee a staff of 120 people.
They arranged the space in a gymnasium: 20 beds for people with severe cases—a provisional place where these patients either recover, hold on long enough to be transferred to a hospital, or…
This clinic is here not just to help the locals. We are near an asylum-seeker camp with 2,000 displaced people who are stranded in limbo at the border between Mexico and the United States.
They come from all over: Honduras, Belize, Guatemala, southern Mexico. And they are forced to live in tents…hoping that the U.S. will reopen the border. So, they camp there on the other side of the Rio Grande River from Texas.

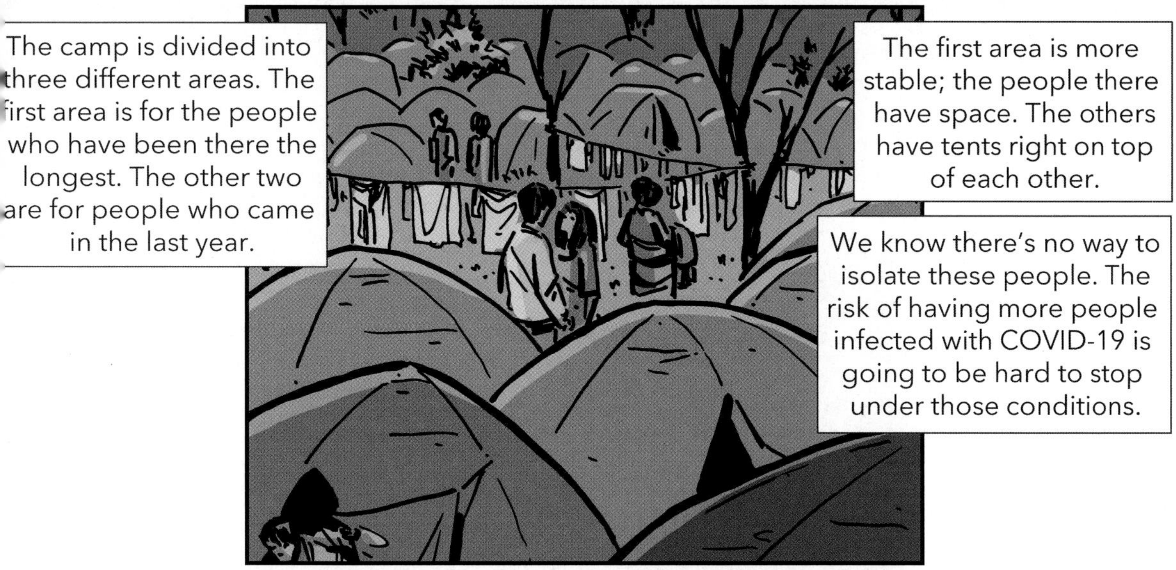
The camp is divided into three different areas. The first area is for the people who have been there the longest. The other two are for people who came in the last year.
The first area is more stable; the people there have space. The others have tents right on top of each other.
We know there's no way to isolate these people. The risk of having more people infected with COVID-19 is going to be hard to stop under those conditions.

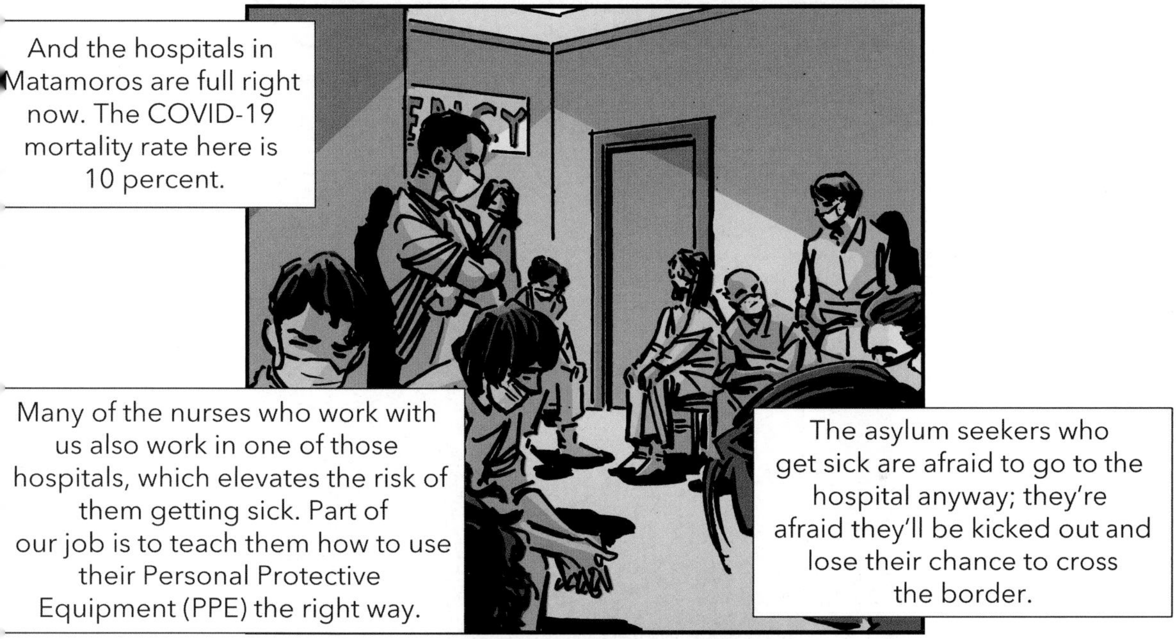
And the hospitals in Matamoros are full right now. The COVID-19 mortality rate here is 10 percent.
Many of the nurses who work with us also work in one of those hospitals, which elevates the risk of them getting sick. Part of our job is to teach them how to use their Personal Protective Equipment (PPE) the right way.
The asylum seekers who get sick are afraid to go to the hospital anyway; they're afraid they'll be kicked out and lose their chance to cross the border.

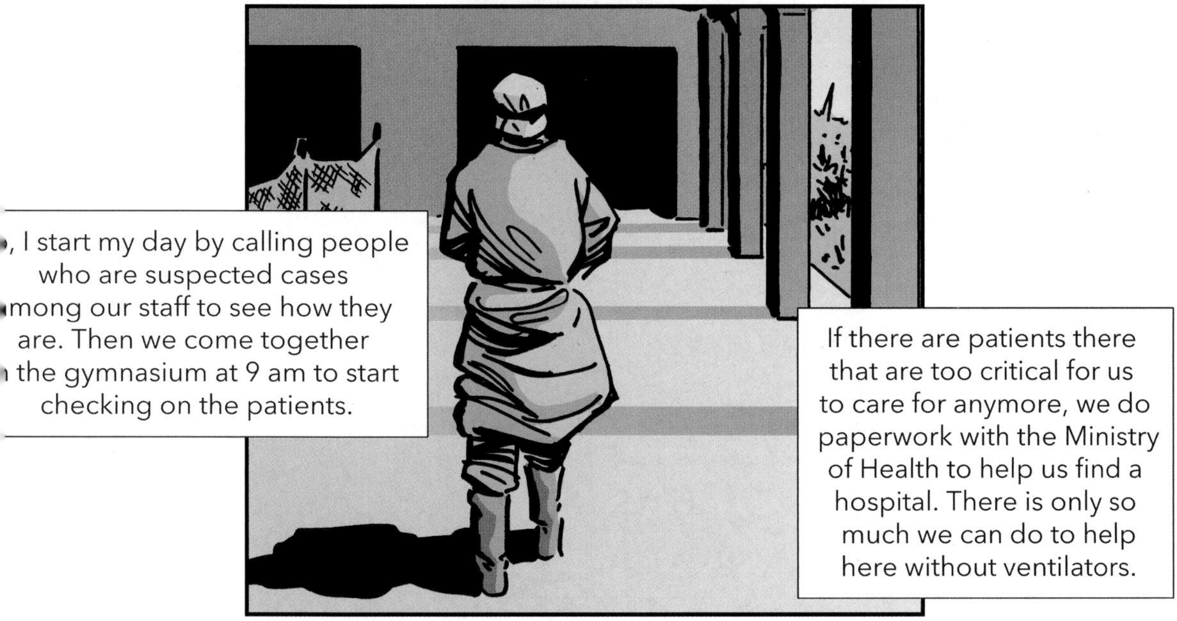
, I start my day by calling people who are suspected cases mong our staff to see how they are. Then we come together the gymnasium at 9 am to start checking on the patients.
If there are patients there that are too critical for us to care for anymore, we do paperwork with the Ministry of Health to help us find a hospital. There is only so much we can do to help here without ventilators.

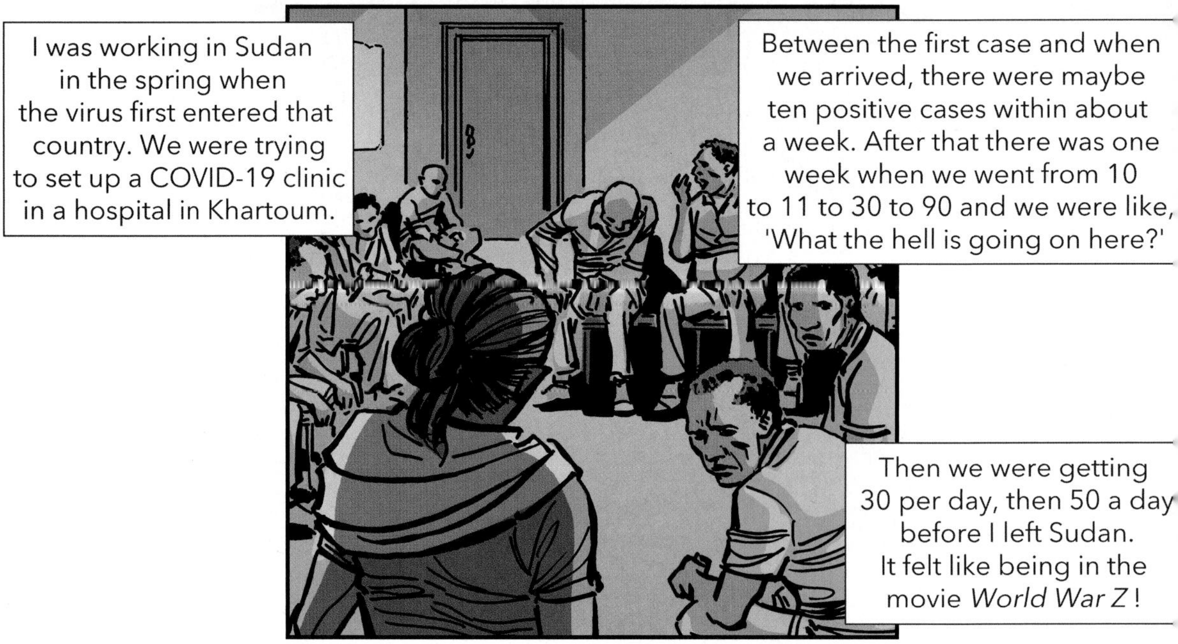
I was working in Sudan in the spring when the virus first entered that country. We were trying to set up a COVID-19 clinic in a hospital in Khartoum.
Between the first case and when we arrived, there were maybe ten positive cases within about a week. After that there was one week when we went from 10 to 11 to 30 to 90 and we were like, 'What the hell is going on here?'
Then we were getting 30 per day, then 50 a day before I left Sudan. It felt like being in the movie *World War Z* !

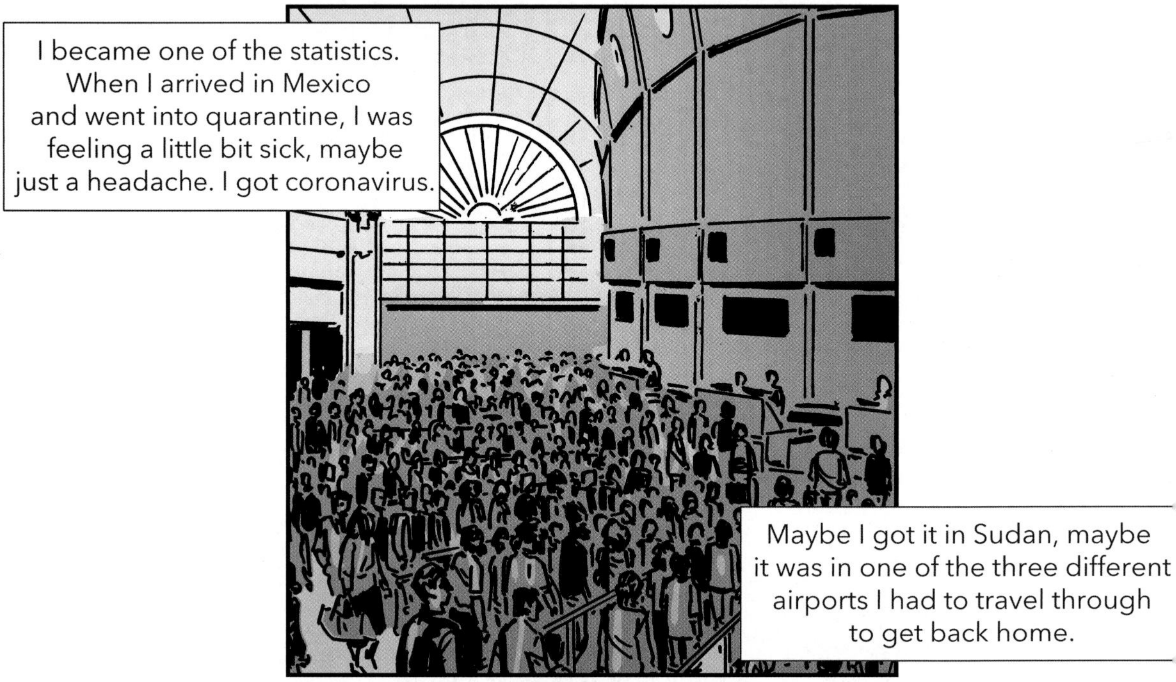
I became one of the statistics. When I arrived in Mexico and went into quarantine, I was feeling a little bit sick, maybe just a headache. I got coronavirus.
Maybe I got it in Sudan, maybe it was in one of the three different airports I had to travel through to get back home.

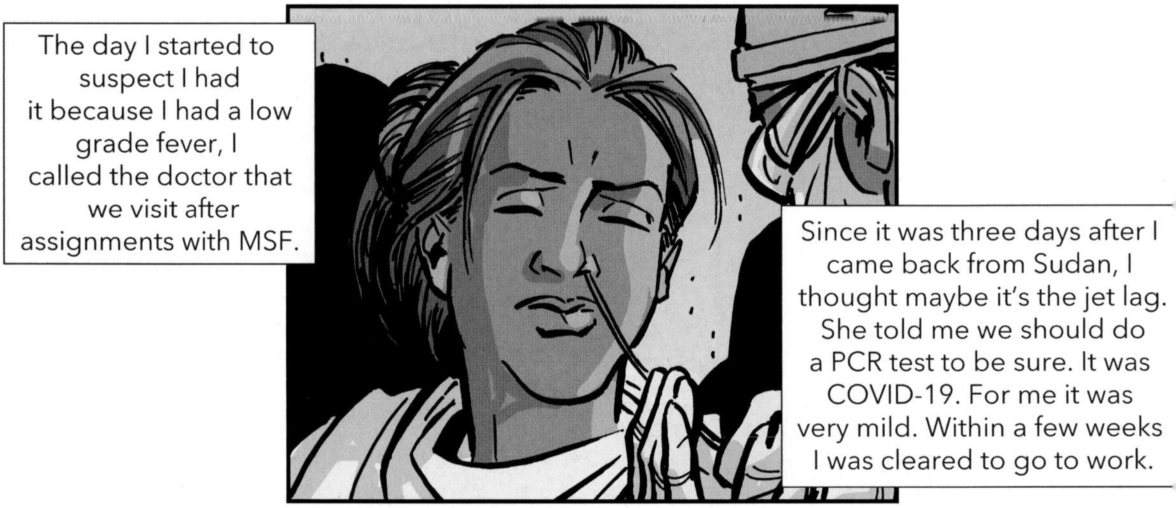
The day I started to suspect I had it because I had a low grade fever, I called the doctor that we visit after assignments with MSF.
Since it was three days after I came back from Sudan, I thought maybe it's the jet lag. She told me we should do a PCR test to be sure. It was COVID-19. For me it was very mild. Within a few weeks I was cleared to go to work.

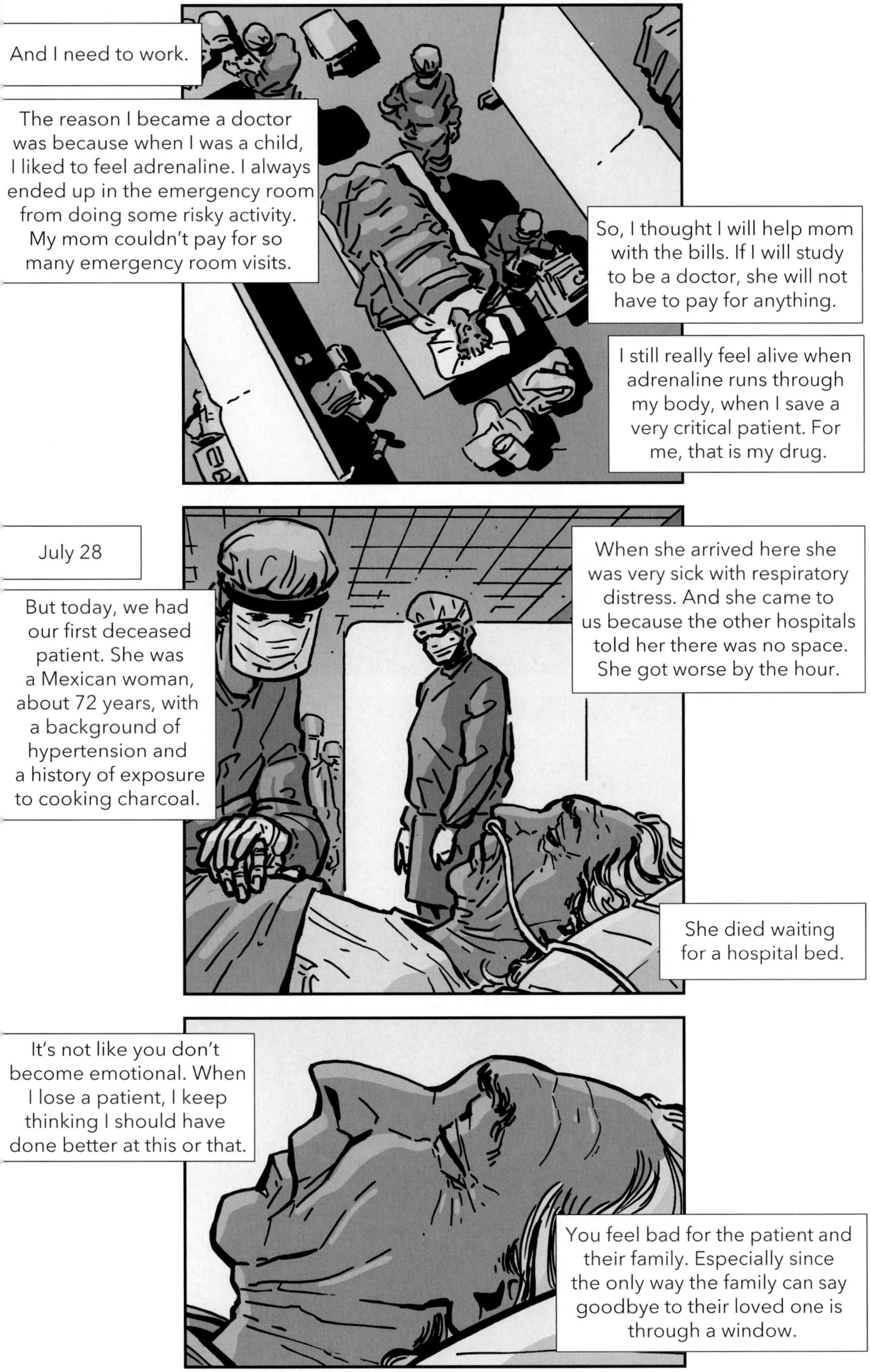
And I need to work.
The reason I became a doctor was because when I was a child, I liked to feel adrenaline. I always ended up in the emergency room from doing some risky activity. My mom couldn't pay for so many emergency room visits.
So, I thought I will help mom with the bills. If I will study to be a doctor, she will not have to pay for anything.
I still really feel alive when adrenaline runs through my body, when I save a very critical patient. For me, that is my drug.
July 28
But today, we had our first deceased patient. She was a Mexican woman, about 72 years, with a background of hypertension and a history of exposure to cooking charcoal.
When she arrived here she was very sick with respiratory distress. And she came to us because the other hospitals told her there was no space. She got worse by the hour.
She died waiting for a hospital bed.
It's not like you don't become emotional. When I lose a patient, I keep thinking I should have done better at this or that.
You feel bad for the patient and their family. Especially since the only way the family can say goodbye to their loved one is through a window.

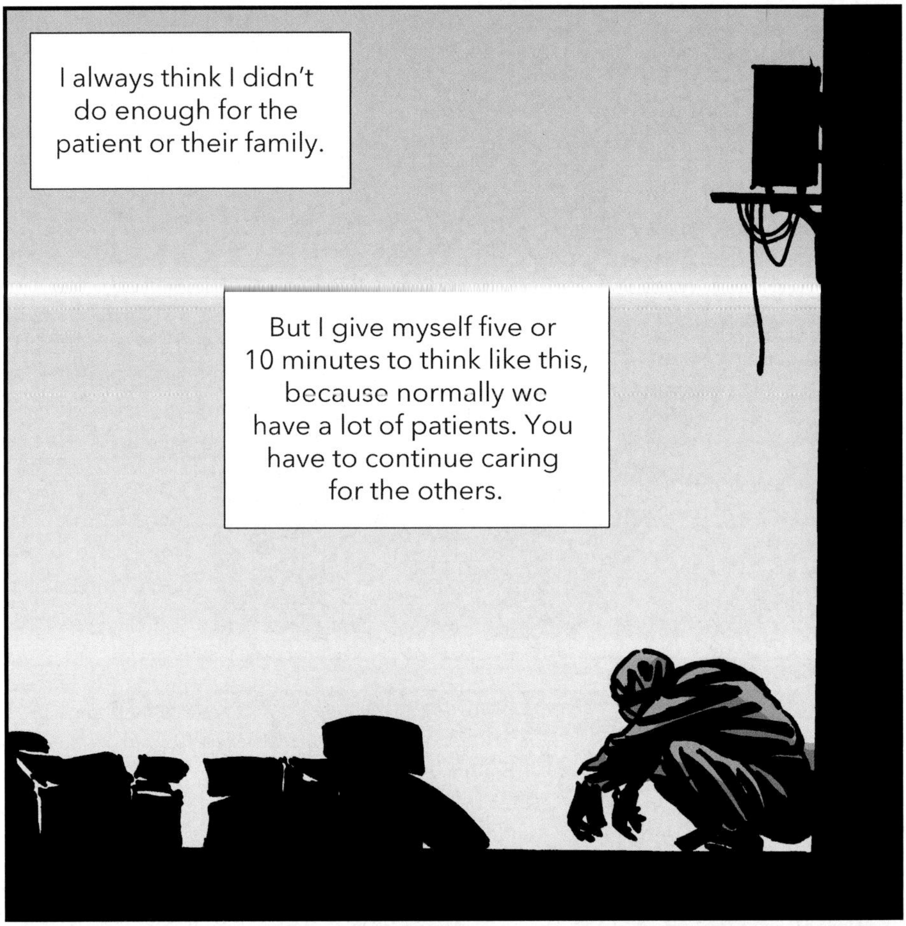
I always think I didn't do enough for the patient or their family.
But I give myself five or 10 minutes to think like this, because normally we have a lot of patients. You have to continue caring for the others.
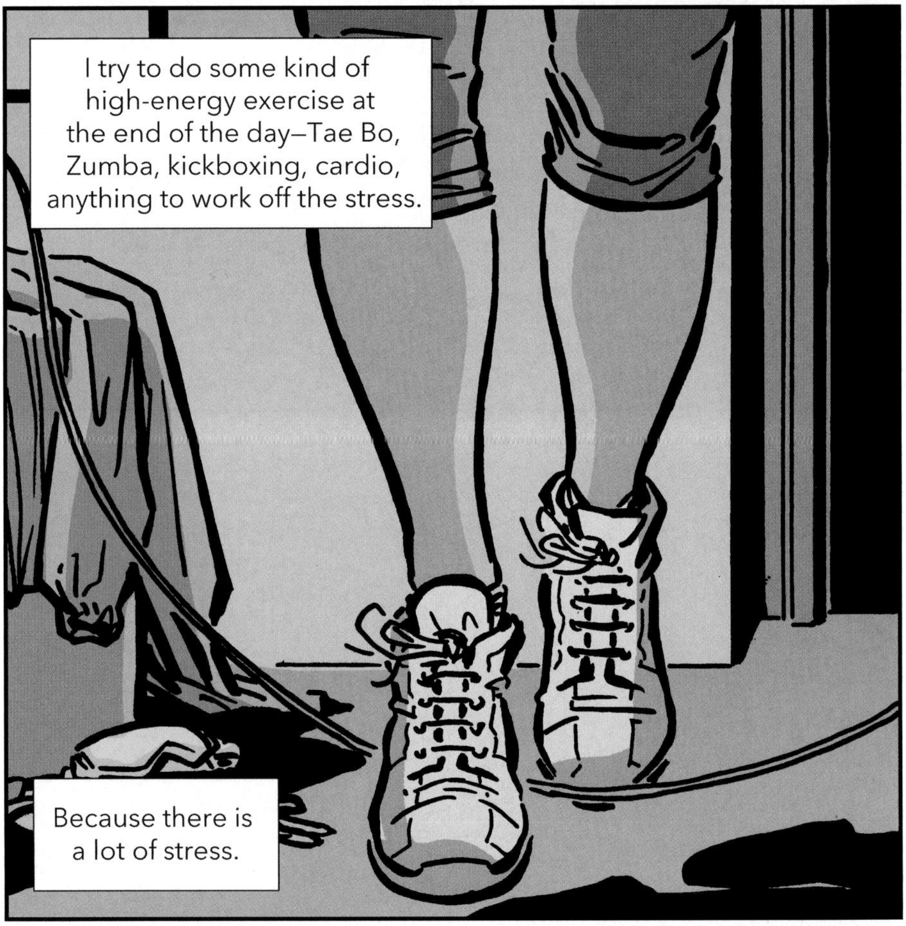
I try to do some kind of high-energy exercise at the end of the day—Tae Bo, Zumba, kickboxing, cardio, anything to work off the stress.
Because there is a lot of stress.

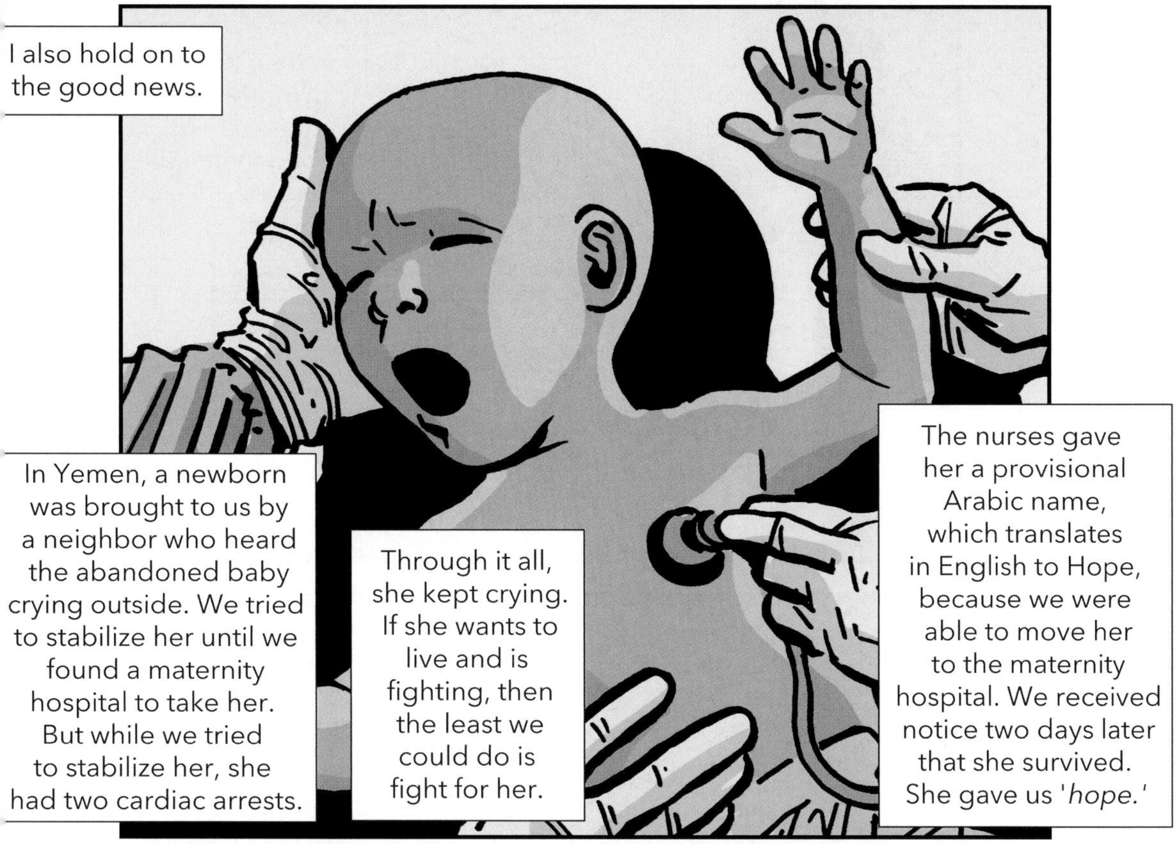
I also hold on to the good news.
In Yemen, a newborn was brought to us by a neighbor who heard the abandoned baby crying outside. We tried to stabilize her until we found a maternity hospital to take her. But while we tried to stabilize her, she had two cardiac arrests.
Through it all, she kept crying. If she wants to live and is fighting, then the least we could do is fight for her.
The nurses gave her a provisional Arabic name, which translates in English to Hope, because we were able to move her to the maternity hospital. We received notice two days later that she survived. She gave us '*hope.*'

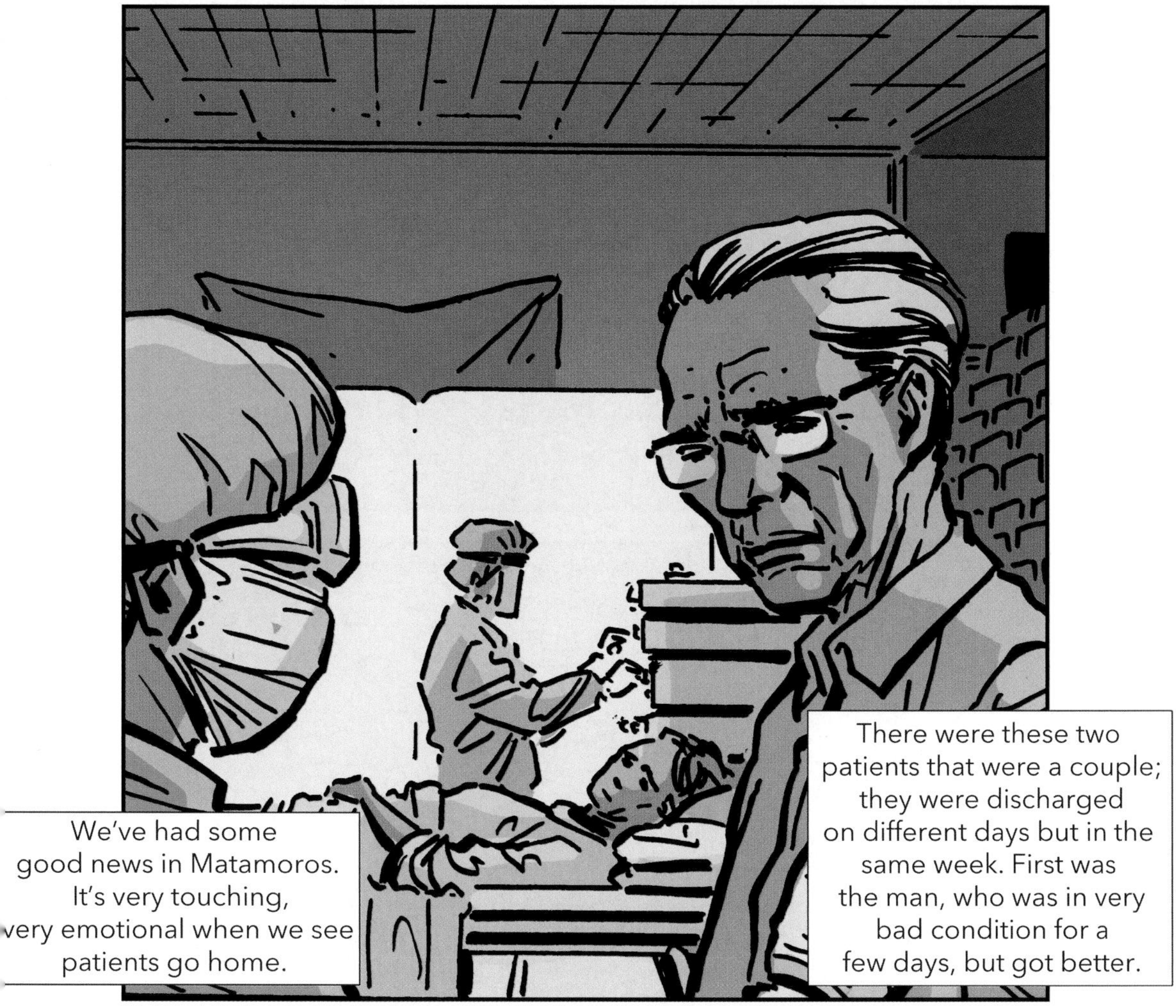
We've had some good news in Matamoros. It's very touching, very emotional when we see patients go home.
There were these two patients that were a couple; they were discharged on different days but in the same week. First was the man, who was in very bad condition for a few days, but got better.

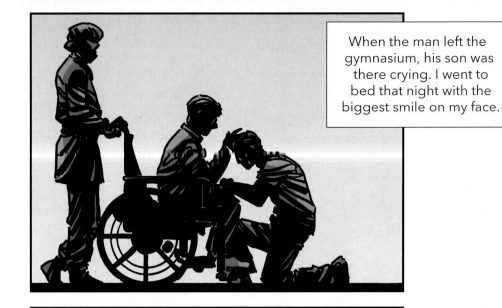

When the man left the gymnasium, his son was there crying. I went to bed that night with the biggest smile on my face.

After some more days, the wife came out of the clinic, and she was very emotional, too.

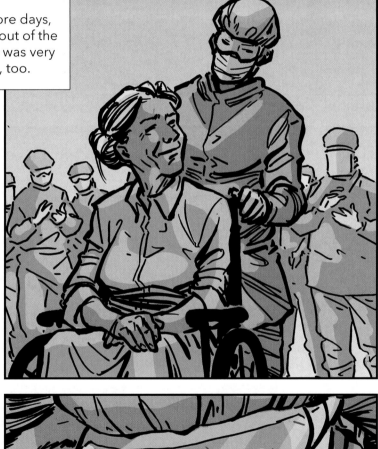

She told us, 'You are some angels and I appreciate what you did for us.'

That made me so happy. Because today we made a difference, even if it's one or two lives.

CHAPTER 10

THREE SCIENTISTS RACE TO TRACK DEADLY PATHOGEN IN THEIR CITY

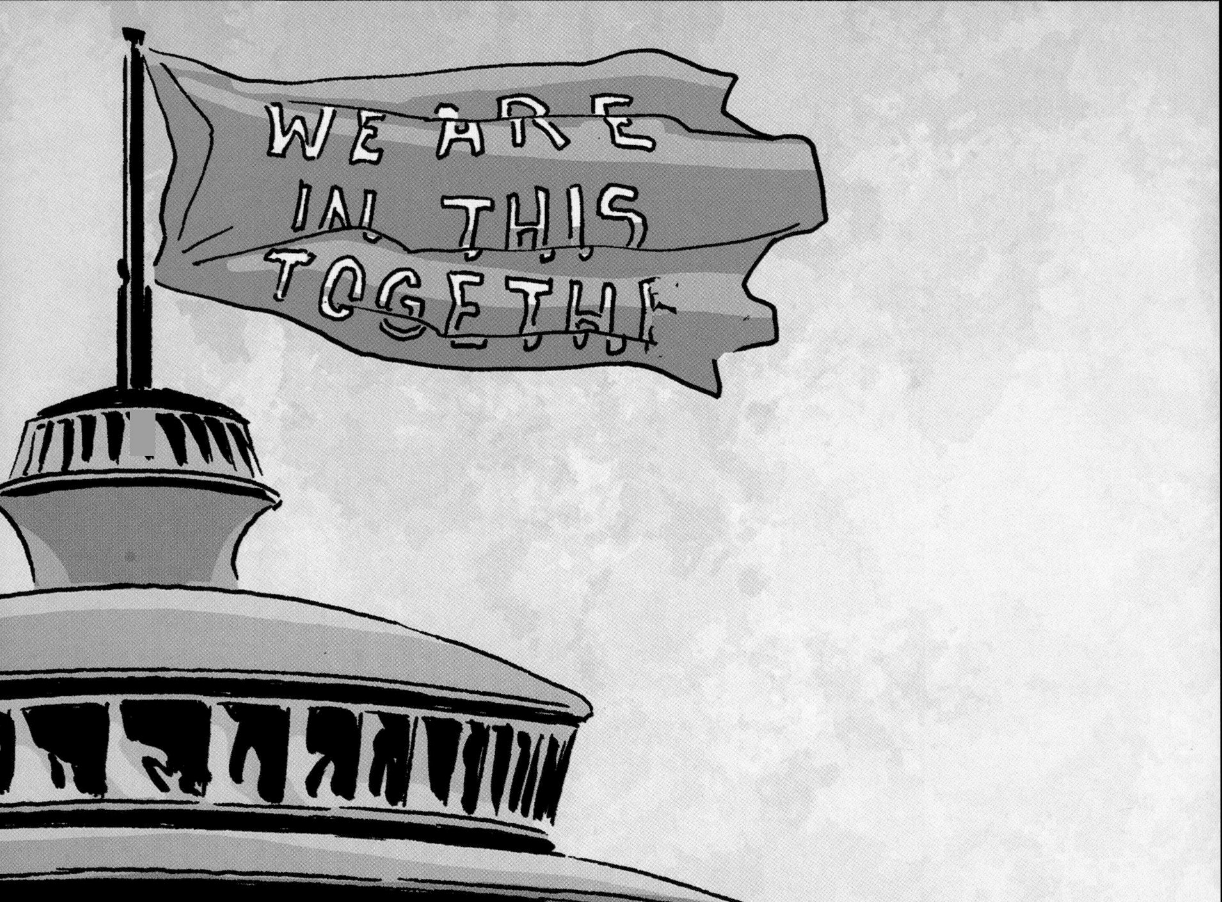
WE ARE
IN THIS
TOGETHE

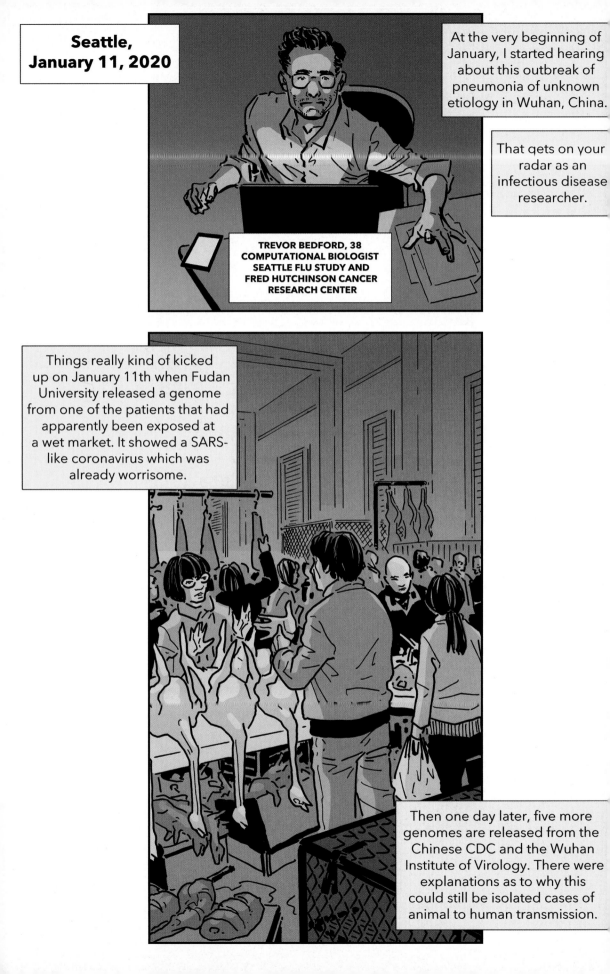

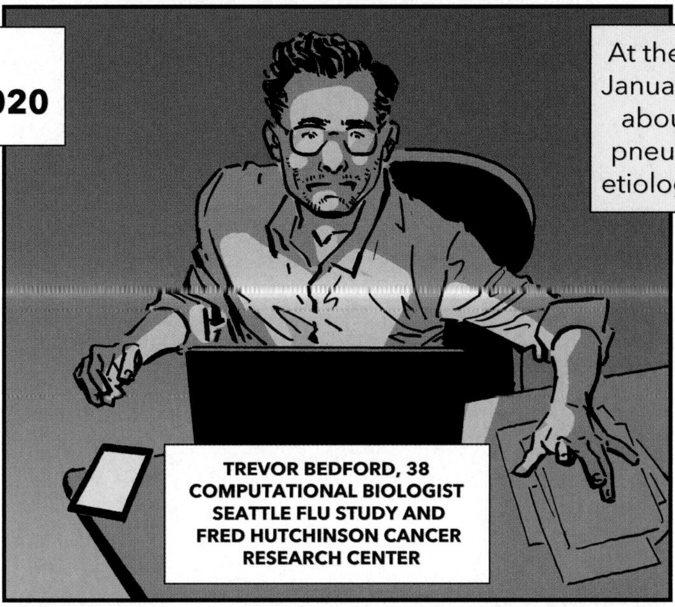
Seattle, January 11, 2020
At the very beginning of January, I started hearing about this outbreak of pneumonia of unknown etiology in Wuhan, China.
That gets on your radar as an infectious disease researcher.
TREVOR BEDFORD, 38
COMPUTATIONAL BIOLOGIST
SEATTLE FLU STUDY AND
FRED HUTCHINSON CANCER RESEARCH CENTER

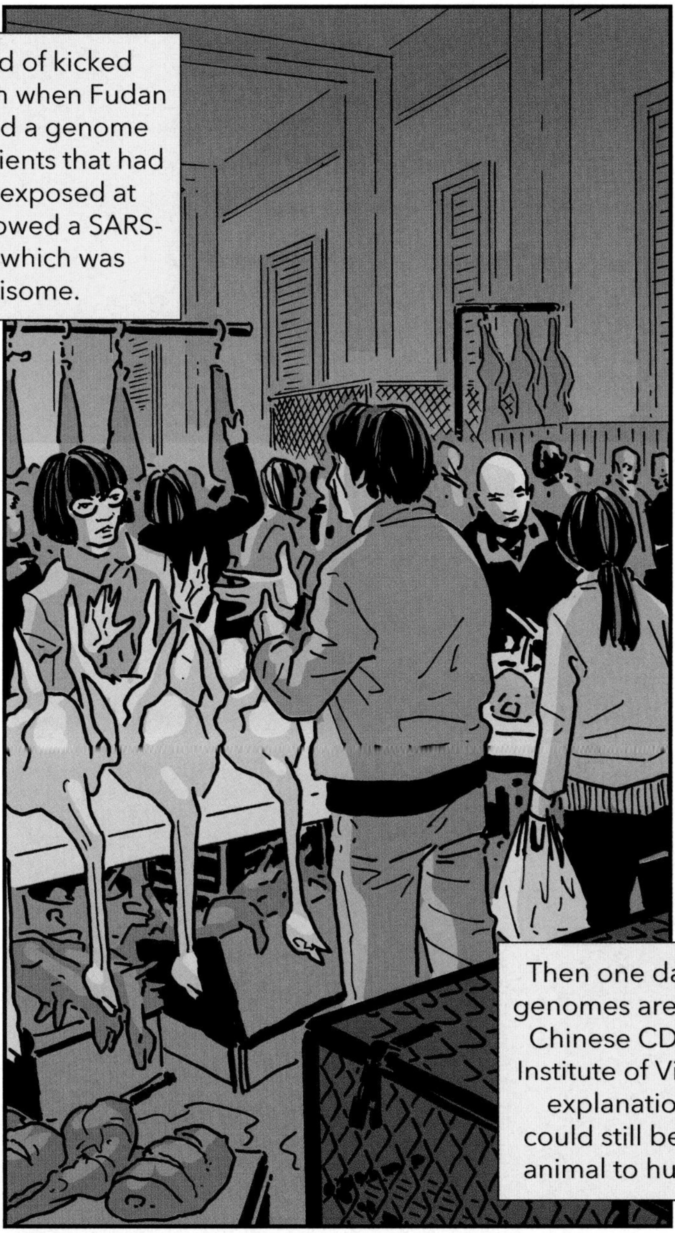
Things really kind of kicked up on January 11th when Fudan University released a genome from one of the patients that had apparently been exposed at a wet market. It showed a SARS-like coronavirus which was already worrisome.
Then one day later, five more genomes are released from the Chinese CDC and the Wuhan Institute of Virology. There were explanations as to why this could still be isolated cases of animal to human transmission.

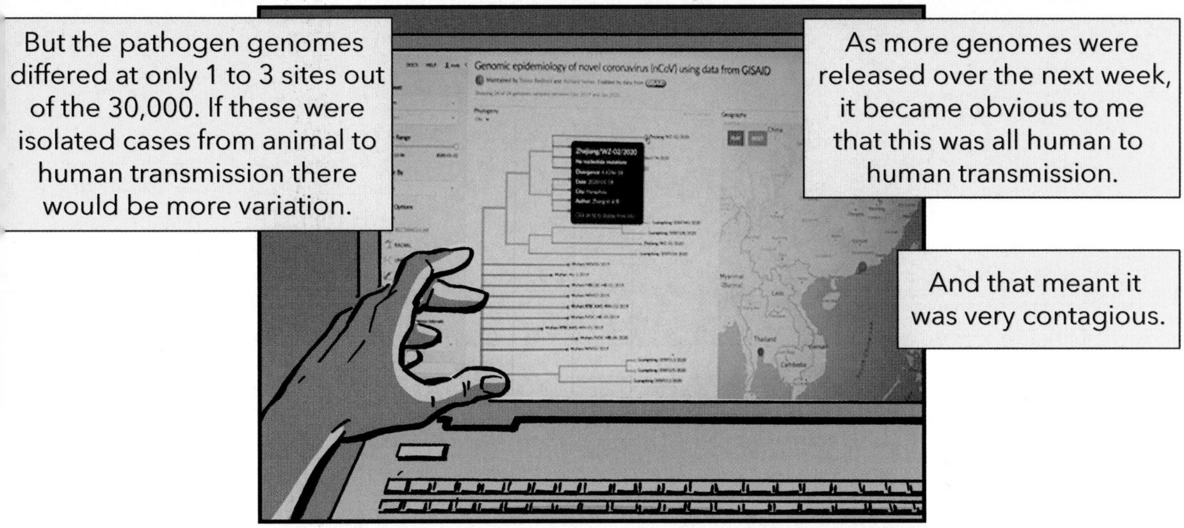
But the pathogen genomes differed at only 1 to 3 sites out of the 30,000. If these were isolated cases from animal to human transmission there would be more variation.
Genomic epidemiology of novel coronavirus (nCoV) using data from GISAID
As more genomes were released over the next week, it became obvious to me that this was all human to human transmission.
And that meant it was very contagious.

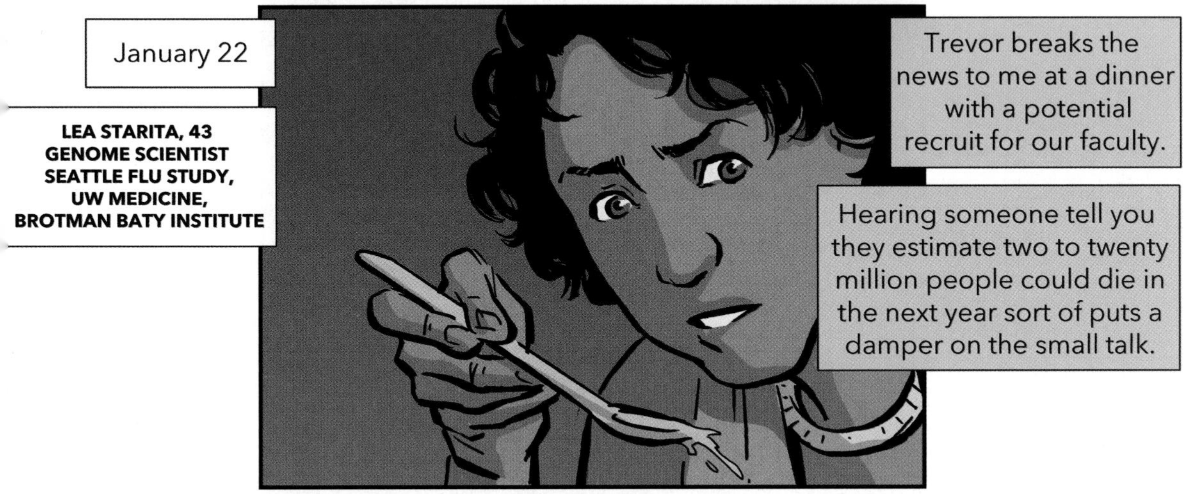
January 22
LEA STARITA, 43
GENOME SCIENTIST
SEATTLE FLU STUDY,
UW MEDICINE,
BROTMAN BATY INSTITUTE
Trevor breaks the news to me at a dinner with a potential recruit for our faculty.
Hearing someone tell you they estimate two to twenty million people could die in the next year sort of puts a damper on the small talk.

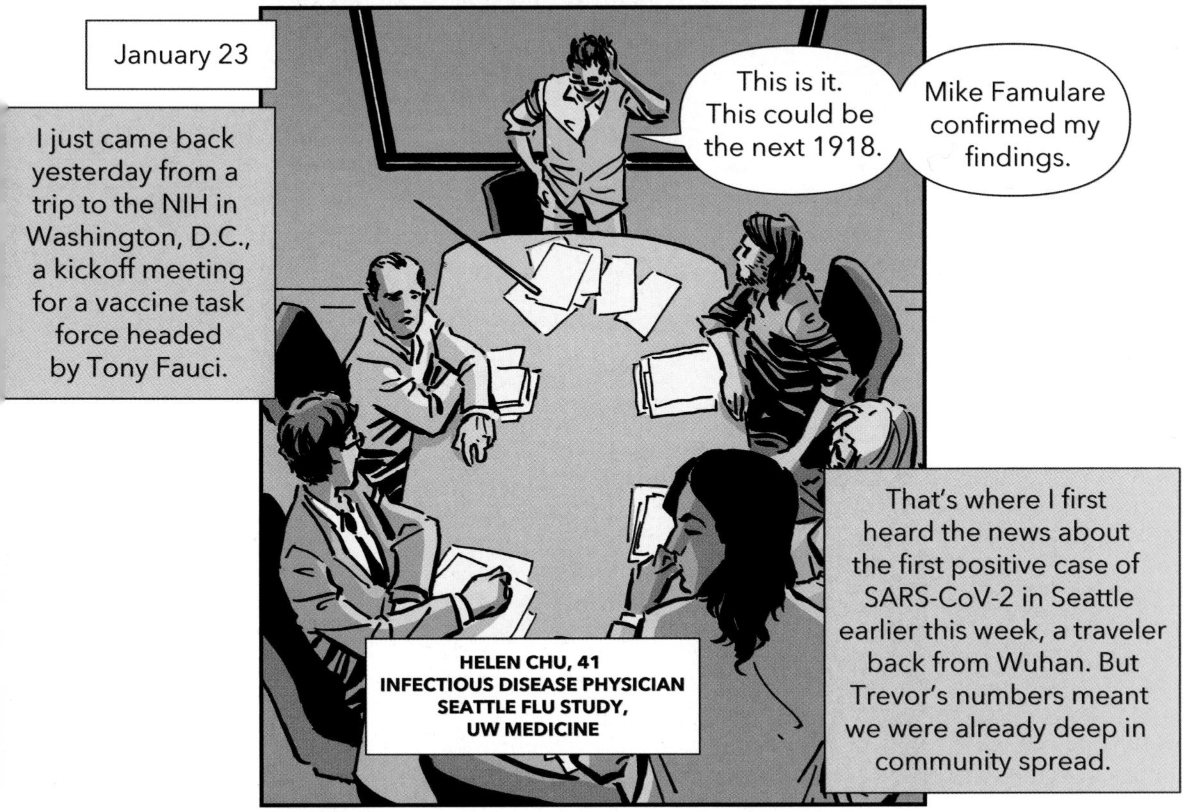
January 23
I just came back yesterday from a trip to the NIH in Washington, D.C., a kickoff meeting for a vaccine task force headed by Tony Fauci.
This is it. This could be the next 1918.
Mike Famulare confirmed my findings.
HELEN CHU, 41
INFECTIOUS DISEASE PHYSICIAN
SEATTLE FLU STUDY,
UW MEDICINE
That's where I first heard the news about the first positive case of SARS-CoV-2 in Seattle earlier this week, a traveler back from Wuhan. But Trevor's numbers meant we were already deep in community spread.

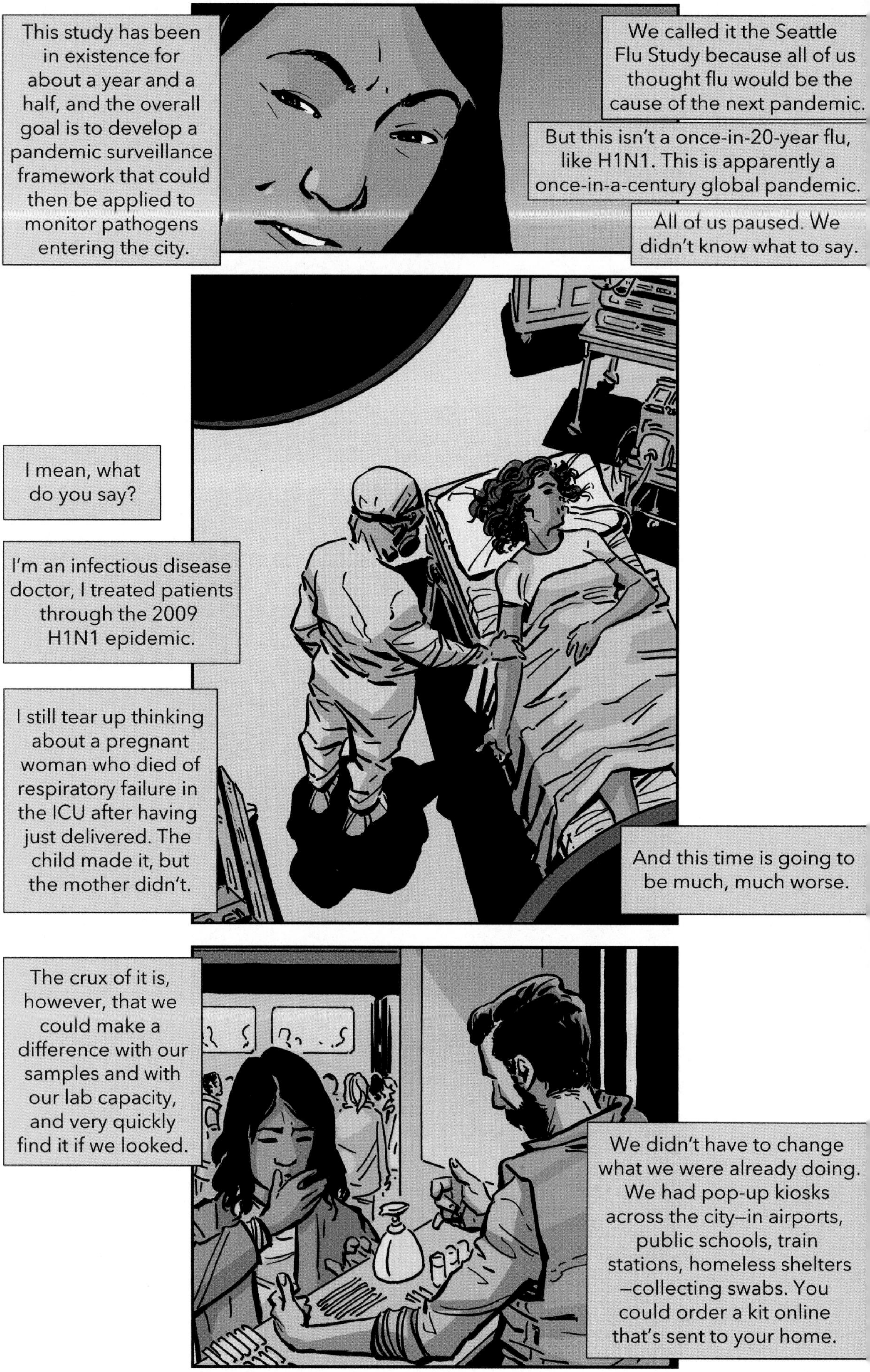
This study has been in existence for about a year and a half, and the overall goal is to develop a pandemic surveillance framework that could then be applied to monitor pathogens entering the city.
We called it the Seattle Flu Study because all of us thought flu would be the cause of the next pandemic.
But this isn't a once-in-20-year flu, like H1N1. This is apparently a once-in-a-century global pandemic.
All of us paused. We didn't know what to say.
I mean, what do you say?
I'm an infectious disease doctor, I treated patients through the 2009 H1N1 epidemic.
I still tear up thinking about a pregnant woman who died of respiratory failure in the ICU after having just delivered. The child made it, but the mother didn't.
And this time is going to be much, much worse.
The crux of it is, however, that we could make a difference with our samples and with our lab capacity, and very quickly find it if we looked.
We didn't have to change what we were already doing. We had pop-up kiosks across the city—in airports, public schools, train stations, homeless shelters—collecting swabs. You could order a kit online that's sent to your home.

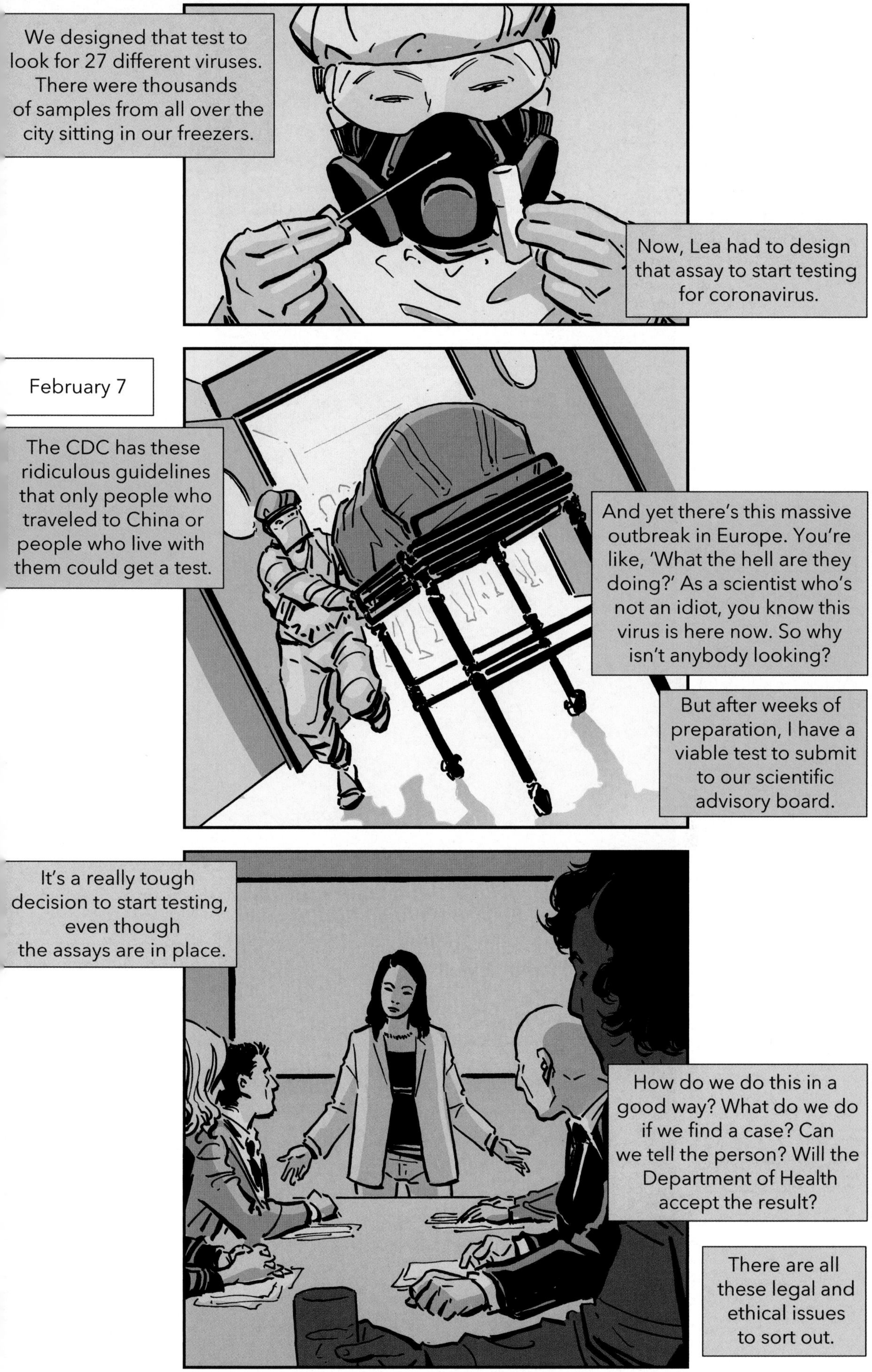
We designed that test to look for 27 different viruses. There were thousands of samples from all over the city sitting in our freezers.
Now, Lea had to design that assay to start testing for coronavirus.
February 7
The CDC has these ridiculous guidelines that only people who traveled to China or people who live with them could get a test.
And yet there's this massive outbreak in Europe. You're like, 'What the hell are they doing?' As a scientist who's not an idiot, you know this virus is here now. So why isn't anybody looking?
But after weeks of preparation, I have a viable test to submit to our scientific advisory board.
It's a really tough decision to start testing, even though the assays are in place.
How do we do this in a good way? What do we do if we find a case? Can we tell the person? Will the Department of Health accept the result?
There are all these legal and ethical issues to sort out.

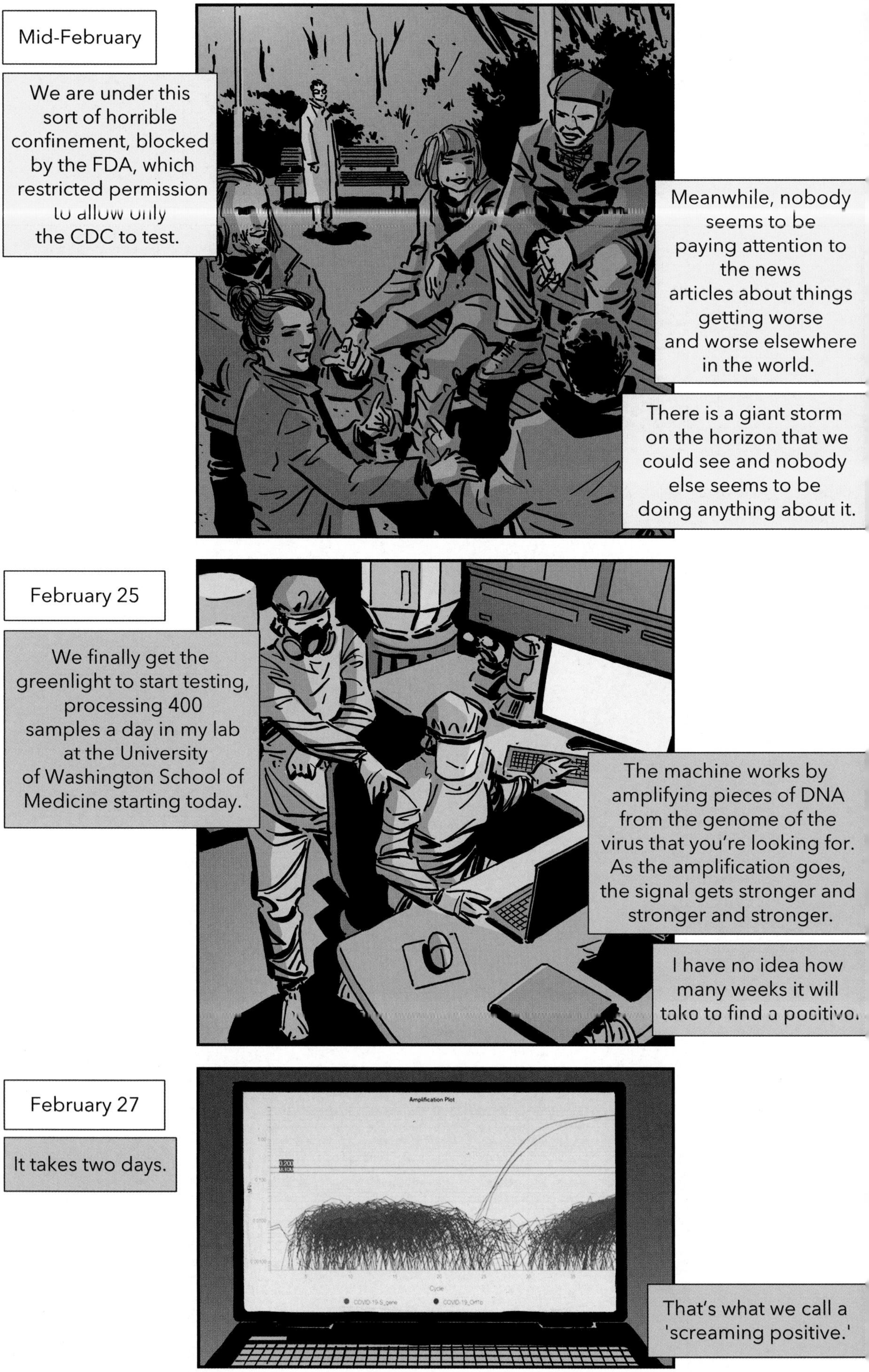

Mid-February
We are under this sort of horrible confinement, blocked by the FDA, which restricted permission to allow only the CDC to test.
Meanwhile, nobody seems to be paying attention to the news articles about things getting worse and worse elsewhere in the world.
There is a giant storm on the horizon that we could see and nobody else seems to be doing anything about it.
February 25
We finally get the greenlight to start testing, processing 400 samples a day in my lab at the University of Washington School of Medicine starting today.
The machine works by amplifying pieces of DNA from the genome of the virus that you're looking for. As the amplification goes, the signal gets stronger and stronger and stronger.
I have no idea how many weeks it will take to find a positive.
February 27
It takes two days.
Amplification Plot
Cycle
That's what we call a 'screaming positive.'

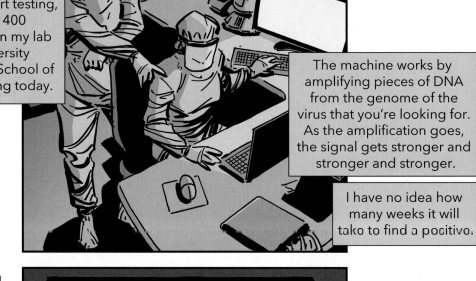

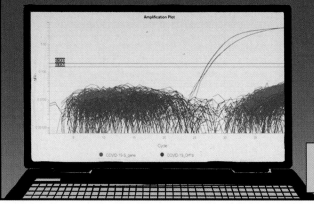

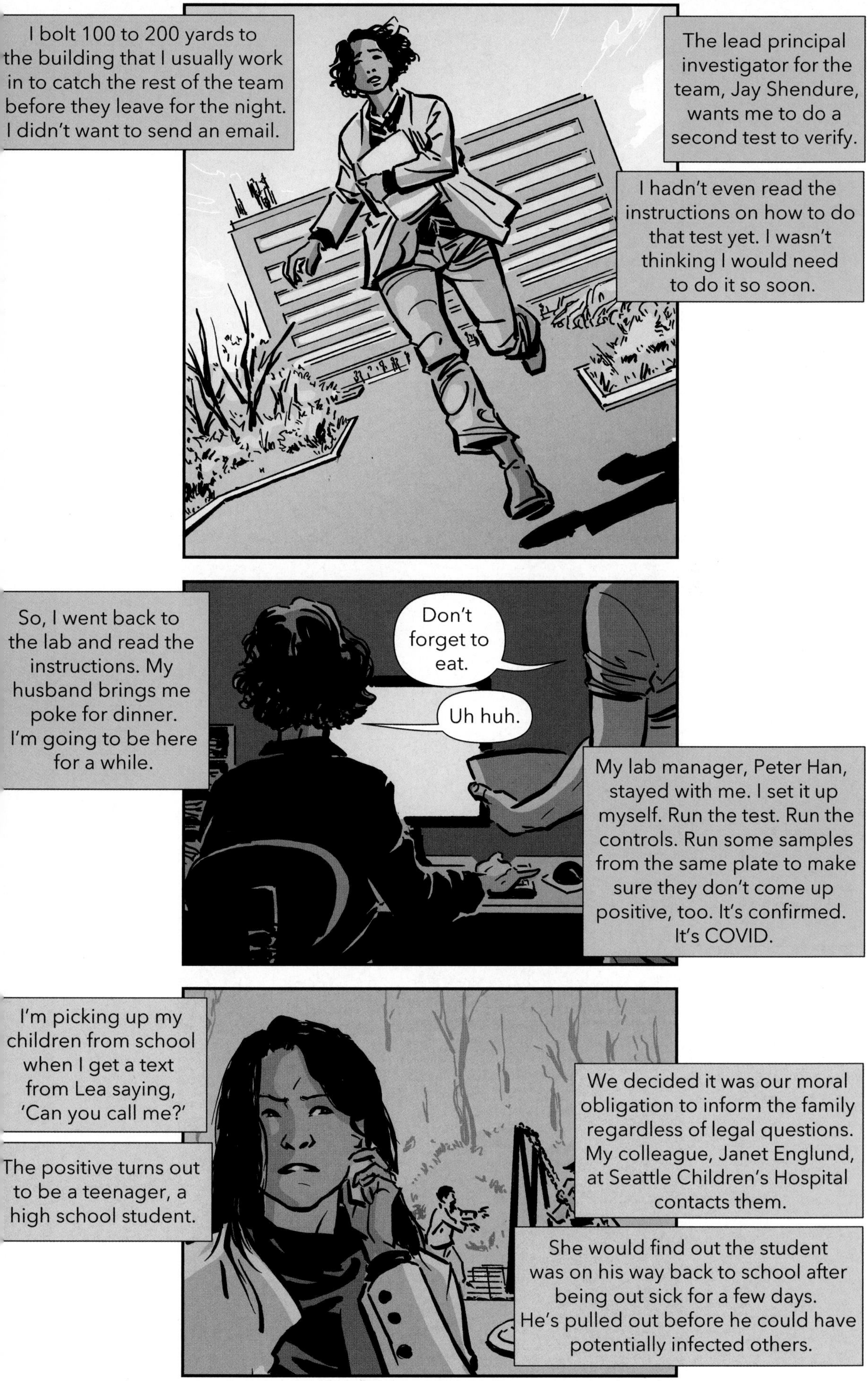
I bolt 100 to 200 yards to the building that I usually work in to catch the rest of the team before they leave for the night. I didn't want to send an email.
The lead principal investigator for the team, Jay Shendure, wants me to do a second test to verify.
I hadn't even read the instructions on how to do that test yet. I wasn't thinking I would need to do it so soon.
So, I went back to the lab and read the instructions. My husband brings me poke for dinner. I'm going to be here for a while.
Don't forget to eat.
Uh huh.
My lab manager, Peter Han, stayed with me. I set it up myself. Run the test. Run the controls. Run some samples from the same plate to make sure they don't come up positive, too. It's confirmed. It's COVID.
I'm picking up my children from school when I get a text from Lea saying, 'Can you call me?'
The positive turns out to be a teenager, a high school student.
We decided it was our moral obligation to inform the family regardless of legal questions. My colleague, Janet Englund, at Seattle Children's Hospital contacts them.
She would find out the student was on his way back to school after being out sick for a few days. He's pulled out before he could have potentially infected others.

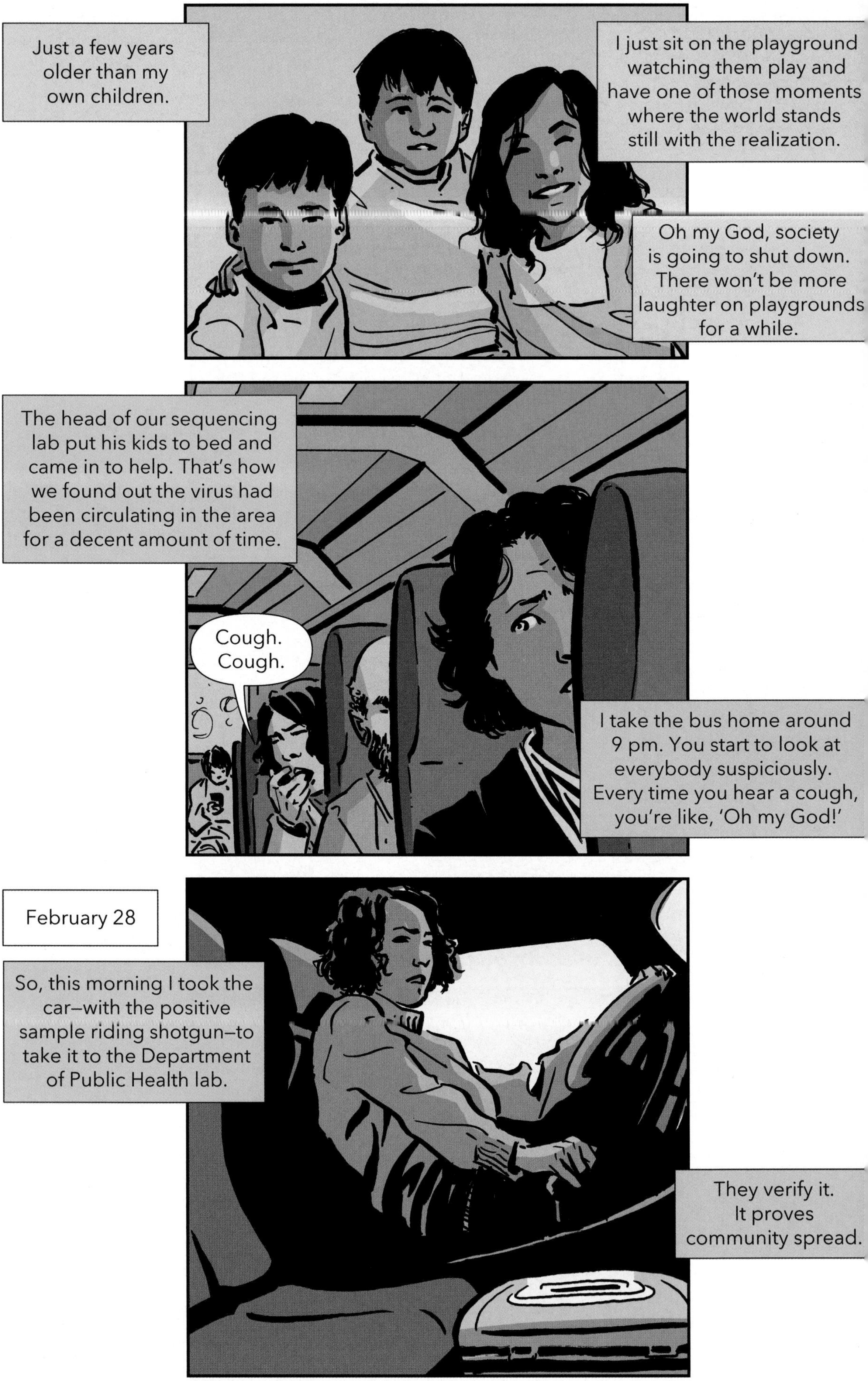
Just a few years older than my own children.
I just sit on the playground watching them play and have one of those moments where the world stands still with the realization.
Oh my God, society is going to shut down. There won't be more laughter on playgrounds for a while.
The head of our sequencing lab put his kids to bed and came in to help. That's how we found out the virus had been circulating in the area for a decent amount of time.
Cough. Cough.
I take the bus home around 9 pm. You start to look at everybody suspiciously. Every time you hear a cough, you're like, 'Oh my God!'
February 28
So, this morning I took the car—with the positive sample riding shotgun—to take it to the Department of Public Health lab.
They verify it. It proves community spread.

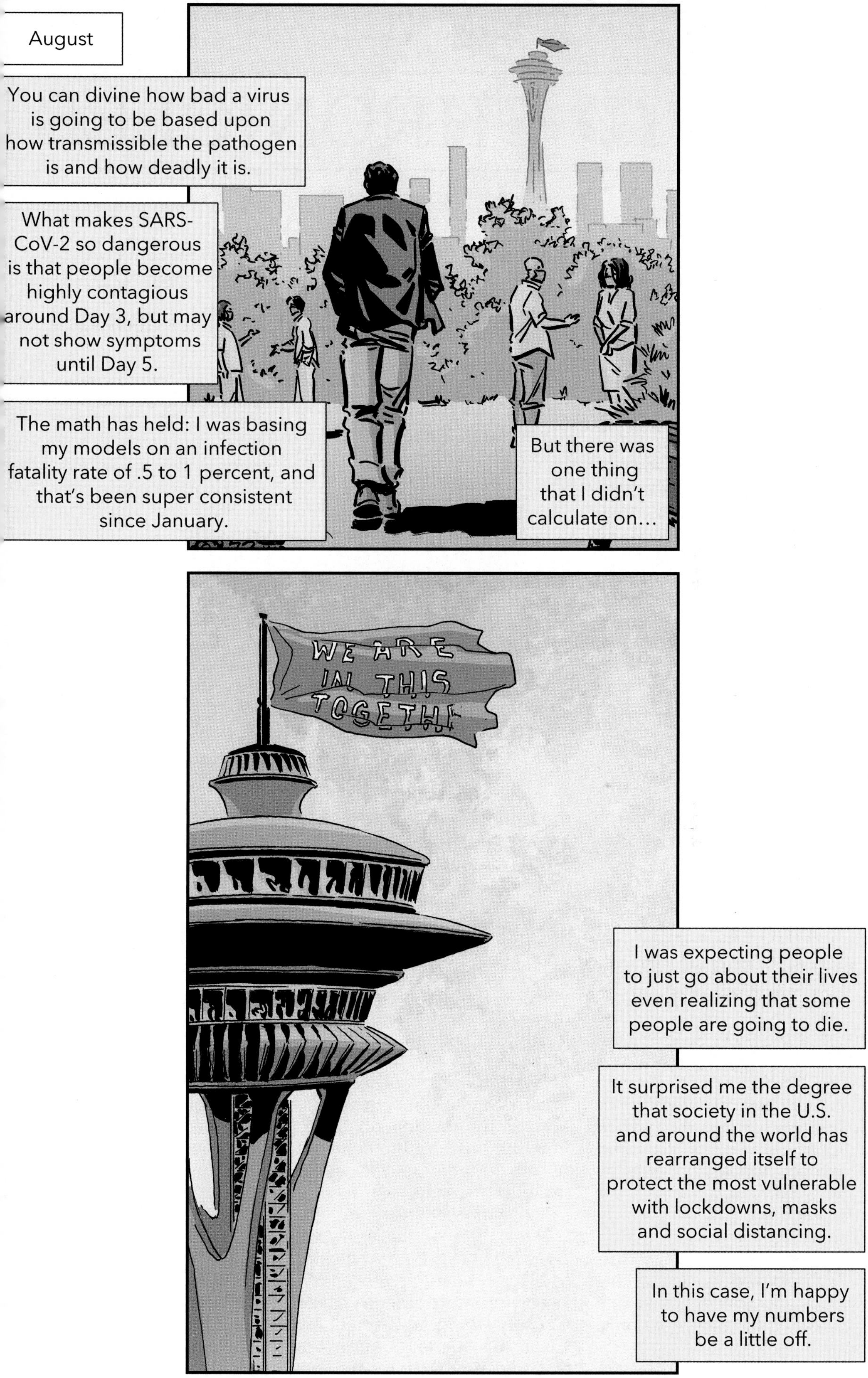
August
You can divine how bad a virus is going to be based upon how transmissible the pathogen is and how deadly it is.
What makes SARS-CoV-2 so dangerous is that people become highly contagious around Day 3, but may not show symptoms until Day 5.
The math has held: I was basing my models on an infection fatality rate of .5 to 1 percent, and that's been super consistent since January.
But there was one thing that I didn't calculate on…
WE ARE IN THIS TOGETHE
I was expecting people to just go about their lives even realizing that some people are going to die.
It surprised me the degree that society in the U.S. and around the world has rearranged itself to protect the most vulnerable with lockdowns, masks and social distancing.
In this case, I'm happy to have my numbers be a little off.

A LETTER FROM THE WRITER OF

COVID CHRONICLES

by Ethan Sacks

As much of the country shut down in mid-March under the crush of a once-in-a-century pandemic, the comic book industry also was mired in limbo.

Comic book stores closed under health guidelines; the major distributor shuttered; printing presses went cold. This could have been a dark time for Upshot Studios, part of the brand-new publisher AWA Studios, which had just launched its first critically-acclaimed comics into the world. Among Upshot's first batch of books: *The Resistance*, an all-too-timely series that revolves around a global pandemic.

Then COVID-19 enveloped New York City, which Upshot CCO Axel Alonso and

Photo by Nina Lin

> **Our heroes were now the real-life healthcare workers and grocery store clerks who kept the city running at great risk to themselves.**

most of the AWA Studios staff call home. No matter where you lived, a never-ending succession of ambulance sirens punctuated the night as they ferried coronavirus victims to overwhelmed hospital emergency rooms. New York earned the moniker, "The City That Never Sleeps," for the most devastating of reasons.

And this was no longer the kind of speculative fiction that you read in the pages of comic books.

Our heroes were now the

real-life healthcare workers and grocery store clerks who kept the city running at great risk to themselves.

So Axel decided the world needed to see and hear their stories. And rather than sit still and wait for the printing presses to be turned on again, he decided to get these stories out there as quickly as possible online. More people needed to understand the sacrifices that were quietly being made and the heroism quietly being shown in the midst of this crisis, even as we couldn't look away from the crush of the numbers of the dying. Comics could make a difference.

Then he called me.

Three years earlier, Axel changed my life by bringing me to Marvel, where he was editor-in-chief, to write a series called *Old Man Hawkeye*. Before then, I was a full-time journalist for the *New York Daily News*. Axel

wanted a reporter who knew how to write comic scripts to write *COVID Chronicles*, and the overlap in that Venn diagram is very small. But I had also been reporting on COVID for NBC News part-time since even before that fateful March phone call.

For art, he brought in Dalibor Talajić, a Croatian artist who had collaborated with Axel and ABC News a few years ago on *Madaya Mom*, a nonfiction account of a mother trapped in the conflict in Syria, the closest to a prototype we had. I call his

> **More people needed to understand the sacrifices that were quietly being made and the heroism quietly being shown in the midst of this crisis.**

art "emotional realism," as I've never seen an artist in comics who does a better job of expressing feelings.

My goal was to attack this assignment like I would report out any important news story. By reporting, of course. But the format would give us an advantage because we could actually get inside the heads of the subjects and tell their story from their point of view in a way

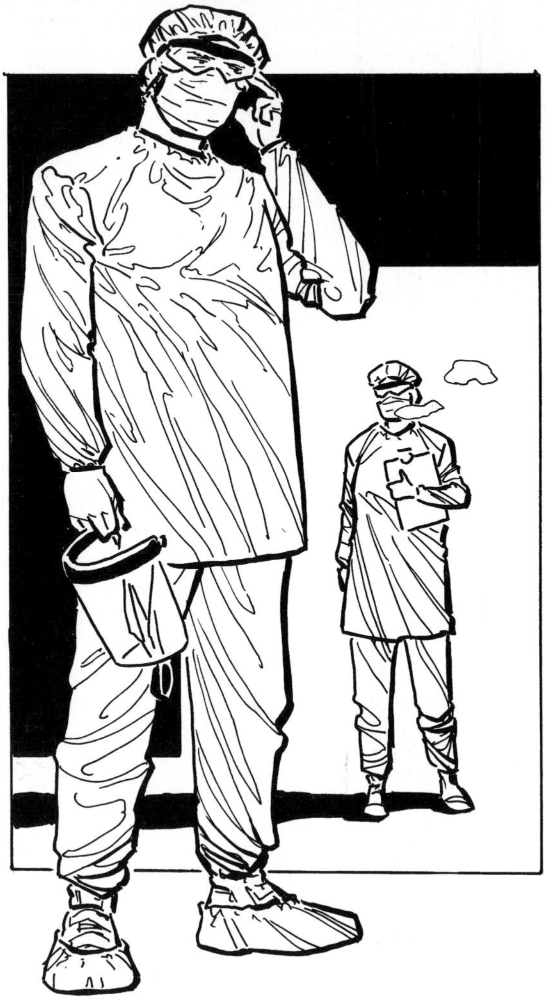

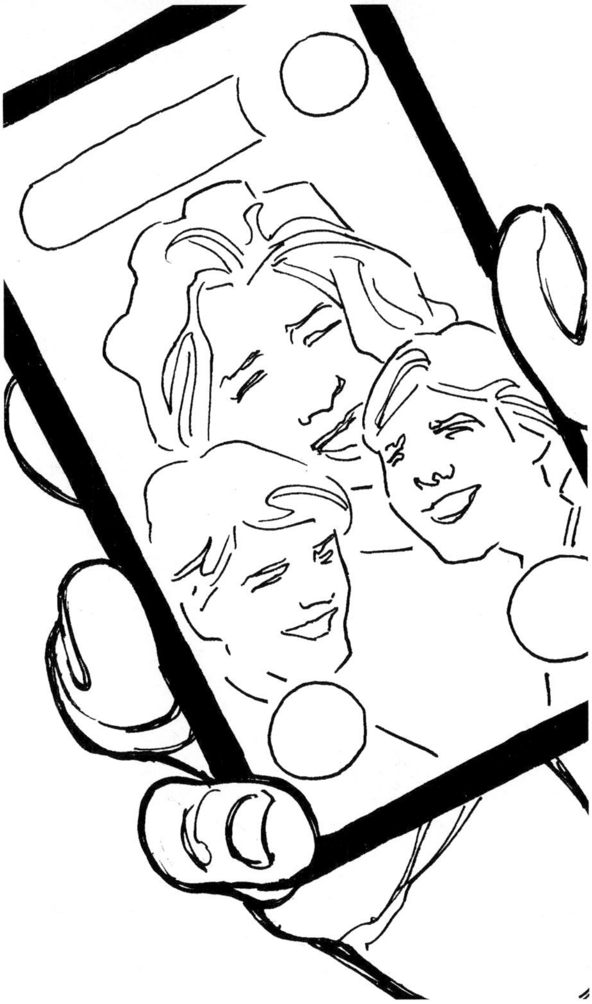

ːould never do before as a jour-
ıalist. It would require hours of
nterviews, personal photos,
ınd input at every stage of de-
ʼelopment. These were emo-
ıonally devastating interviews
vith a lot of tears shed. Some
ɔy me.

For the first two installments
wrote, I used one of my best

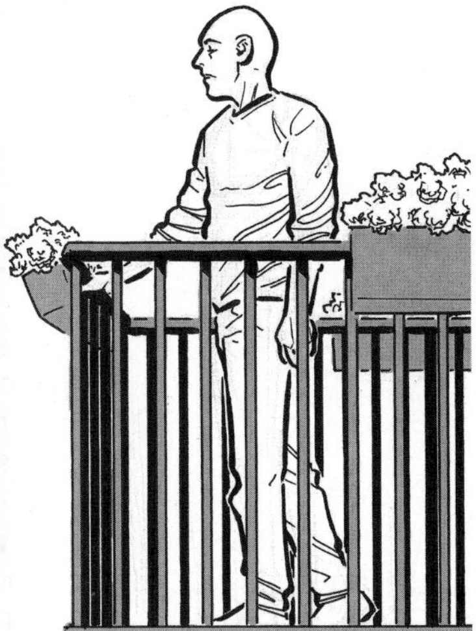

friends, Raj Waghmare, an emergency room doctor in Toronto, and an old *Daily News* colleague, Kerry Burke. I knew they had compelling stories as they were working right in the midst of the pandemic, but also knew that they would give me the access, interview time and personal photos I needed to give Dalibor for art references. (Chanelle, the Brooklyn mom who beat COVID, is also someone I knew previously.) Once I had those to show strangers, particularly once they witnessed Dalibor's art, I felt they would understand the project.

For the others, I scoured social media, local articles, talked to acquaintances and contacted medical organizations. There are obviously billions of potential subjects, but the ones I gravitated towards were ones which would be relatable no matter who was reading the story or where they were reading the story. There were some who said no, not ready to publicly share their private pain. But I stumbled on Jessica, the nurse that opens the book, in a video for a charity raising money for badly needed PPE for healthcare workers in the early days of the pandemic. She was so articulate about the problem that I knew she would make a great subject.

"It would require hours of interviews, personal photos, and input at every stage of development. These were emotionally devastating interviews with a lot of tears shed. Some by me."

I wanted to find someone caught in the original outbreak in Wuhan, China. Xi Lu, a London resident who found himself trapped in Wuhan during a planned two week visit to his parents, ran a lockdown Facebook group. He turned out to be the perfect guide, patiently taking me through the conditions on the ground. The New York office of Doctors Without Borders put me in touch with Guadalupe, the Mexican doctor running a COVID clinic near a displaced persons camp. An acquaintance told me about his best friend, Jack, an Orlando-based respiratory therapist who intubated patients with the virus, got sick himself, nearly died, was saved in the very hospital in which he worked, and eventually returned there to go back to saving others.

While we were working on *COVID Chronicles*, another seismic news story of 2020 broke. After the killing of George Floyd led to a national reckoning on racism in this country, we saw protests across the country that drew millions—even amid the pandemic. But why weren't the BLM protests leading to major spikes in COVID-19? I found an answer courtesy of Apollonia Piña, who was profiled in an article on Indian Country and explained to me the tremendous steps taken by her and her fellow street medics to keep protesters masked and safe as best as they could.

Most of the subjects were not household names, but we did want to document several of the unlikely celebrities who emerged in the first half of 2020. There was Italian opera singer Maurizio Marchini, who started by serenading his neighbors from his balcony in Florence, to keep their spirits up during quarantine—and then did the same for the rest of the world when the video went viral. Finally, there were the scientists of the Seattle Flu Study who used their knowledge and experience to track down the first documented case of community spread in the U.S. at the time.

Many thanks to everyone at AWA who made this possible—both as a vertical scroll internet comic and a graphic novel: Senior Editor Michael Coast, Associate Editors Dulce Montoya and Jaime Coyne, Managing Editor Will Graves, Production Manager Chris Burns, hard-working Art Director Stan Chou, Production & Design Assistant Bosung Kim, who formatted and lettered all the stories, and colorist Lee Loughridge, who colored this whole collection on short notice. Gratitude as well to marketing wiz Lisa Y. Wu, who helped draw attention to this project. This was a true labor of love.

NBC News, my part-time employer—and in particular editors Catherine Kim, David Firestone, Anna Brand, and Kara Haupt—saw the potential of *COVID Chronicles* early on and committed to publishing these first on their national web platform. Their faith, and the backing of one of the largest and most prestigious news organizations in the world, allowed us to tell our stories to a potential audience of 120 million sets of eyeballs each month. Hopefully together we convinced some skeptics to wear masks.

The final goal, however, was always to have the printed record you now hold in your hands. Axel's original cocktail napkin idea is now 144 pages. Long after science and the human spirit vanquishes COVID-19, and it will be vanquished one day, we hope the legacies of these ordinary heroes who faced extraordinary circumstances won't be forgotten.

COVID CHRONICLES

New York City – April 2, 2020

PAGE ONE (FIVE PANELS)

Panel 1. Open with a view through a car windshield, looking at a Caucasian woman, 23, who is facing the reader. She's in the driver's seat of the car, gripping the steering wheel tightly. This is JESSICA, an ICU nurse, and the anxiety is written on her face. (See the reference of the real-life Jessica below.)

CAPTION: (Background color/ text differs from internal narration captions)
JESSICA, 23, ICU NURSE

CAPTION: (Internal narration)
I arrive at the hospital parking lot 15 minutes before the start of my night shift.

CAPTION: (Internal narration)
I need that time to psych myself up to leave the car.

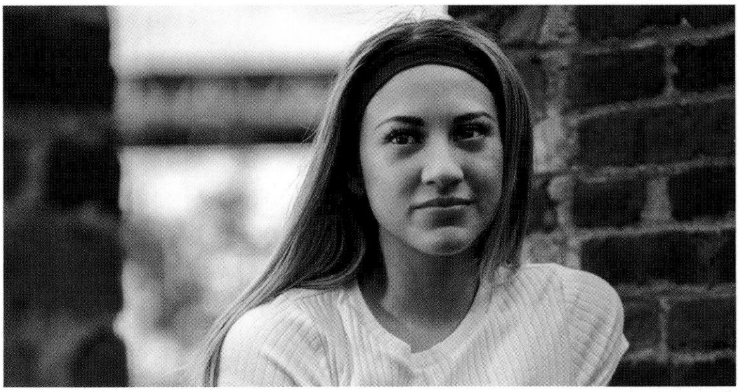

Panel 2. A view from behind as Jessica walks towards the hospital entrance. She is pinning her hair in place so we can see a flower tattoo on her neck. This is an important detail for later. There are no identifying landmarks to indicate which New York hospital it is. There should, however, be a hospital sign with a red cross to indicate the nature of the building.

> CAPTION: (Internal narration)
> Everything has changed in the last 11 days… since the first COVID-19 case hit our ICU.

> CAPTION: (Internal narration)
> Now, all 20 beds in my unit are filled. Now, they're converting every ward except maternity and oncology to more ICU space.

Panel 3. Inside the hospital, Jessica is in the background as a doctor, wearing a mask, rushes past her in the foreground. It can be a blur. The goal is to convey that she's going into a very busy hospital that's in crisis mode.

> CAPTION: (Internal narration)
> In 11 days, our lives have been turned upside down.

> CAPTION: (Internal narration)
> We went from being relaxed to scared, not knowing how it's transmitted.

> CAPTION: (Internal narration)
> The fear that we're going to bring it home with us.

Panel 4. Inside the ward, Jessica pulls out a plastic bag from a box — it's her PPE, already used the past two days.

> CAPTION: (Internal narration)
> I live with my 62-year-old mom and the idea that I could infect her… I couldn't live with *that.*

> CAPTION: (Internal narration)
> And this PPE that I've been reusing the last three days in a row is the only thing that protects both of us.

Panel 5. A tight shot of Jessica's hand holding an N95 regulator mask. It is clearly soiled.

CAPTION: (Internal narration)
The instructions on the N95 box says we're supposed to dispose and use a new one after every interaction with a patient. I've used this three days in a row.

CAPTION: (Internal narration):
I'm pretty sure it's not supposed to look or *smell* like this.

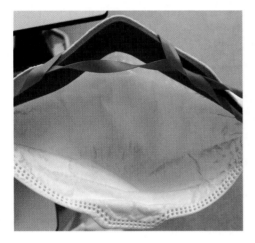

Panel 6. Jessica starts putting on her PPE. She's almost done getting geared up. We can try to replicate the picture below.

CAPTION: (Internal narration)
Still, every piece of PPE counts.

CAPTION: (Internal narration)
Every piece gives me a fighting chance of not bringing anything home.

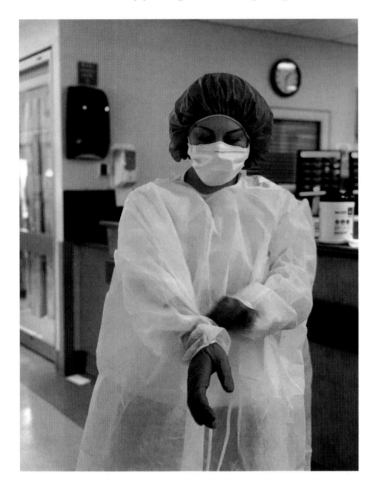

Panel 7. Tight shot of Jessica from the shoulder's up as she puts on her face-shield. (See reference below.)

CAPTION: (Internal narration)
Of not bringing anything home to my mother and sister.

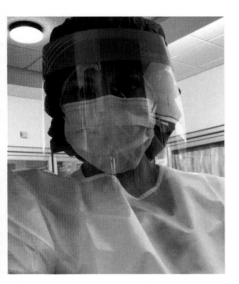

Panel 8. Cut to a quick flashback. In the absence of coloring to indicate that it's a flashback, we should play with the margins or the soften the art to differentiate it from the rest of the strip. Another nurse not wearing a mask is trying to hold down with a patient laying on a hospital bed trying to pull out the ventilator that snakes into his throat.

CAPTION: (Internal narration)
The nurses know what's at stake… My coworker risked herself to rush in before she could get all her gear on…

CAPTION: (Internal narration)
…to stop a COVID patient from pulling out his respirator.

Panel 9. The flashback continues with an almost identical layout as last panel. Only the bed is covered with a body in a body bag.

CAPTION: (Internal narration)
He died a few days later anyway.

Panel 10. From behind as Jessica, all geared up, enters an ICU hospital room.

CAPTION: (Internal narration)
I could quit. I could stay safe.

PAGE THREE (FIVE PANELS)

Panel 11. The patient is a 70-something Caucasian man, who is also on the ventilator, sedated and unconscious. He's been on the ventilator for days and there's no change. Which is not a good thing as the days tick off. Jessica is pressing on the screen of a smartphone.

> CAPTION: (Internal narration)
> But I *have* to be here. For them. For their families.

> JESSICA:
> Hello? It's Jessica, your dad's nurse.

> JESSICA:
> I'm here with him now.

Panel 12. Jessica holds the phone near the unconscious man's ear. Her eyes, visible through her face-shield, are welling up with tears.

> FROM PHONE:
> D-dad? We can't wait for you to come home...

> FROM PHONE:
> ...we're going to take back you to the beach you love so much in the summer.

> FROM PHONE:
> Please-please come home, dad.

Panel 13. Tight shot of Jessica as she hangs her head down as she clicks off the phone.

> SFX:
> Click.

> CAPTION: (Internal narration)
> I...I think they know he's not going to see that beach again.

> CAPTION: (Internal narration)
> Oh, God, it's all just too much!

Panel 14. In almost identical panel as Panel 10, Jessica enters another ICU room.

CAPTION: (Internal narration)
I *won't* bring any of this back home.

CAPTION: (Internal narration)
I *won't* put my mom in one these beds

Panel 15. Inside there is a Hispanic woman lying unconscious on the bed, also hooked up to a respirator. The vital signs on the monitor look shaky. From Jessica's body-language, she looks scared.

CAPTION: (Internal narration)
This patient is just 38. A mom with two young kids.

CAPTION: (Internal narration)
I thought young people were supposed to be safe from the virus.

CAPTION: (Internal narration)
Maybe no one is safe.

Panel 16. Jessica is manipulating some dials on the regulator.

> CAPTION: (Internal narration)
> She's crashing!

> CAPTION: (Internal narration)
> I stay in the room for more than an hour trying everything I can, fixing her Sedation levels, checking her blood pressure meds.

Panel 18. Jessica watches as a doctor, kitted up the same way she is, rushes into the room.

> CAPTION: (Internal narration)
> It's just emotionally exhausting to see people deteriorate right in front of your eyes — despite all of your efforts.

Panel 19. Tight shot of Jessica's glove hand holding the sedated patient's hand. We can see the wrist and it has an almost identical tattoo to Jessica's – the one from Panel 2. Maybe the flower is a similar shape, but different color.

> CAPTION: (Internal narration)
> Especially when you feel a personal connection to them.

> CAPTION: (Internal narration)
> She'll survive today. I hope she'll still be here when I'm back in two days.

Panel 20. Close with a mirror image of panel 1, looking again through the car windshield at Jessica, who is again sitting in the driver's seat of the car and gripping the steering wheel tightly. This time tears are visible on her cheeks.

> CAPTION: (Internal narration)
> I sit in the hospital parking lot for 15 minutes at the end of my night shift.

> CAPTION: (Internal narration)
> I need every second to psych myself up to return home to my mother and sister.

COVID CHRONICLES #9

Guadalupe Garcia, 36, Doctor, Matamoros

Panel 1. Open with a shot of the protagonist of this chapter, GUADALUPE GARCIA, during a previous mission for Doctors Without Borders in YEMEN. She's trying to desperately stabilize an injured Yemeni man. Please use the photo below for reference. This is a flashback panel, one of four in this chapter, so let's make it look different than the ones set in the present.

CAPTION:
Guadalupe Garcia, 36, trauma doctor

CAPTION:
I trained in my home country of Mexico as an emergency room doctor long before I started working for Médecins Sans Frontières, or Doctors Without Borders, in 2017.

CAPTION:
But this job always surprises you. If I close my eyes, I can still see the Yemeni man who was hit by stray bullets on the table as I tried to figure out which hole to close first, to give him a chance to survive long enough to get him to an intensive care unit…

CAPTION:
They don't teach you that in medical school."

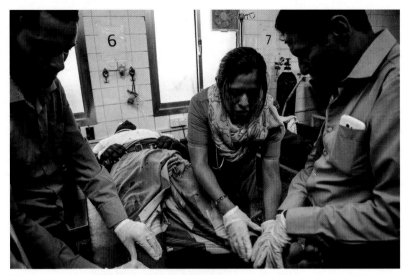

(Photo courtesy of Agnes Virraine-Leca)

Panel 2. In an almost identical layout, Guadalupe is now geared up in PPE and helping a nurse "prone" an elderly male Mexican COVID patient from lying on her back to position him on his front to help the breathing. The doctor is in the same position as the previous panel to help the transition.

CAPTION:

I did important work in Yemen and Sudan. But my friends and family kept asking me, 'Why do you go out of your country when we have needs here?'

CAPTION:

Now, because of COVID-19 pandemic, I have the opportunity to do something for Mexico.

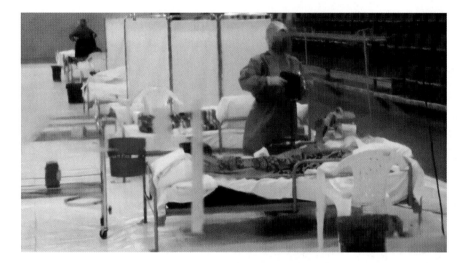

Panel 3. Pull back to show an aerial view of the gymnasium which has been reconfigured to be the Doctors Without Borders makeshift COVID clinic. Beds line two rows along the floor, with nurses and doctors caring for the patients. A "Medicos Sin Fronteras" banner hangs on the back wall.

CAPTION:

June 29, 2020

CAPTION:

I'm now in the city of Matamoros working at a COVID-19 center that Doctors Without Borders opened the week before I arrived. I oversee a staff of 120 people.

CAPTION:

They arranged the space in a gymnasium: Twenty beds for people with severe cases —a provisional place where these patients either recover, hold on long enough to be transferred to a hospital, or …

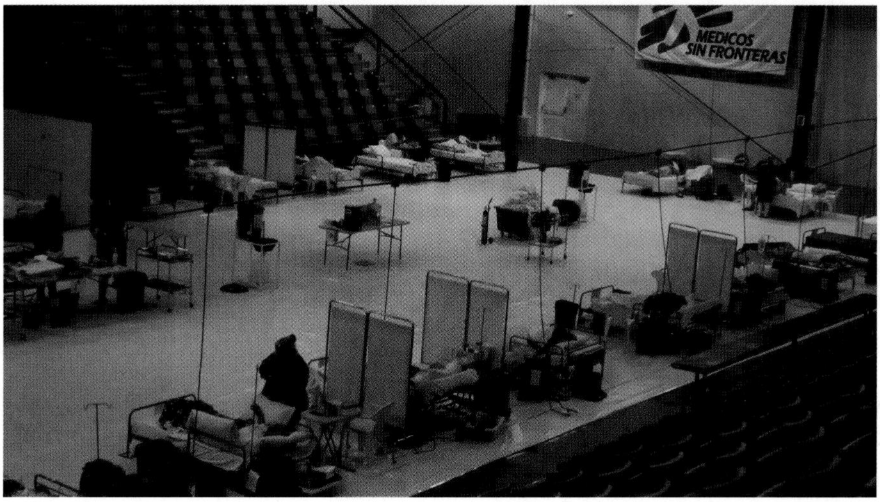
MEDICOS
SIN FRONTERAS

Panel 4. Cut to the refugee camp near the U.S. border to show some children playing in the dirt near the Rio Grande river, the U.S. border visible on the other side. This is helping to set the geography.

CAPTION:
This clinic is here not just to help the locals. We are near an asylum seeker camp with 2,000 displaced people who are stranded in limbo at the border between Mexico and the United Statess.

CAPTION:
They come from all over: Honduras, Belize, Guatemala, southern Mexico. And they are forced to live in tents … hoping that the U.S. will reopen the border. So, they camp there on the other side of the Rio Grande River from Texas.

Panel 5. Cut to a more crowded part of the refugee camp, showing how the tents are right up against each other. It's not the most sanitary of conditions. Social distancing is virtually impossible.

CAPTION:
The camp is divided in three different areas. The first area is the people who have been there the longest. The other two are for people who came in the last year.

CAPTION:
The first area is more stabilized; the refugees have space. The others have tents right on top of each other.

CAPTION:
We know there's no way to isolate these people. The risk of having more people infected with COVID-19 is going to be hard to stop under those conditions.

Panel 6. Cut to an overcrowded emergency room in Matamoros. We see why the Doctors Without Borders put the clinic in this region.

CAPTION:
And the hospitals in Matamoros are full right now. The COVID-19 mortality rate here is 10 percent.

CAPTION:
The refugees who get sick are afraid to go to the hospital anyway; they are afraid they'll be kicked out and lose their chance to cross the border.

CAPTION:
Many of the nurses who work with us also work in one of those hospitals, which elevates the risk of them getting sick. Part of our job is to teach them how to use their personal protective equipment (PPE) the right way.

Panel 7. Guadalupe is shown from behind as she heads to the gymnasium entrance in her own PPE. A reference photo of the entrance is below.

CAPTION:
So, I start my day calling people who are suspected cases among our staff to see how they are. Then we come together in the gymnasium at 9 am to start checking on the patients.

CAPTION:
If there are patients there that are too critical for us to care for anymore, we do paperwork with the Ministry of Health to help us find a hospital. There is only so much we can do to help here without ventilators.

Panel 8. Cut to a flashback of Guadalupe in a hospital in Khartoum, in South Sudan, where she's in the background, looking at an emergency room full of COVID patients. Photo reference choices below.

CAPTION:
I was working in Sudan in the spring when the virus first entered that country. We were trying to set up a COVID-19 clinic in a hospital in Khartoum.

CAPTION:
Between the first case and when we arrived, there were maybe 10 positive cases within about a week. After that there was one week when we went from ten to 11 to 30 to 90 and we were like, 'What the hell is going on here?'

CAPTION:
Then we were getting 30 per day, then 50 a day before I left Sudan. It felt like being in the movie, 'World War Z!'

Panel 9. Guadalupe is in the Khartoum airport, wearing a mask, waiting in a long line of people waiting to pass through a gate.

CAPTION:

I became one of the statistics. When I arrived in Mexico and went into quarantine, I was feeling a little bit sick, maybe just a headache. I got Coronavirus.

CAPTION:

Maybe I got it in Sudan, maybe it was in one of the three different airports I had to travel through to get back home.

Panel 10. Still in flashback mode, Guadalupe gets a nasal swab test from a doctor in full PPE upon her return to Mexico. She looks feverish, but is persevering.

CAPTION:

The day that I start to suspect it was because I have a little fever, so I called the doctor that we visit after assignments with MSF.

CAPTION:

Since it was three days after I came back from Sudan, I thought maybe it's the jet lag. She told me we should do a PCR test to be sure. It was COVID-19. For me it was very mild. Within a few weeks I was cleared to go to work.

Panel 11. Back to a medium shot of the healthcare workers taking care of patients inside the gymnasium.

CAPTION:
And I need to work.

CAPTION:
The reason I became a doctor was when I was a child, I liked to feel adrenaline. I always ended up in the emergency room from doing some risky activity. My mom couldn't pay for so many emergency room visits.

CAPTION:
So, I thought I will help mom with the bills. If I will study to be a doctor, she will not have to pay for anything.

CAPTION:
I still really feel alive when adrenaline runs through my body, when I save a very critical patient. For me, that is my drug.

Panel 12. Cut to inside the gymnasium, an elderly Mexican woman is hooked to an oxygen tank. Her eyes are half open. A nurse is holding her hand. Guadalupe is there at bedside, too.

> CAPTION:
> July 28

> CAPTION:
> But today, we had our first deceased patient. She was a Mexican woman, about 72 years old, with a background of hypertension and a history of exposure to cooking charcoal.

> CAPTION:
> When she arrived here she was very sick with respiratory distress. And she came to us because the other hospitals told her there was no space. She got worse by the hour.

> CAPTION:
> She died waiting for a hospital bed.

Panel 13. An almost identical shot shows the woman now with her eyes closed, clearly having died. Guadalupe and the nurse have their heads bowed a little to convey their sadness.

> CAPTION:
> It's not like you don't become emotional. When I lose a patient, I keep thinking I should have done better at this or that.

> CAPTION:
> You feel bad for the patient and their family. Especially since the only way the family can say goodbye to their loved one is through a window.

Panel 14. Guadalupe, still in her PPE, leans against the wall, allowing herself five minutes to mourn.

> CAPTION:
> I always think I didn't do enough for the patient or their family.

> CAPTION:
> But I give myself five or 10 minutes to think like this, because normally we have a lot of patients. You have to continue caring for the others.

Panel 15. Cut to Guadalupe in her apartment later in workout clothes, a blur as she does some kind of aerobic exercise to vent her feelings after losing the patient.

> CAPTION:
> I try to do some kind of high-energy exercise at the end of the day – Tae Bo, Zumba, kick-boxing, cardio, anything to work off the stress.

> CAPTION:
> Because there is a lot of stress.

Panel 16. Cut to another Flashback, this time back to one of her tours of duty in Yemen. Guadalupe and other healthcare workers are busy trying to help stabilize an infant girl.

> CAPTION:
> I also hold on to the good news.

> CAPTION:
> In Yemen, a newborn was brought to us by a neighbor who heard the abandoned baby crying outside. We tried to stabilize her until we found a maternity hospital to take her. But while we tried to stabilize her, she had two cardiac arrests.

> CAPTION:
> Through it all, she kept crying. If she wants to live and is fighting, then the least we could do is fight for her.

> CAPTION:
> The nurses gave her a provisional Arabic name, which translates in English to Hope, because we were able to move her to the maternity hospital. We received notice two days later that she survived. She gave us *hope*.

Panel 17. Cut back to the present, in the gymnasium. In the foreground, an elderly male COVID patient is in the foreground. In the background, there's a very sick female COVID patient watches him. Guadalupe is on the side of the panel listening to the man.

> CAPTION:
> We've had some good news in Matamoros. It's very touching, very emotional when we see patients go home.

> CAPTION:
> There were these two patients that were a couple, they were discharged on different days but in the same week. First was the man, who was in very bad condition for a few days, but got better.

Panel 18. The man is wheeled out to his appreciative adult son, who is visibly emotional.

> CAPTION:
> When the man left the gymnasium, his son was there crying. I went to bed that night with the biggest smile on my face.

Panel 19. Days later, the wife is wheeled out past a line of clapping health care workers still dressed in their PPE.

> CAPTION:
> After some more days, the wife came out of the clinic, and she was very emotional, too.

Panel 20. The old woman leans in closer to tell Guadalupe something.

> CAPTION:
> She told us, 'You are some angels and I appreciate what you did for us.'

> CAPTION:
> That made me so happy. Because today we made a difference, even if it's one or two lives.

PHOTO REFERENCE

CHAPTER 4: REPORTER

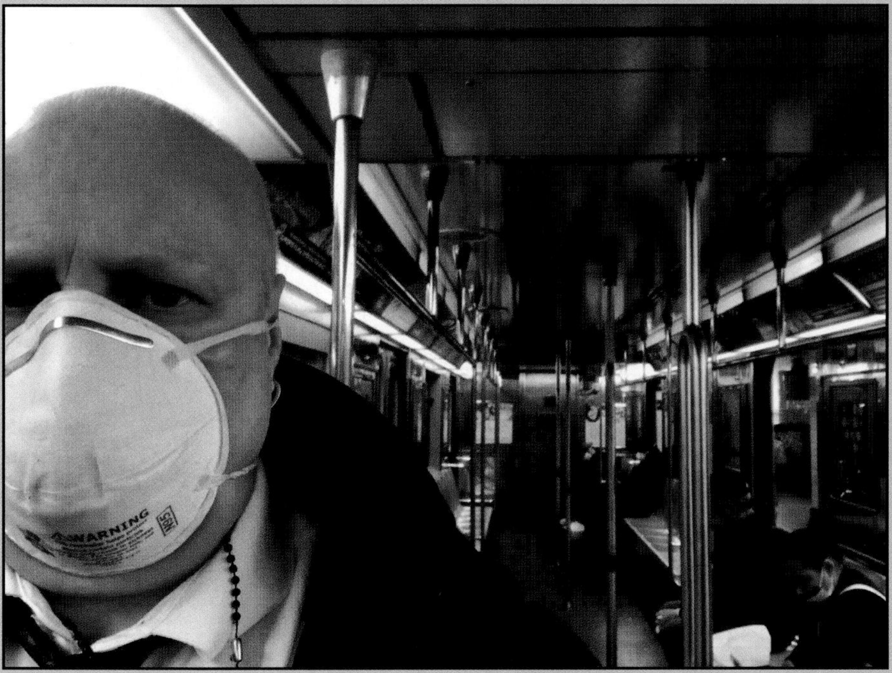
WARNING

CHAPTER 5: TORONTO

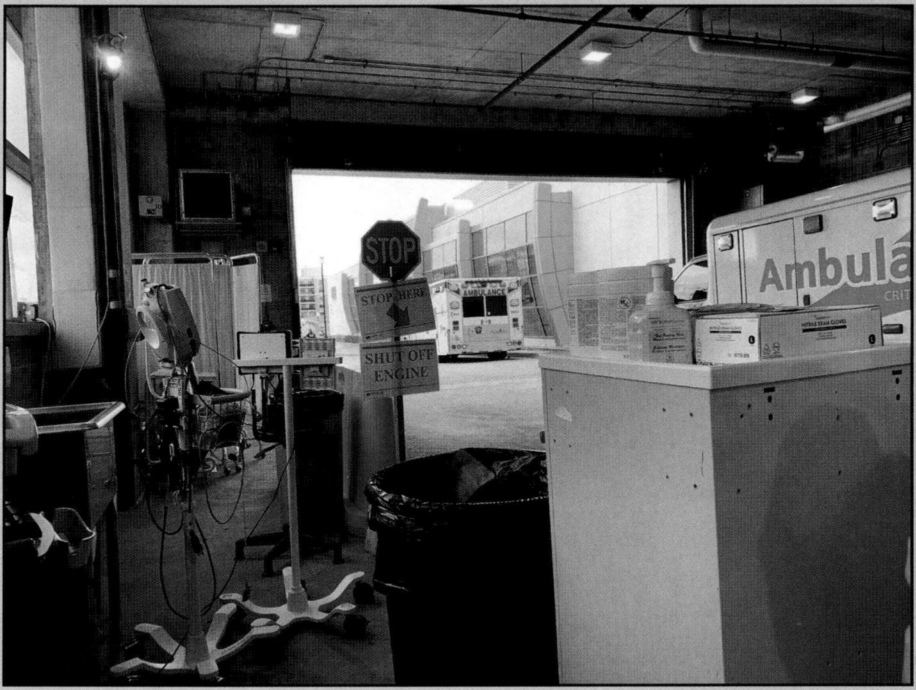
STOP
STOP HERE
SHUT OFF ENGINE
AMBULANCE
Ambula

PHOTO REFERENCE

CHAPTER 7: TULSA

CHAPTER 10: SEATTLE

Amplification Plot
1.00
0.200
0.100
0.0100
0.00100
ΔRn
5
10
15
20
25
30
35
40
Cycle
COVID-19-S_gene
COVID-19_Orf1b

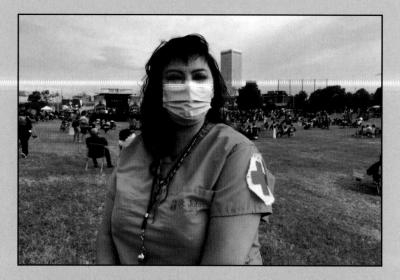

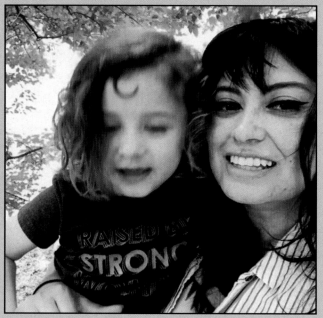

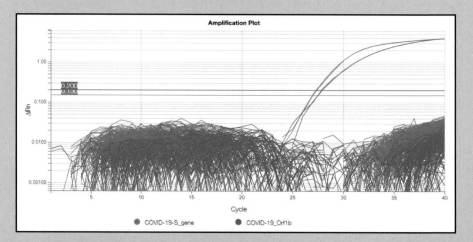

ART PROCESS FOR *COVID CHRONICLES*

Rough Layout by Dalibor Talajić

Inked Panel by Dalibor Talajić

Gray Tones for NBC News web version
by Dalibor Talajić

Colors by Lee Loughridge
for print version

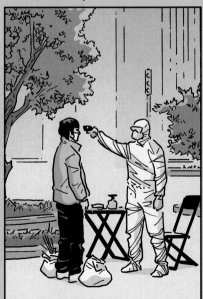

ART PROCESS FOR *COVID CHRONICLES*

Rough Layout by Dalibor Talajić

Inked Panel by Dalibor Talajić

Gray Tones for NBC News web version
by Dalibor Talajić

Colors by Lee Loughridge
for print version

ART PROCESS FOR *COVID CHRONICLES*

Rough Layout by Dalibor Talajić

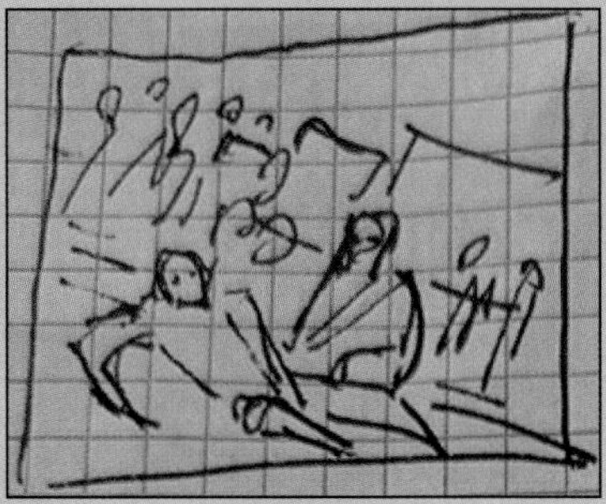

Inked Panel by Dalibor Talajić

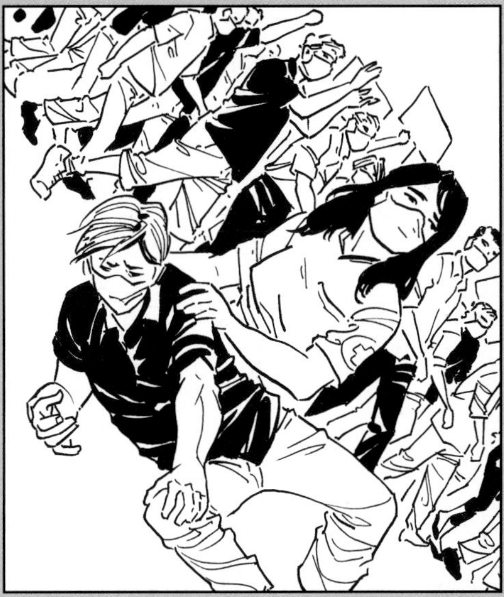

Gray Tones for NBC News web version
by Dalibor Talajić

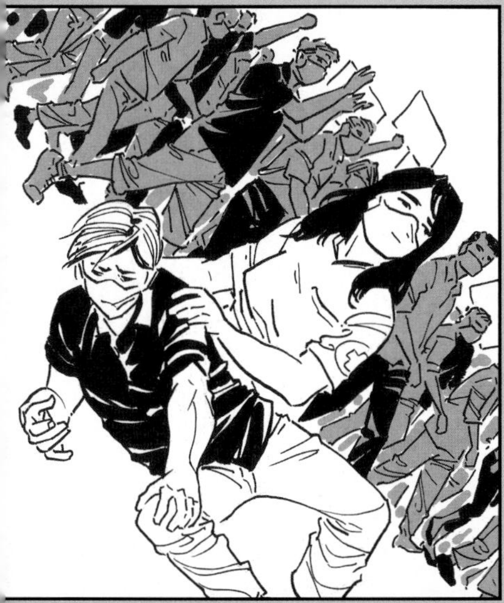

Colors by Lee Loughridge
for print version

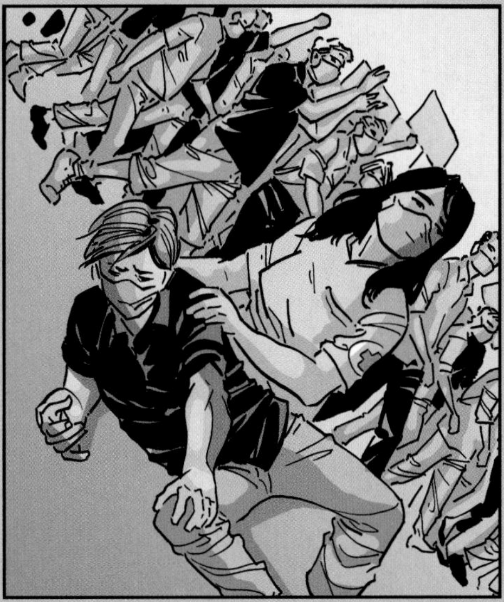

ART PROCESS FOR *COVID CHRONICLES*

Rough Layout by Dalibor Talajić

Inked Panel by Dalibor Talajić

Gray Tones for NBC News web version
by Dalibor Talajić

Colors by Lee Loughridge
for print version

ART PROCESS FOR *COVID CHRONICLES*

Rough Layout by Dalibor Talajić

Inked Panel by Dalibor Talajić

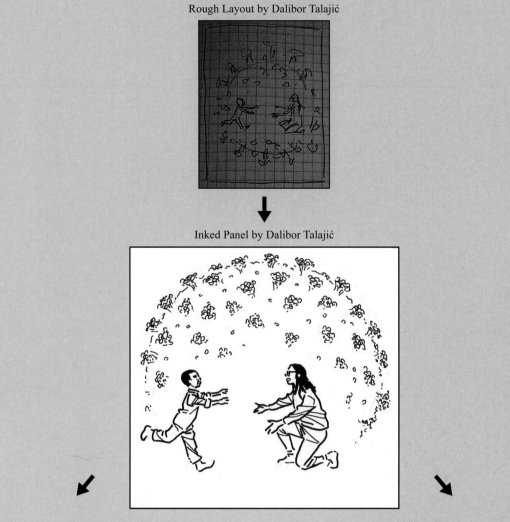

Gray Tones for NBC News web version
by Dalibor Talajić

Colors by Lee Loughridge
for print version

ART PROCESS FOR *COVID CHRONICLES*

Rough Layout by Dalibor Talajić

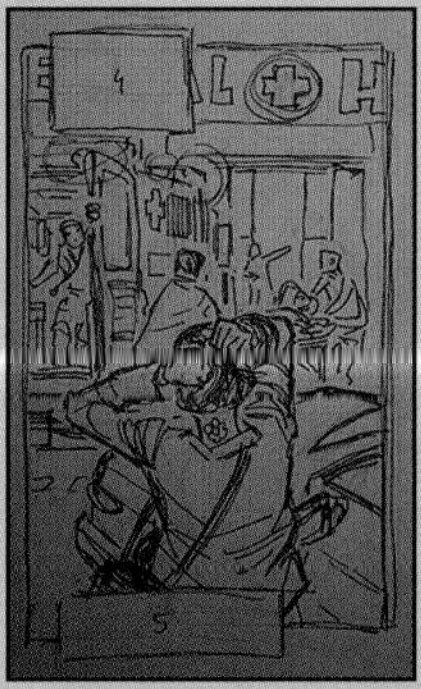

Inked Panel by Dalibor Talajić

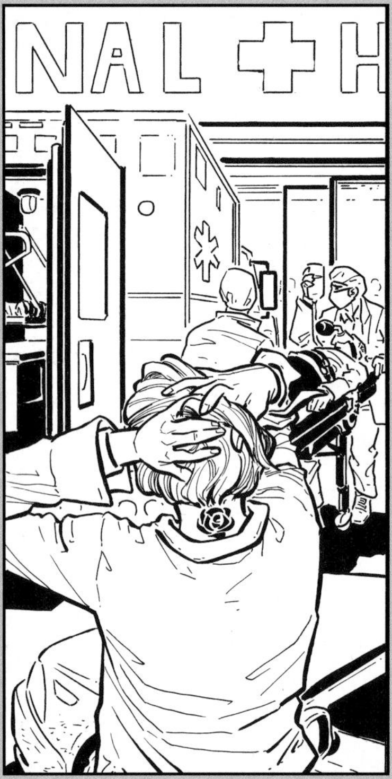
NAL H

Gray Tones for NBC News web version
by Dalibor Talajić

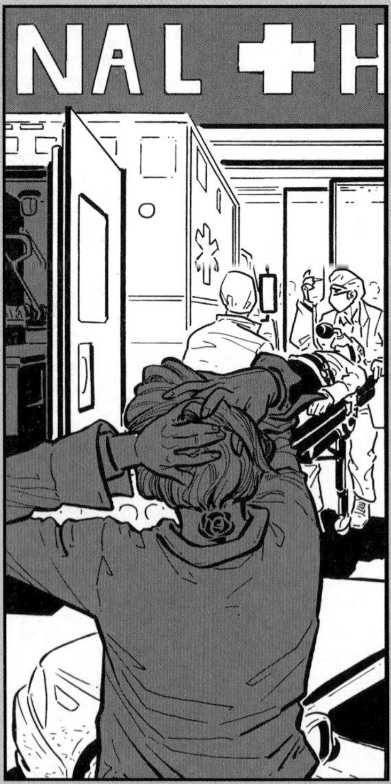
NAL H

Colors by Lee Loughridge
for print version

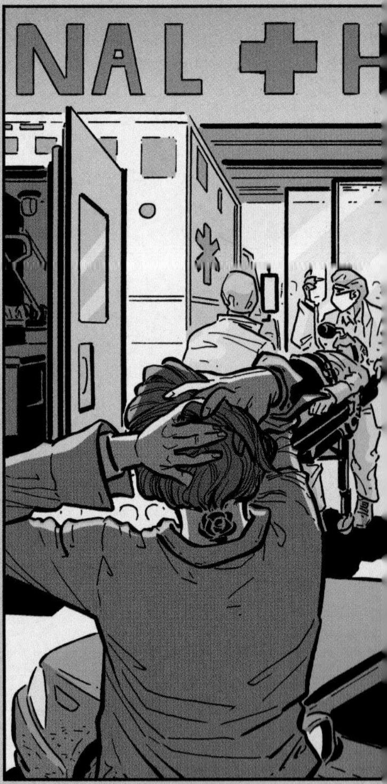
NAL H